Human Resource Management in Irish Organisations

Practice in Perspective

Patrick Gunnigle

Michael Morley

Noreen Clifford

Thomas Turner

with

Noreen Heraty

Marian Crowley

Oak Tree Press

Dublin

in association with

Graduate School of Business

University College Dublin

Oak Tree Press
Merrion Building
Lower Merrion Street
Dublin 2, Ireland

A catalogue record of this book is
available from the British Library.

ISBN 1-86076-054-6

Printed in Ireland by Colour Books Ltd.

CONTENTS

ABOUT THE CONTRIBUTORS

PATRICK GUNNIGLE is Professor of Business Studies at the University of Limerick and Director of the Employment Relations Research Unit.

MICHAEL MORLEY lectures in personnel management and industrial relations at the University of Limerick.

NOREEN CLIFFORD is a researcher based in the Employment Relations Research Unit at the University of Limerick.

THOMAS TURNER lectures in industrial relations and organisational behaviour at the University of Limerick.

NOREEN HERATY lectures in human resource management at the University of Limerick.

MARIAN CROWLEY is a graduate of the University of Limerick and University College Cork and is currently employed in a multinational organisation in Munich.

LIST OF TABLES

LIST OF FIGURES

ACKNOWLEDGMENTS

This book is the result of a tremendous collaborative effort by people from both within and outside the University of Limerick. Work first began on this project in 1991 and has continued ever since due to the efforts of a number of people to whom we extend our thanks.

Faculty and staff in the Centre for European Human Resource Management, Cranfield University, have effectively supported our work in all respects. We would therefore like to thank Professor Chris Brewster, Araine Hegewisch, Leslie Mayne, Olga Tregaskis and Sarah Atterbury for their efforts on our behalf.

In Ireland our initial work in this field was supported by the Department of Enterprise and Employment. We thank them for this support, particularly Martin Territt, Ronald Long, Kevin Bonner and Padraig Cullinane. The Labour Relations Commission also facilitated our work and again we would like to thank Kieran Mulvey and Sean Healy. As Sean has recently retired we would particularly like to acknowledge his support for, and contribution to, independent research in the field of industrial relations and human resource management, and to wish him well in his future activities.

Our work has benefited immensely from the comments and involvement of colleagues in other universities. Of particular note have been the contributions of Professor Philip Beaumont, University of Glasgow, Professor Bob McKersie, Massachusetts Institute of Technology, Professor Bill Roche, University College Dublin, Professor Shaun Tyson, Cranfield University, Dr. Jim Walsh, University College Cork and Dr. Kathy Monks, Dublin City University.

Oak Tree Press have provided great support for our work. They have encouraged our research and continue to provide an invaluable outlet for research based publications on aspects of Irish business. We would particularly like to acknowledge the role of David Givens.

Within the University of Limerick a number of people helped both materially and in kind. Professors Whelan, Dineen, and Andreosso helped provide infrastructure and material support which is necessary for any research effort. This work was also aided by a grant from the University of Limerick Research Seed Fund which has been supported by gifts from the General Electric Fund and others donors. We would particularly like to thank Professor Stuart Hampshire and Eamon Cregan for their support in this regard.

On the fieldwork side, Geraldine Floyd provided tremendous administrative support and direction. We would like to thank her for her efforts and for also helping to keep us all in line! We would also like to acknowledge the administrative support of Deirdre O'Dwyer, Margaret Corbett and Margaret Fennessy.

At the risk of embarrassing my co-authors, I would like to mention two particular contributions. Noreen Clifford joined the research team in 1995. Since then she has undertaken in a most professional manner the onerous task of data analysis. Her efforts have been unstinting and I would like to acknowledge her immense contribution to this research effort. I would like to mention Mike Morley who oversaw the initial sample selection and managed the questionnaire distribution and collation. Mike carries an huge workload and, to his great credit, does so with both good humour and great competency. Without his contribution this work would not have been possible.

Finally, I would like to mention other colleagues in the University of Limerick who have contributed in various ways. Bernard Delany and Haaris Sheikh helped with the fieldwork. Others provided advice and assistance and we would like to acknowledge the contributions of Daryl D'Art, Patrick Flood, Noreen Heraty, Tom Garavan, Sarah Moore and Joe Wallace.

Paddy Gunnigle, February 1997
(On behalf of the research team)

Chapter 1

HUMAN RESOURCE MANAGEMENT IN IRELAND: AN OVERVIEW

Noreen Clifford, Thomas Turner, Patrick Gunnigle & Michael Morley

INTRODUCTION

This book examines human resource management (HRM) practice in Ireland. It is the product of an analysis of data generated by the second Cranfield/University of Limerick (CUL) study of HRM in Irish organisations, administered in 1995. The study forms part of the *Price Waterhouse Cranfield Project on International Strategic Human Resource Management in Europe*, first established in 1989 and currently involving some 19 participating countries. The purpose of this project is to generate an overall picture of HRM in European organisations by examining the nature of human resource management at organisational level. The first Irish survey was carried out in 1992 and results of this initial study were reported in *Continuity and Change in Irish Employee Relations* (Gunnigle et al., 1994). This current text, based on 1995 data, makes reference to the previous findings in order to bring into focus any major changes which have occurred since the first study in 1992.

The introductory chapter has three objectives. Firstly, it attempts to synthesise current debates on HRM by considering the international literature and contemporary developments in the field. Secondly, it reviews the key findings of our first (1992) study on HRM in Ireland and compares these to the study findings on HRM in other European countries. Finally, the research methodology employed in this study is described. It is hoped that this approach will help position our analysis of HRM in Ireland within an appropriate conceptual, comparative and methodological frame-work. We begin by considering how developments in the structure of competition affects the nature of HRM in organisations.

HUMAN RESOURCE MANAGEMENT AND COMPETITION

Changes in product markets, technology and the occupational composition of labour markets have increased the importance of human resource utilisation in modern economies. The growing competition from late industrial starters such as Korea, Singapore and China and the further dismantling of trade barriers following the General Agreement on Tariffs and Trade (GATT) have, on the one hand, sharpened the competition between firms for international markets but, on the other, have also provided new opportunities through the expansion of markets. These new opportunities are often in product and service areas where the application of technologies is central to gaining competitive advantage in supplying a consumer market characterised by attention to product variety, reliability and quality.

According to Piore and Sabel (1984), these developments herald a new industrial revolution and a major restructuring of capitalism. The economic viability of firms depends on their ability to restructure in order to withstand increased global competition and the fragmentation of mass markets (Marshall, 1992). In the 1970s and 1980s both firms and national economies that were capable of offering more diverse and customised products fared better than more traditional producers of standardised mass products (Streeck, 1992). While claims of a new industrial revolution may be exaggerated there have been substantial changes in what organisations produce, the way they produce and in the delivery of goods and services to the marketplace. The altered economic conditions of the 1980s and 1990s have prompted firms to change their traditional structures and policies for managing human resources. These new structures and policies centre on developing three key factors at firm level: product quality, productivity and labour flexibility. Human resource utilisation has therefore become a critical feature for those firms where human resources are a potential asset in the search for competitive advantage. The potential for competitive advantages from human resources is related to four features of a firm's human resources:

1. A firm's workforce must add value to the product or service provided

2. Levels of individual performance must matter

3. A firm's human capital investment cannot be easily imitated

4. A firm's human resources must not be subject to replacement by technological advancements or other substitutes if they are to provide a source of sustainable competitive advantage.

Employees in commercial organisations operating in a competitive market are by definition employed to add value and individual performance has some impact. However, it is the latter characteristics of imitation and substitutability which are important determinants of the potential of human resources to give firms a competitive advantage. In general, the more skilled and knowledgeable a work force the greater the potential for competitive advantage, which in turn depends on the way the firm manages its human resources. In the developed industrial economies the proportion of occupations in the professional and skilled categories has steadily increased at the expense of the unskilled and semi-skilled category. Between 1971 and 1990, skilled occupations grew more rapidly than semi/unskilled occupations in Ireland. Professional and associate professional occupations increased by 84 per cent and skilled maintenance, clerical and sales workers had moderate increases in the range from 20 per cent to 50 per cent. In contrast, labourers decreased by 40 per cent, transport workers by approximately 3 per cent and skilled production workers remained unchanged (Corcoran et al., 1992). There are some indications that firms in Ireland are giving a higher priority to the management of human resources. The membership of the Institute of Personnel and Development provides a measure of the trend in the number qualified in the area of human resource management. Total membership of the institute increased from 427 in 1976 to approximately 2200 by 1996.

However, the human resource policies and practices of Irish organisations remained relatively unexamined, with little systematic research against which to judge policies and practices. The 1992 Cranfield/University of Limerick (CUL) study of human resource practices and policies in Irish firms reported in *Continuity and Change in Irish Employee Relations* (Gunnigle et al., 1994) attempted to remedy this lacuna in studies of Irish management.

MANAGING EMPLOYEES: THE HUMAN RESOURCE MANAGEMENT DEBATE

Managing human resources is one of the key elements in the coordination and management of work organisations. Without labour, capital is inert, and without capital, labour is inert. In all commercial organisations human resources add some value to the production process. Thus, the way employees are managed, the policies and practices used to co-ordinate the production effort is essential to organisational performance. Arguably the changes in the economic context discussed above point to new demands and challenges for the management of human resources. In the academic literature the changing economic context and the consequent effect on the management of human resources has initiated a debate on the most appropriate style and system of policies and practices which are consistent with organisational success in the 1990s. The models of HRM which have emerged form this debate have tended to contrast (either empirically or prescriptively) the past methods of managing employees with either contemporary methods or possible future approaches. There is considerable conflict, however, among academics as to the substance and nature of the shift in the way employees are managed (Beardwell and Holden, 1994). However, there is a consistently sanguine theme evident in many of the models of HRM. Changes in employment relations are perceived or modelled in terms of a shift from a low to a high commitment approach to managing human resources (Walton, 1985a); from low trust to high trust (Fox, 1974); from an emphasis on the use of employees in a flexible and cost-effective manner to viewing human resources as an asset (Storey, 1989). The dichotomous states in these models are defined according to the nature and implementation of employee policies such as rewards, human resource flows, employee communication and the way work is organised (Table 1.1).

Table 1.1: HRM Models and Associated Practices

HRM MODELS		
Low commitment	⇒	High commitment
Low trust	⇒	High trust
Labour as a commodity	⇒	Labour as an asset

HUMAN RESOURCE PRACTICES

Rewards

Standard rate for the job		Pay contingent on employee performance
Bonus systems	⇒	Gain sharing through share-holding and profit sharing for employees

HR flows

Low investment in training		High investment in training
Underdeveloped internal labour market:	⇒	Developed internal labour market:
No security of employment; No career ladders; High use of atypical employment		High security of employment; career ladders; low use of atypical employment

Communications

Little information conveyed to employees about the organisation	⇒	Employees briefed on strategic and financial issues
No mechanisms for upward communication of employee voice to management		A variety of mechanisms allowing employee preferences to be communicated

Work organisation

Explicit job demarcation		High functional flexibility across jobs
Low task discretion	⇒	High task discretion
Low employee participation		High employee participation
High level of employee supervision		Low level of supervision

Much of the empirical research on human resource management focuses on the human resource practices outlined in Table 1.1. An optimistic prediction in the human resource management literature is that an integrated approach to the implementation of those practices leads to a high-commitment, high-trust organisation which in turn is associated with higher levels of organisational performance as measured by such outcomes as absenteeism, labour turnover, productivity and product quality. A necessary element linking practices and performance is the strategic capacity of management to relate the needs and performance of the business with the way that employees are managed. Thus one of the prominent features of the human resource management debate is the emphasis on the concept of strategy. Storey (1992) notes that an important emergent theme in the personnel management literature is a desire to address what he terms the dilemmas in workforce management. Essentially this is reflected in a shift away from the tendency to prescribe the "how to" in managing employees to an approach which takes a more contingent view of the personnel management practices considered suitable for particular organisations. Consequently, survey research in human resource management has tended to address three critical areas: human resource management strategy; human resource policies and practices; and organisational performance.

REVIEW OF 1992 FINDINGS

Before considering the findings of our second study of HRM practice in Irish organisations, it is useful to review the findings of our first study conducted in 1992. The three central aims of the 1992 study were: (i) to detail existing human resource practices in Irish firms; (ii) to assess the evidence for change (using the extant research in the area) in the management of employees; and (iii) to provide a basis for comparing HRM policies and practices in Ireland in a European context. The rationale for such an assessment was prompted by the macro-level changes in the environment discussed above as they related to Ireland. Increased unemployment during the 1980s, the growth of the service sector, atypical forms of employment and the growing dominance of foreign firms in the manufacturing sector appeared to pose a challenge to the dominant traditional model of employee management through collective bargaining (Roche and Geary, 1995; Turner et al., 1997). Collectivism in employee relations incorporates the extent to which management acknowledges the right of employees to collective representation and the involvement of the collective in influencing management decision-making (Gunnigle, 1995a; Purcell, 1987). Thus, high collectivism is manifested in the establishment, recognition and incorporation of mechanisms for employee representation, particularly trade unions, as a vehicle in the conduct of establishment-level employee relations, while at the other extreme, low collectivism is manifested in managerial opposition to collective employee representation (Gunnigle, 1995a).

However, the results of the study tended to indicate the continued robustness of the traditional model for managing employee relations (Gunnigle et al., 1994). Indicators of union presence such as union recognition and density were high in the organisations studied. An average of 56 per cent of employees were unionised and 79 per cent of organisations recognised a trade union. The specific policies and practices used to manage employees also appeared to confirm the general continuing stability of the dominant collective bargaining model. Although many organisations had developed direct avenues of communication with the individual employee alongside the formal union channels, the use of techniques such as profit-sharing and flexible employment practices remained low, indicating a pattern of continuity rather than change. Gunnigle et al. (1994) concluded that organisations are adopting a piecemeal and pragmatic approach to the management of human resources. Where new initiatives in the management of human resources occur it is, they suggest, alongside, rather than in place of, collective bargaining. Not all of these practices, though, are compatible with trade unions. The implicit threat of performance-related pay to individualise the employment relationship and undermine collectivism is supported by the negative relationship found between the use of performance-related pay and unionisation (see Roche and Turner, 1994; Turner, 1994). The results of the study indicated an increasing tendency, particularly in the private sector, to link the performance of employees more closely with the performance of the organisation through the use of variable pay schemes like performance-related pay. US-owned organisations in particular were more likely to use performance-related pay for all employees than were their Irish or UK counterparts. A further threat to the traditional model of employee management is the preference of many newly established organisations to remain non-union (Gunnigle, 1995a). While these firms make up only a small proportion of the established organisations, their increasing visibility holds the possibility of a viable non-union sector based on sophisticated human resource management practices as an alternative to the traditional collective bargaining model.

Overall, Gunnigle et al. (1994) concluded that there remained a strong sense of continuity in employment relations despite the increasing tendency to individualise the employment relationship and the trend towards the non-unionisation of new organisations. They suggested that the evidence more appropriately fitted a dual framework, with new initiatives in HRM co-existing with the established collective bargaining system, than the imposition or establishment of a completely new order. It is questionable whether such an arrangement can remain stable. Contemporary trends in the management of human resources indicate that the development of an individualist orientation in management–employee interactions is one of the most important developments in employee relations in the past decade (Kochan et al., 1986; Guest, 1987; McLoughlin and Gourlay, 1992; Bacon and Storey, 1993). The focus of many human resource practices is on forging a closer relationship between the organisation/management and the employee through direct communication; between performance and pay through contingent reward systems; and between organisation loyalty/commitment and career progression through rigorous appraisal of the individual employee. The consequent individualising of the employment relationship is generally inimical to the collectivism associated with collective bargaining. In a study of greenfield sites established in Ireland between 1987 and 1992, a negative relationship was found between almost every measure of individualism and collectivism (Gunnigle, 1995a and b). Overall, there was little evidence of dualism in the organisations studied, that is, high levels of individualism and collectivism were present in the same firm and the trend appeared to indicate a decline in collectivism and conversely a pronounced shift in favour of more individualist management styles in industrial relations.

HUMAN RESOURCE MANAGEMENT IN IRELAND AND EUROPE: A COMPARATIVE REVIEW

As previously mentioned, the climate of change in the 1980s in Ireland appeared to pose a threat to the traditional model of employee management, with the introduction of factors such as the increased utilisation of HRM practices, the individualisation of the employment relationship, and the increasing opposition of employers to trade unions. Concomitantly, a debate was also emerging concerning the transformation of personnel management within Europe. However, there was considerable confusion concerning the nature and extent of such change. Some authors argued that, rather than a convergence of practices (due to factors such as the internationalisation of markets, and the development of the European Union), there was instead increasing divergence between employee management systems in Europe due to the historical divisions which exist between countries, in economic, legislative, political, social and cultural conditions (Morley et al., 1996). Due et al. (1991: 91) commented that:

> It is interesting to note that the trend towards convergence in European labour markets does not appear to have been very prevalent. Most of today's member states have thus been members of the Community for 20–30 years, sharing in many fields the same market and technological base, without producing any general homogenisation of industrial relations.

These factors may constitute difficulties in relation to an analysis of the European situation, as comparability may become an issue. However, with the growth of international trading blocs, particularly the EU itself, it is useful to examine Ireland within a European context[1]. This analysis will focus on three principal areas: 1) changes in the institutional arrangements governing employee relations; 2) the integration of HRM with business strategy; 3) the utilisation of HR practices generally associated with individualising the employment relationship.

---

[1] It is important to consider that in this section only organisations with more than 200 employees throughout Europe are considered (see Figure 1.1).

Institutional Arrangements Governing Employee Relations

Changes in institutional arrangements are often seen as a benchmark for change in other areas of HR. Throughout the 1980s and early 1990s many authors had pointed to the decline in trade union membership that had taken place across Europe. As Hyman (1992: 38) notes:

> It is certainly true that in a number of the countries of Western Europe, the 1980s and the 1990s have seen an abrupt loss of trade union membership and influence, and a new assertiveness on the part of management. This has been connected to a questioning of traditional forms of regulation external to the firm, whether by law or by sectoral collective agreements.

While the findings of the Cranfield study highlighted large differences between European countries, the prevailing situation was still quite a positive one from the perspective of trade unions. Although in some European countries trade unions have experienced losses, more than 70 per cent of employers in Ireland, the Scandinavian countries and Turkey, reported union density rates of more than 50 per cent of their workforce (see Figure 1.1). (The proportion of employees in Sweden and Finland was as high as 95 per cent.) One of the factors which may have influenced the relatively high levels of membership in Ireland could be the traditional political and social acceptance of trade unions in this country. Von Prondzynski (1992: 71), argues that "Ireland's traditionally centralised collective bargaining system has shown little movement towards decentralisation during the last decade". Figure 1.2 illustrates the extent of pay determination at a national level in Ireland for manual workers, at over 70 per cent with only the Scandinavian countries and the Netherlands reporting a greater level of pay determination at this level.

Figure 1.1: Organisations Reporting more than 50 per cent of the Workforce Unionised (1992)

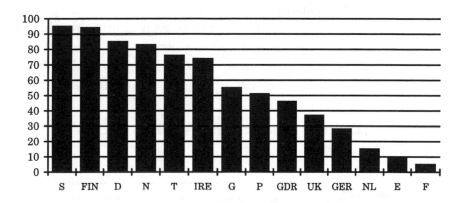

Figure 1.2: Level of Pay Determination at National Level — Manual Workers (1992)

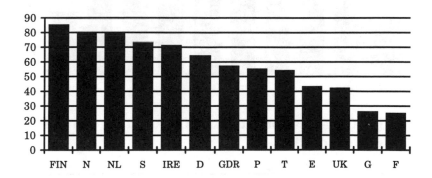

Source: Price Waterhouse Cranfield Project 1992.

While trade union density is an important measure of the industrial relations situation, an equally important factor is trade union recognition[2]. On the whole, levels of union recognition in Europe have remained stable (see Figure 1.3). Even in the UK where trade union membership has decreased significantly in the

---

[2] The question of trade union recognition was not included in the Cranfield survey in certain countries, due to the almost universal recognition in organisations of more than 200 employees in these countries.

last decade, levels of recognition remain relatively high (7 in 10 employers recognise a trade union). The Netherlands is the only country reporting low levels of recognition with less than four in ten employers recognising a trade union.

The Cranfield study also attempted to gain an insight into any perceived changes in trade union influence over the previous three years. The findings indicate a reasonable level of stability (see Figure 1.4), with more than half of the organisations from the

Figure 1.3: Trade Unions Recognised for Collective Bargaining (1992)

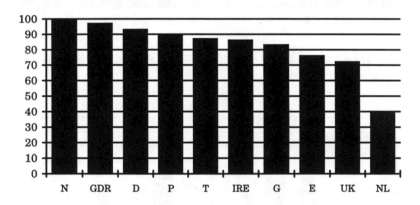

Figure 1.4: Organisations Reporting No Change in Trade Union Influence (1992)

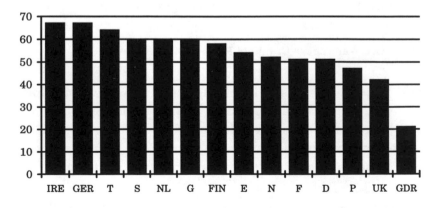

Source: Price Waterhouse Cranfield Project 1992.

majority of European countries reporting no change (the exceptions being the UK, GDR and Portugal). Two-thirds of the organisations operating in Ireland reported no change in this area.

In summary, in examining the changes taking place in institutional arrangements across Europe it is important to remember that many countries in Europe, including Ireland, have a tradition of collectivism, which gives trade unions a legitimate social role. Brewster and Hegewisch (1994: 5) state that:

> Clearly, the European evidence suggests that managements can see the unions, for example, as social partners with a positive role to play in human resource management: and the manifest success of many European firms which adopt that approach shows the, explicit or implicit, anti-unionism of many American views to be culture bound.

As mentioned previously, one of the main findings of the 1992 study in Ireland was the continuing robustness of the traditional collective model of employee management. In addition, in a European context, Irish trade unions appear to be relatively strong at establishment level in terms of recognition, density and influence.

HRM Strategy: A European Comparison

One of the difficulties inherent in any discussion on HRM is distinguishing it from "traditional personnel management". This is a complex issue in itself given the fact that HRM is not a homogenous concept. However, one generally accepted defining feature put forward by Hendry and Pettigrew (1990: 36) is "HRM as a perspective on employment systems, characterised by their close alignment with business strategy". Therefore, in the context of the Cranfield study there are some important measures worthy of analysis, namely: HR representation at board level; HR involvement in strategy formulation; and the existence of a personnel/human resource (P/HR) strategy.

HR representation at board level may be seen as a crude indicator of the level at which personnel operates within organisations. In Ireland the number of organisations reporting the head of P/HR with a seat on the board of directors is average to low in the European context, and very comparable to the UK (see Figure

1.5). This contrasts with countries such as Sweden and France where more than 80 per cent of organisations report P/HR representation at board level.

Figure 1.5: Organisations where the Head of HR has a Seat on the Board of Directors (1992)

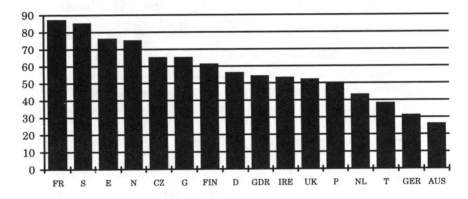

Source: Price Waterhouse Cranfield Project 1992.

In relation to the level of participation of the P/HR function in the strategic process and the existence, or otherwise, of a written P/HR strategy in Irish organisations, the findings broadly mirror those on board level representation (see Figures 1.6 and 1.7). This would seem to indicate that where the organisational structure

Figure 1.6: HR Involvement in Corporate Strategy from the Outset (1992)

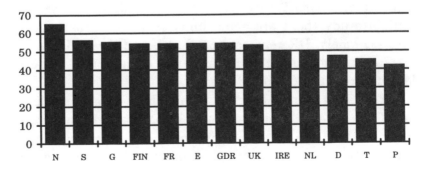

Source: Price Waterhouse Cranfield Project 1992.

exists, allowing representation at board-level, it is likely that there will be P/HR involvement in corporate strategy formulation from the outset. A slightly lower percentage of Irish organisations report a written P/HR strategy.

Figure 1.7: Organisations with a P/HR Strategy (1992)

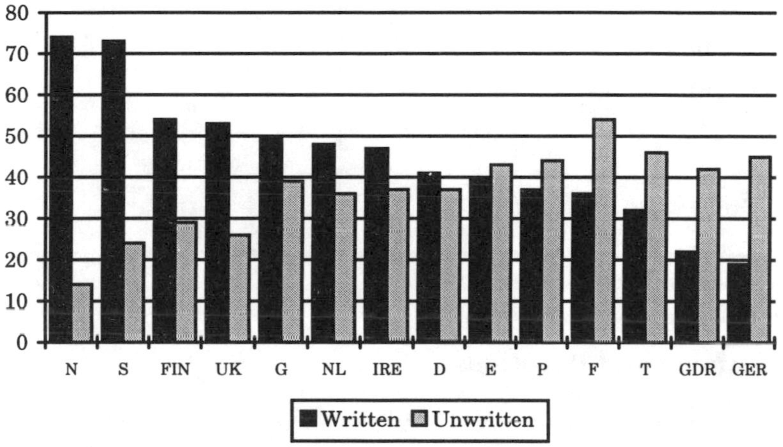

Source: Price Waterhouse Cranfield Project 1992.

On the basis of his analysis of the Price Waterhouse Cranfield data, Brewster (1994) developed a ranking of European countries from those where organisations were most likely to integrate HRM and business strategy, to those least likely to do so (1994: 30). Brewster's analysis reflects the findings of this section, with organisations in Sweden, Norway and France having well integrated HR departments (see Table 1.2). On the basis of his analysis and the findings in this section, it can be concluded that organisations in Ireland and the UK are less likely to integrate HRM and business strategy.

Table 1.2: HR Integration Ranking for Europe

Group 1 (most integrated)	Sweden
	Norway
	France
Group 2	Switzerland
	Spain
	Finland
	Netherlands
Group 3	UK
	Ireland
	Denmark
	Portugal
	Turkey
Group 4 (least integrated)	Germany
	Italy

Source: Adapted from Brewster (1994).

HR Policies and Practices

In the following section the four main functional areas — rewards, human resource flows, employee communications and the organisation of work — are compared. The analysis centres around the adoption or otherwise of practices often associated with a high commitment approach to the management of human resources.

Rewards

The reward system which an organisation adopts is often seen as a strong indicator of the preferred approach to workforce management. The utilisation of gainsharing or employee share option schemes, for example, are sometimes seen as emphasising the development of a "shared vision" within the organisation.

In general there is little utilisation of employee share option schemes across Europe. There is, though a relatively high proportion of Irish organisations offering these schemes, with only the UK and Norway reporting greater usage (see Figure 1.8). The same proportion of organisations in Ireland use profit-sharing as a payment system. However, Ireland rates as an average to low user as profit-sharing is a more popular payment system in Europe (see Figure 1.9).

Figure 1.8: Employee Share Options Offered to Manual Employees (1992)

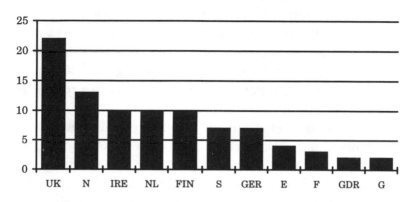

Figure 1.9: Existence of a Profit Sharing System for Manual Employees (1992)

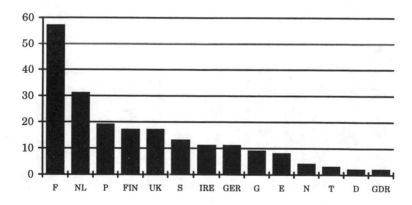

Source: Price Waterhouse Cranfield Project 1992.

Overall, in relation to the area of variable pay, Ireland had the highest proportion of respondents reporting no change, while also showing the lowest number of organisations with an increase in variable pay over the previous three years. One of the factors which may have caused this is the "relatively well functioning incomes policy operating in Ireland" (Filella and Hegewisch, 1994: 97) since the mid-1980s.

HR Flow

The development of internal labour markets and an emphasis on human resource planning and training and development is often associated with the high commitment HRM model. By examining variables such as the incidence of human resource planning, performance appraisal, and spending on training and development, an insight is gained into organisational approaches to managing the internal flow of the workforce.

There is a high level of human resource planning across European organisations, with more than 80 per cent of Irish organisations engaging in human resource planning. The incidence of performance appraisal is also very high, and although over 70 per cent of the organisations operating in Ireland regularly use performance appraisal, in the European context this is an average figure (see Figure 1.10).

Figure 1.10: Performance Appraisal Utilised (1992)

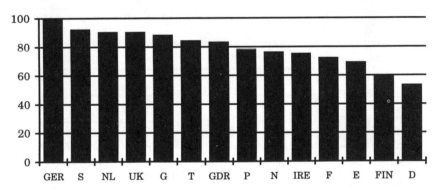

Source: Price Waterhouse Cranfield Project 1992.

Almost one-in-four Irish organisations spend more that 2 per cent of the wages/salaries bill on training. While this does not compare very favourably with a country such as France, where almost 80 per cent of organisations spend more than 2 per cent on training, it is a fairly typical proportion across Europe (see Figure 1.11).

It would seem, therefore, that when compared to their European counterparts, organisations in Ireland conform to the norm in their utilisation of human resource planning and associated techniques.

Figure 1.11: Organisations spending more than 2 per cent of the Wages/Salaries Bill on Training and Development (1992)

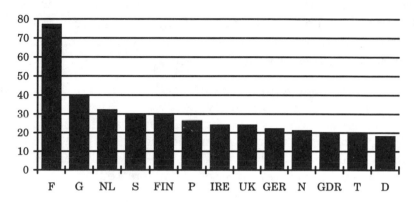

Source: Price Waterhouse Cranfield Project 1992.

Employee Communication

In relation to communication, Ireland rates very well in the communication of strategic issues to employees. Only Norway and Finland have a higher proportion of organisations communicating on these issues. However, the situation is not quite as positive in relation to the communication of financial information (see Figure 1.12).

Figure 1.12: Employee Communication (Manual)

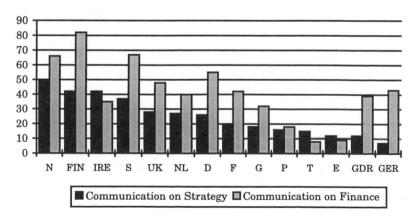

Source: Price Waterhouse Cranfield Project 1992.

An emphasis on direct communication with employees is a practice often associated with individualising the employment relationship. Overall, within Europe there were massive increases in direct communication across all countries, both written and verbal. However, a substantial number of organisations also reported an increase in their use of collective channels of communication. The picture which emerges is one where:

> the evidence supports those that would argue that HRM as a concept is being increasingly adopted in Europe and that HRM would include greater communication with employees. It does not support those who would argue that this should be done through individual communication at the expense of collective channels (Brewster et al., 1994b: 162).

Work Organisation

The way in which work is organised can also indicate particular approaches to the management of employees. Changes in the specification of jobs, including the emergence of broader, more flexible jobs has recently been an area of much interest and speculation. Data from the Price Waterhouse Cranfield study indicates that jobs are becoming wider, particularly within organisations operating in Sweden, Finland and the UK. Ireland also reports an increase in this area, but in less than 30 per cent of respondent organisations (see Figure 1.13).

The importance attached to team principles of work organisation may be inferred by an emphasis on management training in team building. Ireland rated relatively highly with 50 per cent of organisations reporting training in this area (see Figure 1.14). Only Finland and Greece have a greater percentage of organisations engaging in this form of training.

Figure 1.13: Jobs Made Wider/More Flexible (Manual Employees — 1992)

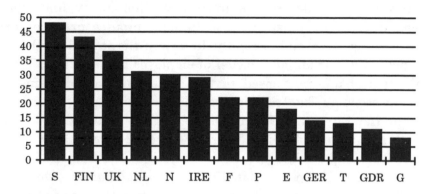

Figure 1.14: Management Trained in Team Building

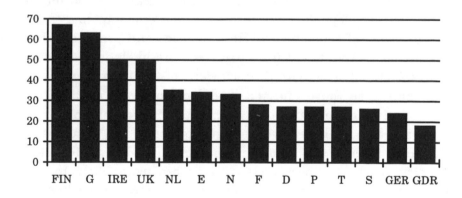

Source: Price Waterhouse Cranfield Project 1992.

Overall, the findings indicate that trade unions remain strong at establishment level in Ireland. There is some evidence of the adoption, in Irish organisations, of certain P/HR practices normally associated with a high trust, high commitment approach to HRM. However, in a European context, Irish organisations seem not to have incorporated HRM at a strategic level, which is evident from Table 1.2 above, outlining a HR integration ranking for Europe.

THE 1995 STUDY: AIMS AND CONTEXT

As in the analysis of the 1992 study, the two central objectives which we seek to address are, firstly, to outline and evaluate the range, scope and sophistication of human resource practices in Irish organisations and, secondly, to assess the impact of these practices on the traditional model of employee management. This evaluation should be viewed in the context of an increasingly buoyant economy. The Irish economy is the fastest growing economy in the European Union. The real gross national product growth rate increased from 3.5 per cent in 1992 to over 6 per cent in 1995. Unemployment (seasonally adjusted) fell from 15.5 per cent in 1992 to 12.2 per cent in 1995 (*Statistical Bulletin*, December 1996). A consequence of economic success is that many firms have potentially more resources available for investment in human resources. Whether these extra resources are invested in human resources is, it can be argued, a critical question for the continued development and success of the economy. In general, the diffusion of sophisticated HRM policies and practices which require some investment from firms is more likely in the kind of buoyant economic climate characteristic of the Irish economy. At the same time the traditional model of employee management characterised by collective bargaining and the recognition of trade unions is also likely to have been strengthened by the success of the economy as trade union membership is directly affected by changes in the business cycle. Unions are more likely to gain members when unemployment declines or conversely when the numbers employed increase (Bain and Elsheikh, 1976). Union membership in Ireland increased from approximately 479,400 in 1992, to 485,700 in 1993 (*Industrial Relations News*, 1995).

Furthermore, the involvement of the trade union movement in social partnership agreements since 1987 has delivered relatively modest wage increases and industrial peace which can be seen as a positive inducement to employers to deal with unions. The interaction of these various factors on the way in which employees are managed can only be gauged through empirical research. In the following chapters a number of specific HRM areas are addressed. Chapter 2 focuses on the P/HR function in Irish organisations, examining recent changes in the functional profile and role of the function. Chapter 3 examines current practices in recruitment and selection. Chapter 4 considers trends in the organisational usage of various forms of flexible working practices. In particular, findings in relation to the utilisation of non-standard forms of employment and changes in the specification of jobs for all employee categories are examined. We also assess the extent to which these changes represent a planned strategic approach to long-term workforce management. Chapter 5 gives a detailed analysis of recent developments in training and employee development. Chapter 6 focuses on compensation and benefits, highlighting recent innovations. Chapter 7 reviews recent developments in employee relations and focuses specifically on trade union density and recognition, and changes in employee–management communications and employee participation. Finally, Chapter 8 summarises the research findings and considers the implications for HRM in Ireland.

DATA AND RESEARCH METHODOLOGY

The sample frame used for the 1995 Cranfield/University of Limerick (CUL) Study in Ireland was the *Business and Finance Top 2000 Trading and Non-trading Bodies* in the Republic of Ireland. Organisations are ranked according to level of turnover, financial institutions by the size of their assets, and non-trading bodies by the number of their employees. If one excludes organisations employing less than 50 employees, the size distribution of establishments in the sample is similar to the size distribution in the relevant population. The rationale behind eliminating these organisations was that their size might not warrant the existence of a specialist personnel function or the adoption of more formal HR policies and practices; therefore, incorporating these questionnaires might distort the findings of the study. A questionnaire addressed to either the personnel manager or chief executive was posted to 1,212 organisations and a total of 261 were returned giving a response rate of 21.5 per cent. While there is a slight bias in the sample towards large organisations, compared with the population, these differences are small and the sample can be considered reasonably representative of the overall population.

Table 1.3: Size Distribution of Organisations

Size	Sample	Population
50–100	46 (18%)	376 (31%)
101–200	68 (27%)	346 (28%)
201–500	74 (29%)	286 (24%)
501–1000	36 (14%)	118 (10%)
1000+	30 (12%)	86 (7%)
Total	254*(100%)	1,212**

* 7 respondents did not indicate size and 103 organisations had less than 50 employees and are not included in the above table

** 936 organisations with less than 50 employees have been excluded

Source: Cranfield/University of Limerick Project 1995.

Table 1.3 gives a breakdown of the number of organisations in each industrial sector from the sample, and compares this with the population. The results clearly illustrate the close similarity between both.

Table 1.4: Sectoral Distribution Of Establishments

Industry	Sample	Population
Agriculture	1.1%	1.8%
Energy and water	0.8%	0.01%
Non-energy chemicals	9.2%	7.2%
Metal manufacture	14.9%	12.4%
Other manufacturing	20.3%	23%
Building and civil engineering	2.7%	5%
Distributive trades	7.3%	11.6%
Transport and communications	3.8%	3.2%
Banking and finance	11.5%	7.3%
Health	6.5%	8.7%
Other services	3.8%	4.4%
Education	6.1%	6.4%
Local and Central govt.	4.9%	6.4%
Other	6.1%	2.4%
	n=259	n=1,212

Two organisations failed to answer this question

Establishments with less than 50 employees are excluded

Source: Cranfield/University of Limerick Project 1995.

Using the Census of Industrial Production (1989), we can calculate the number of foreign-owned firms in the industrial sector where the vast majority of these firms are located. A total of 893 firms are foreign-owned, representing 19 per cent of all firms; of these 46 per cent are US-owned, 43 per cent from EU countries, and 11 per cent are owned by other countries. In the Cranfield/ University of Limerick sample 46.3 per cent of firms were foreign-owned, with 51 per cent US-owned, 39 per cent from EU[3] countries and 10 per cent were from the rest of the world.

Explaining Variation in HR at Organisational Level

A critical issue in analysing human resource management is the extent of variation which occurs between organisations. In addition to examining key aspects of HRM such as the role of the specialist P/HR function or the incidence of particular pay systems, it is useful to consider some of the main factors which might explain variations in organisational approaches. In a review such as this we can "only speculate" as to possible explanatory factors which influence patterns of HRM, and it is beyond the scope of this book to engage in detailed quantitative analysis to establish the significance of relationships between variables.

A range of factors has been advanced to explain variations in human resource management and employee relations, such as size, technology, labour costs, performance and sector (Beaumont, 1986, 1992; Beaumont and Harris, 1994; Roche and Turner, 1994; Storey and Sisson, 1994). However, while the extant literature identifies a range of factors which may explain variations in HRM approaches at the level of the organisation, there is widespread consensus on the relative significance of these factors (Beaumont, 1985, 1993; Kochan et al., 1986; Roche and Turner, 1994). While it is beyond the scope of this text to engage in the extent of analysis necessary to identify statistically significant relationships, the subsequent chapters attempt to tease out potential explanations of variance in HRM between organisations. This approach allows us to speculate in an informed fashion on those factors which best

---

[3] In comparing EU countries the 1995 survey includes Finland, Sweden and Austria, which were not members in 1992.

explain variations in HRM patterns in Irish organisations. Indeed, Ireland is a particularly appropriate testing site for evaluating the impact of different explanatory factors on variations in HRM. It has a high level of inward investment, and the Irish socio-political context provides a stark contrast to that of the US and UK where much of the contemporary literature on developments in employee relations emanates (see, for example, Roche, 1992; Gunnigle, 1995b).

To allow a useful degree of analysis of potential explanatory variables, it is necessary to be selective in our choice of variables for investigation. We have chosen a few commonly used areas for investigation and used these in all the key content chapters. This selection is of course somewhat arbitrary and we acknowledge that factors other than those we have chosen may significantly impact on variations in HRM in Irish organisations.

To evaluate the main explanatory factors potentially impacting upon variations in HR and employee relations in Irish organisations, the following independent variables were utilised. Their selection is based on the extant literature as well as our experience in the 1992 study (see Gunnigle et al., 1994; Roche and Turner, 1994). The main variables used were (i) organisation size; (ii) sector (private v. public); (iii) country of ownership; and (iv) union recognition. It is useful to consider briefly the rationale for the selection of these variables.

Organisation size has figured prominently as an important explanatory factor impacting on variation in patterns of HRM (Curran and Stanworth, 1981a and b; Marchington, 1982; Blyton and Turnbull, 1994). Most of these studies note the positive relationship between size and trade union recognition, the presence of a specialist personnel function, and the level of HR policy sophistication (Millward and Stevens, 1986; Millward et al., 1992). This current study only covered establishments employing over 50 employees. The rationale for this decision was based on a desire to exclude very small firms. In an attempt to identify the impact of size on HRM in Irish organisations, it was further decided to classify the companies studied into "small to medium" organisations (50–199 employees) and "large" organisations (over 200 employees). This classification into "small to medium" and "large" organisations was used to analyse the impact of size on variations in HRM.

Location in either the public or private sector is seen as a particularly important factor impacting on variation in HRM. This is particularly the case in Ireland where a high percentage of the workforce are employed in the public sector and where that sector is currently experiencing considerable pressures for change in the HRM sphere (see, for example, Hastings, 1994; Hourihan, 1994; Roche and Gunnigle, 1995).

Area of activity is also identified as an important factor impacting upon variations in HRM (Beaumont, 1985; Kochan et al., 1986; Guest, 1987; Turner, 1994). The most prominent issue in this literature is the suggestion that "high-technology" sectors are positively associated with more "individualist" and "strategic" HRM approaches and negatively associated with "collectivist" employee relations (particularly in relation to levels of trade union recognition and density).

Country of ownership is essentially used as a proxy variable to assess the impact of managerial values on variations in HRM. This is based on the rationale that managerial preferences in HRM will closely reflect underlying managerial values associated with country of ownership (Poole, 1986; Guest and Rosenthal, 1992; Gunnigle, 1995b). Ownership might be expected to be an important explanatory factor in the context of an Irish economy which is characterised by particularly high levels of direct foreign investment. This text addresses the impact of ownership categories (particularly Irish, UK, US, other European, Asian and other organisations) to investigate the impact of ownership on HRM.

Finally, the impact of trade union recognition is used to evaluate whether different HRM patterns are discernible in unionised and non-union organisations. Again this variable is well established in the literature and was an important factor in explaining different patterns of HRM in the 1992 study (see Gunnigle et al., 1994; also see Guest, 1987; Roche and Turner, 1994).

Chapter 2

THE PERSONNEL/HUMAN RESOURCE FUNCTION

Patrick Gunnigle & Noreen Clifford

INTRODUCTION

Since its initial development during the Industrial Revolution in Britain, the role of the personnel department has evolved to become an important aspect of the managerial infrastructure of most medium to large organisations. While in Ireland the emergence of formal personnel departments did not take place on a widespread basis until the late 1960s or early 1970s, it is clear that they quickly became an established feature of most larger organisations (Shivanath, 1987; Gunnigle and Flood, 1990). It is also clear that, traditionally, the primary role of personnel departments and personnel practitioners concerned industrial relations (Shivanath, 1987; Monks, 1992). The dominant model of the personnel function in Ireland equated to what Tyson (1987) termed the "contracts manager": essentially the personnel function assumed responsibility for managing relations with trade unions while also undertaking activities such as personnel administration, recruitment and training (see Gunnigle, 1996).

However, there is now evidence that significant change has been occurring in personnel management in Ireland, particularly since the 1980s (see, for example, Hastings, 1994; Roche and Gunnigle, 1995). The intensification and globalisation of competition in product and service markets created pressures to optimise the utilisation of human resources. We can also point to evidence of important changes such as greater strategic integration of the personnel/human resource function, a movement away from traditional industrial relations and collective bargaining, a growth in atypical forms of employment and a greater emphasis on other aspects of personnel activity, particularly training and development (see, for example, Shivanath, 1987; Monks, 1991; Gunnigle and Morley, 1993; Gunnigle et al., 1994; Foley and Gunnigle, 1995). The 1980s also saw the emergence of *Human Resource Management*, and an associated emphasis on a more individualistic approach to industrial relations. It has been suggested that, during the period since the early 1980s, organisations were introducing new, innovative approaches to workforce management in an effort to become more efficient (Hannaway, 1992). Associated with this change was a move in some organisations to incorporate human resource issues and the personnel/human resource function at a strategic level.

However, although change has evidently taken place it has not been homogenous across organisations and the nature and extent of such change is by no means clear. This chapter reviews evidence on the current nature of human resource management (HRM) in Ireland. In particular, it considers empirical findings on the nature and role of the specialist personnel/human resource (P/HR) function.

THE PERSONNEL/HUMAN RESOURCE FUNCTION IN IRISH ORGANISATIONS

Historically, the role of the personnel function in organisations has been plagued by debates as to its ambiguity and lack of a demonstrable contribution to the "bottom line" (see, for example, Legge, 1978; Tyson, 1979). In spite of such criticisms, the personnel function appears to have achieved considerable status in the managerial infrastructure of organisations (Tyson, 1987; Guest, 1987; Shivanath, 1987). To evaluate the current nature and role of the specialist personnel/human resource (P/HR) function in Irish organisations a number of indicators may be used, particularly those concerning: (a) functional profile — incorporating issues such as the presence of a formalised P/HR function, scale, etc.; (b) functional role — incorporating issues such as organisational status and board-level involvement. In Ireland, we are fortunate in that we can evaluate contemporary developments in relation to the findings of two important previous studies of the P/HR function in Ireland (Shivanath, 1987; Monks, 1991) as well as to findings of the last Cranfield/University of Limerick Study (Gunnigle et al., 1994).

PROFILE OF THE PERSONNEL/HUMAN RESOURCE FUNCTION IN IRISH ORGANISATIONS

In this section the role of the specialist P/HR function will be examined by looking at issues such as the actual presence of the function within organisations, the size of the function, the activities engaged in and the level at which P/HR function operates in Irish organisations. Factors such as organisation size and country of ownership are also examined in order to assess the effect, if any, they may have on the profile of the P/HR function in Ireland.

Presence of the P/HR Function

Before outlining the study findings on the existence of a formalised P/HR function, it is necessary to begin with a caveat. The number of organisations reporting the existence of a specialist P/HR function is obviously an important bottom-line indicator of the nature and role of human resource management (HRM) within organisations. However, one must be circumspect in interpreting such findings. The presence or otherwise of a personnel department is only one indicator of the HRM role and conclusions should only be drawn in the light of other factors. The existence of a specialist function, while certainly positive, does not indicate the precise role of the P/HR function or the level at which it operates in the organisation. Equally, the absence of a P/HR department is not necessarily indicative of a lack of concern with personnel issues. There are other defining factors: for example, some organisations may not warrant the existence of a specialist P/HR function due to their (small) size or particular Chief Executive Officers (CEOs) may feel they should carry responsibility for personnel matters.

Turning to the actual study findings, the results indicate that the existence of a specialist P/HR function is increasing in importance in Irish organisations, with over three-quarters of respondent organisations reporting the presence of a formal P/HR function (a 6 per cent increase on the previous study in 1992: see Table 2.1).

Table 2.1: Presence of a Personnel/HR Department

	1992	1995
Yes	70% (160)*	76% (199)
No	29% (66)	22% (56)
Missing	1% (2)	2% (6)
	n=228	n=261

*Actual numbers in parentheses
Source: Cranfield/University of Limerick Survey, 1995.

It is widely accepted that the presence of a formalised personnel function is positively correlated with organisation size. This was certainly the case with the present study: almost all organisations (96 per cent) employing two hundred or more employees reported the presence of a P/HR department, compared to only 55 per cent of organisations employing less than two hundred (see Figure 2.1). This finding reflects an "economy of scale" logic: the greater volume of personnel-related work in larger organisations warrants the existence of a specialist P/HR department and the availability of resources to facilitate it. In contrast, smaller organisations tend to have a less formalised approach to personnel and may not be able to "afford" a specialist function. Therefore, in a small organisation responsibility for personnel issues may be

Figure 2.1: Size as a Determinant of the Presence of P/HR Function

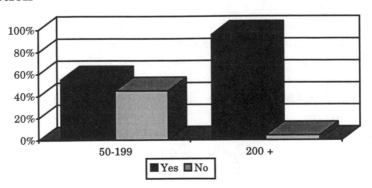

Source: Cranfield/University of Limerick Survey, 1995.

given to another functional head, or, alternatively, the CEO or equivalent may take responsibility for personnel matters. The sector from which the organisation originates also influences the existence of a P/HR function, with 89 per cent of public compared with 75 per cent of private sector organisations reporting the presence of a specialist function.

There is also a clear link between ownership of the organisation and the existence of a P/HR function (see Figure 2.2). Multinational companies constitute a significant proportion of Irish industry. Although many such organisations have adopted specific personnel practices in order to accommodate host country norms, some still wish to retain their own overall "home country" HR philosophy. It has been held, for example, that US organisations consider human resource issues of strategic importance and therefore would favour the existence of a specialist personnel department (Gunnigle, 1996). As indicated in Figure 2.2, the presence of a formalised personnel function is greatest (86 per cent) among US, Asian and other organisations originating outside of the EU. A somewhat lower percentage (72 per cent) of indigenous organisations report the existence of a specialist function. However, when compared to the 1992 figure of 59 per cent, the findings indicate a very positive increase in relation to functional presence in Irish-owned organisations.

Figure 2.2: Ownership as a Determinant of the Presence of P/HR Function

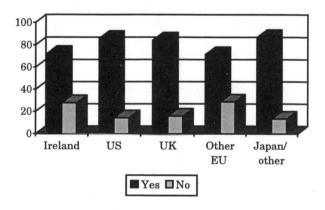

Source: Cranfield/University of Limerick Survey, 1995.

The impact of trade unions on the organisational presence or otherwise of a formalised P/HR function is a matter of some debate. A traditional argument was that the existence of P/HR departments is positively correlated with trade union recognition and density (Thomason, 1984). However, it has also been suggested that a well developed P/HR function is necessary to implement a successful non-union strategy (Foulkes, 1980). The current study examined the impact of trade union recognition on the existence or otherwise of a specialist P/HR function. These findings are outlined in Table 2.2 and do not indicate any dominant pattern: 79 per cent of "unionised" organisations and 76 per cent of "non-union" organisations reported the presence of a P/HR function. However, an important aspect of these findings is the change since 1992, when 72 per cent of unionised and 61 per cent of non-union organisations reported the presence of a P/HR function. While there is an increase in functional presence across organisations, it appears that non-union organisations are establishing a formalised personnel function to an increasing extent. This trend may be associated with increased organisation size: it is widely argued that as organisations grow in size they are more likely to *both* recognise trade unions *and* have a specialist personnel function (Thomason, 1984).

Table 2.2: Unionisation as a Determinant of the Presence of a P/HR Function

	Union	*Non-union*
Yes	79% (157)	76% (38)
No	22% (43)	24% (12)

n=250

Source: Cranfield/University of Limerick Survey, 1995.

Profile of the P/HR Function

In analysing the actual profile of the personnel department this section considers issues such as gender balance, number of people employed (scale) and the division between professional and non-professional staff within the personnel function.

A useful indicator of the role and significance of the specialist personnel function is whether the size of the function in organisations in increasing or decreasing. The study findings on this dimension are outlined in Table 2.3. The results are quite positive, with over 85 per cent of specialist functions either remaining the same or increasing in size. A similar picture emerges in relation to the professionals being employed within the function.

Table 2.3: Change in the Size of the P/HR Function

	Total	Professionals
Expanding	35% (69)	31.8% (50)
Same	50% (98)	56.7% (89)
Contracting	16% (31)	11.5% (18)
	n=198	n=157

Source: Cranfield/University of Limerick Survey, 1995.

Examining the numbers of people employed within personnel provides a crude indication of the role and general workload which P/HR departments are undertaking within organisations. As outlined in Table 2.4, we find the average size personnel function — ten people — is quite large. This finding suggests quite a degree of specialisation *within* the personnel function itself.

Table 2.4: Number of Individuals Employed in the Personnel Function

	1995	1992
1–5	56% (111)	61% (132)
6–10	23% (46)	18% (39)
11–25	11% (21)	14% (30)
26+	10% (20)	6.5% (14)
	n=198	n=215

Source: Cranfield/University of Limerick Survey, 1995.

These study findings on the presence and profile of the P/HR function indicate that personnel departments are an important aspect of the management infrastructure of Irish organisations. To provide a clearer profile of the role of the specialist personnel function it is useful to consider differences between male/female and professional/non-professional staff ratios within P/HR departments. These findings are outlined in Table 2.5 and Figure 2.3.

Table 2.5: Number of Professionals Employed in Personnel

1–5	82% (126)
6–10	12% (18)
11–25	5% (8)
26–900	0.7% (1)

n=153

Source: Cranfield/University of Limerick Survey, 1995.

Figure 2.3: Number of Professional Males and Females Employed in Personnel

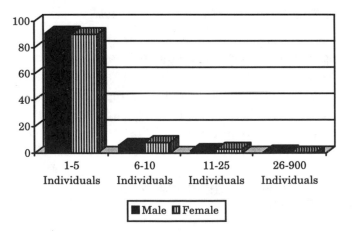

Source: Cranfield/University of Limerick Survey, 1995.

The findings indicate that a greater number of females (average of 6.5) than males (average of 4.43) are employed within the P/HR function. However, when the number of professional males to females is compared, the results show that there is no significant difference (average of 2.63 for both). Thus, while a greater number of females are employed in personnel this is not represented at the higher levels within the P/HR function. This finding points to a traditional male–female dichotomy whereby males are more likely to assume professional/managerial posts and females more likely to undertake non-professional roles (for more discussion on this issue see, for example, Legge, 1995). An associated point supporting this finding is that over three-quarters (76 per cent) of the senior P/HR practitioners who participated in this study were men.

As might be expected, the number of professionals in personnel is positively correlated with organisation size (see Table 2.6). This is most likely associated with the greater volume of work, the greater propensity to have a specialist personnel department in larger organisations, and also the tendency to have more formalised polices and procedures over a range of HR activity areas.

Table 2.6: Number of Personnel Professionals by Organisation Size

	1–5	6–10	11–25	>25
50–199	98% (44)	2% (1)	0	0
>200	76% (80)	16% (17)	8% (8)	1% (1)

n=151

Source: Cranfield/University of Limerick Survey, 1995.

The Personnel Practitioner in Irish Organisations

To explore the role of the personnel practitioner a little further, it is useful to examine specific characteristics in an attempt to develop an accurate profile of the typical practitioner in Irish organisations.

To this end, respondents were firstly asked to indicate the level at which they operated within their organisation. The results indicate that some 71 per cent of respondents were the most senior P/HR practitioner in their organisation. As noted above, over three-quarters of these senior managers were male. Turning to the education level for respondents, it appears that Irish personnel professionals possess high levels of formal education: some 61 per cent of practitioners held a degree, most commonly in business studies.

In evaluating the sourcing pattern of P/HR practitioners, it is interesting that the most senior P/HR managers were recruited either from another functional area within the organisation, or had been a personnel specialist in another company (see Figure 2.4). When organisation size is considered it emerges that 47 per cent of smaller organisations reported recruiting a non-specialist from within the organisation, compared with 18 per cent of large. As organisation size increases it is more likely that the senior HR manager will be a specialist recruited from outside the organisation (26 per cent more large organisations reported this), with a proven track record in personnel.

Figure 2.4: Where the Most Senior P/HR Manager was Recruited

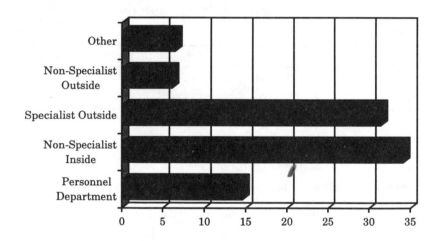

Source: Cranfield/University of Limerick Survey, 1995.

Turning to the level of experience of personnel practitioners, the findings indicate that a higher percentage of practitioners reported having between 11 and 20 years experience than any other category, with the average length of experience being 13 years (see Table 2.7). There is a clear link between organisation size and levels of experience, with notable increases in average levels of experience as organisations become larger. Over half the organisations with 200 or more workers employed a senior personnel specialist with between 11 and 20 years experience compared with a fifth of smaller organisations.

Table 2.7: Number of Years Experience of P/HR Practitioners

1 year	3% (7)
2–5 years	13% (31)
6–10 years	16% (39)
11–20 years	30% (71)
>20 years	9% (22)
Not applicable	29% (69)

n=239

Source: Cranfield/University of Limerick Survey, 1995.

ROLE OF THE PERSONNEL/HUMAN RESOURCES FUNCTION IN THE ORGANISATION

Moving on from the presence and size of the personnel department, it is possible to look at a number of factors which may help define the role which the specialist P/HR function plays in organisations. Of particular concern is the strategic role of the P/HR function, given the extensive debate on the development of human resource management over the past decade. A critical tenet of the HRM literature is that human resource issues are a critical strategic issue for organisations. Consequently, it is argued, organisations need to integrate HR considerations in their strategic decision-making and develop comprehensive and complementary P/HR policies which support the business strategy (see, for example, Fombrun et al., 1984; Beer et al., 1984; Tyson, 1987; Tyson, et al. and 1994; Huselid, 1996). It is therefore interesting to consider study findings on the role of the P/HR function and evaluate the extent or otherwise of strategic involvement.

Board-Level Participation

Analysing the level at which the P/HR function operates, there are a number of factors which may be examined, the first of which is *board-level representation*: that is, the extent to which senior P/HR practitioners are members of their organisation's Board of Directors or equivalent.

While in 1992 almost 48 per cent of respondents were represented at board-level, the figure in the present study has increased to 53 per cent (see Table 2.8). This is quite a positive finding, particularly given that there may be no opportunity for board-level involvement in a number of the respondent organisations. This arises from the fact that some respondent organisations may themselves be subsidiaries of larger, often foreign-owned, corporations. As a consequence, there may not necessarily be scope for board-level involvement in the Irish operation since there may be no Irish board of directors. (Of course, at the corporate level, the P/HR function may indeed be represented at board-level.) In evaluating the significance of these findings on board-level involvement, it is again necessary to sound a note of caution, since the impact of variables such as ownership and organisation size also need to be considered. It is also important to note the difference between *participation* and *influence* in strategic decision-making. Board-level participation clearly facilitates a high level of strategic involvement but does not guarantee it. More detailed qualitative research is necessary to evaluate the extent of influence which the P/HR function exerts in the strategic decision-making process. Finally, it is also important to note that while board-level participation clearly facilitates a personnel input into strategy formulation, being outside the boardroom does not exclude a strategic involvement. Senior P/HR practitioners may have alternative means of influencing strategic decision-making, such as through their relationship with their CEO.

Table 2.8: Head of P/HR with a Seat on the Board of Directors

Yes	53% (109)
No	47% (96)

n=205

Source: Cranfield/University of Limerick Survey, 1995.

Where the head of P/HR does not have a place on the board of directors, the Chief Executive Officer (CEO) is the most likely person on the board to assume responsibility for HR issues (see Table 2.9). Again, this is quite a positive finding: while the P/HR function may not be represented at the highest level in the organisation, HR considerations are represented by the head of the organisation.

Table 2.9: Other Representatives of P/HR on the Board of Directors

Chief Executive	59% (90)
Admin. Director	5% (8)
Finance Director	9% (13)
Company Secretary	7% (11)
Production Director	4% (6)
Other	16% (25)

n=153

Source: Cranfield/University of Limerick Survey, 1995.

As might be expected, board-level participation is positively associated with increases in organisation size: 60 per cent of organisations with 1000 or more employees report personnel representation at board-level or equivalent, compared with only 48 per cent of those with less than 200 (see Table 2.10). There would also seem to be a correlation between board-level representation and trade union recognition. When the results were analysed it emerged that 55 per cent of unionised as opposed to 49 per cent of non-union organisations have P/HR representation at board-level.

Table 2.10: Size as a Determinant of Board-Level Representation

No. of Employees	50–199	200–499	500–999	1000–1999	2000–4999	>5000
Senior P/HR practitioner on board	48% (31)	46% (31)	51% (19)	60% (6)	85% (11)	100% (8)

n=200

Source: Cranfield/University of Limerick Survey, 1995.

While it is difficult to generalise, ownership has in the past been linked to board-level participation, with the US having a particularly high-level of representation (see Figure 2.5). In the current study, the US retains the highest level of participation at 60 per cent, but the increase which has taken place in both Irish- and UK-owned organisations since 1992 is also worth noting.

Figure 2.5: Ownership as a Determinant of Board-Level Participation

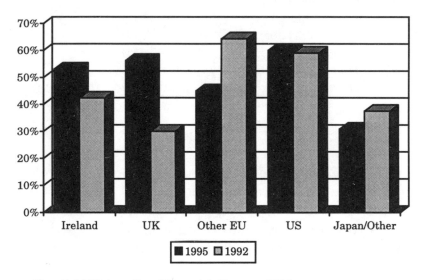

Source: Cranfield/University of Limerick Survey, 1995.

Formal Strategy Development

While the previous findings provide some indication of the level at which the P/HR function operates in organisations, they provide only limited insights into the extent of strategic consideration afforded to HRM issues or the level of involvement of the P/HR function in the strategic process. As previously mentioned, while P/HR practitioners may not have a seat on the board of directors, they may still have an input into strategic decision-making. It is therefore useful to examine the extent to which the P/HR function engages in policy formulation and, generally, its involvement in the strategic planning process.

To consider the extent of formal business and P/HR strategy development it is initially necessary to determine how the organisation itself perceives the importance of strategic planning. If the philosophy does not exist in an organisation, it will be difficult for the P/HR function to have a strategic focus. In this study three indicators of the extent of both formal strategy and of P/HR strategy development ("sophistication") were used: (i) incidence of a mission statement; (ii) incidence of a corporate strategy; and (iii) incidence of a personnel/human resources strategy. The study findings on these dimensions are outlined in Table 2.11.

Table 2.11: Strategy Development in Irish Organisations

	Written		Unwritten		None		Don't know		N	
	1995	1992	1995	1992	1995	1992	1995	1992	1995	1992
Mission statement	74%	57%	5%	10%	21%	30%	0.8%	3.4%	254	207
Corporate strategy	73%	56%	15%	26%	11%	15%	1.5%	3.3%	254	210
P/HR strategy	42%	38%	28%	33%	30%	28%	0.8%	1.4%	252	207

Source: Cranfield/University of Limerick Survey, 1995.

It is clear from Table 2.11 that the vast majority of organisations view it as necessary to have a written mission statement (74 per cent) and corporate strategy (73 per cent). These figures show a substantial increase since 1992. The fact that the increase has taken place in written rather than unwritten mission statements and corporate strategies indicates a trend towards more formalised approaches to strategy formulation.

As might be expected, the extent of formal P/HR strategy development is somewhat lower. Nevertheless, it is significant that over two-thirds of the organisations studied had some form of P/HR strategy and that 40 per cent documented this in written form. These findings indicate a 4 per cent increase in the number of organisations reporting a written P/HR strategy since the last (1992) study. This increase seems to have occurred mainly in organisations that in 1992 reported having an unwritten P/HR strategy. Although the increase is not substantial, it may indeed represent a move towards a more proactive, long-term focus within HRM. Further longitudinal studies are necessary to confirm this trend.

In evaluating the strategic role of HRM, it is useful to consider the impact of size and company ownership on the extent of formal strategy development. The impact of size is outlined in Table 2.12. It is clear that larger organisations are far more likely to engage in formal strategy development. Smaller organisations, on the other hand, adopt a less formal approach, being more likely to have unwritten strategies, or none at all. Looking at the impact of country of ownership, we find that the extent of formal strategy development is highest in US-owned organisations, with almost all such organisations having a mission statement (98 per cent) and corporate strategy (97 per cent) (see Table 2.13). This finding is in line with previous studies on strategy development in US companies (see, for example, Gunnigle et al., 1994; Gunnigle and Morley, 1997). The level of P/HR strategy development is also quite high with almost 60 per cent of US-owned organisations

Table 2.12: Size as a Determinant of Formal Strategy Development

	Mission statement		Corporate strategy		P/HR strategy	
	Written	Unwritten	Written	Unwritten	Written	Unwritten
50–199	65% (69)	8% (9)	65% (69)	20% (21)	30% (31)	27% (28)
200+	81% (113)	3% (4)	79% (111)	11% (16)	50% (70)	29% (41)
	n=140		n=140		n=141	

Source: Cranfield/University of Limerick Survey, 1995.

Table 2.13: Ownership as a Determinant of Formal Strategy Development

	Mission statement		Corporate strategy		P/HR strategy	
	Written	Unwritten	Written	Unwritten	Written	Unwritten
Ireland	67% (72)	7% (7)	65% (70)	19% (21)	32% (35)	28% (30)
US	94% (58)	5% (3)	89% (54)	8% (5)	58% (35)	16% (10)
UK	79% (15)	0%	89% (16)	6% (1)	61% (11)	28% (5)
EU	61% (17)	4% (1)	68% (19)	7% (2)	36% (10)	36% (10)
Japan/ Other	69% (9)	0%	67% (10)	33% (5)	39% (5)	39% (5)
	n=230		n=230		n=228	

Source: Cranfield/University of Limerick Survey, 1995.

having written strategies. The level of formal strategy development in British-owned organisations was also quite high and particularly so in relation to P/HR strategy development with some 90 per cent of British organisations having P/HR strategy in either written or unwritten form. Indigenous Irish organisations and those originating in other EU countries have relatively lower levels of P/HR strategy development.

Role of the P/HR Function in Strategy Development

Having established the priority attached to the development of a strategic focus in organisations in Ireland, it is appropriate to examine the role which P/HR function plays in strategy formulation. This is a useful indicator of the influence of HRM considerations on strategic decision-making.

Figure 2.6 summarises the study findings on the extent of perceived involvement of the P/HR function in the formulation of strategy in respondent organisations. These results indicate quite a positive picture of strategic involvement: more than half (55 per cent) of the respondents report that they are involved in strategy formulation "from the outset". This figure represents an increase of (4 per cent) since the 1992 study. Furthermore, 83 per cent of

Figure 2.6: Involvement of P/HR in Strategy Development

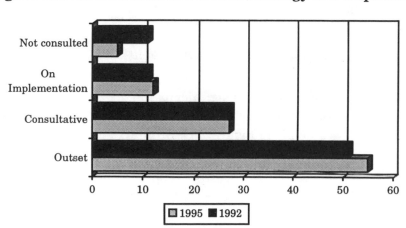

Source: Cranfield/University of Limerick Survey, 1995.

respondents reported their involvement in strategy formulation either "from the outset" or on a "consultative basis". Only 5 per cent of respondents felt that they had no involvement in strategy formulation.

When we tested for the influence of ownership we found that the level of involvement of the P/HR function in strategy formulation *from the outset* was lower in Irish-owned organisations (see Table 2.14). However, as previously mentioned there has been a slight increase in such involvement since 1992. This may indicate a greater awareness of the contribution of HRM in the strategic process. Aggregating the figures to incorporate P/HR involvement on a *consultative* basis provides further support for this contention: 84 per cent of Irish-, 85 per cent of US- and 87 per cent of UK-owned companies report P/HR involvement either from the outset or on a consultative basis.

Table 2.14: Ownership as a Determinant of Personnel Involvement in Strategy Formulation

	Ireland	UK	US	Other EU	Japan/ Other
From the outset	52% (49)	67% (12)	63% (35)	52% (11)	53% (8)
Consultative	32% (30)	22% (4)	20% (11)	19% (4)	20% (3)
Implementation	10% (9)	11% (2)	14% (8)	19% (4)	20% (3)
Not consulted	6% (6)	0%	4% (2)	10% (2)	7% (1)

n=204

Source: Cranfield/University of Limerick Survey, 1995.

Size does not seem to have a significant impact on the level of involvement of the P/HR function in strategy formulation in the organisations studied (see Figure 2.7). Similarly, as in 1992, sector also had little influence.

Figure 2.7: Size as a Determinant of Personnel Involvement in Strategy Formulation

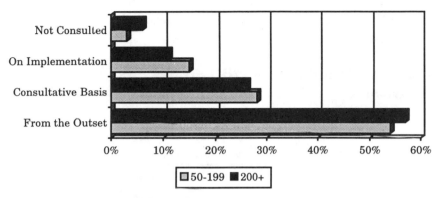

Source: Cranfield/University of Limerick Survey, 1995.

Translation of P/HR Strategy into Work Programmes

While the existence of a formal P/HR strategy is a useful indicator of both the nature of HRM in organisations and of the role of the specialist P/HR function, it is necessary to evaluate the extent to which such strategies impact on the operational role of the personnel function. For example, it may be that strategies are largely aspirational and have little impact on the day-to-day role of the P/HR function. In this study respondents were asked to evaluate the extent to which their organisation's P/HR strategy was translated into work programmes and guidelines for the personnel function. The findings on this issue are summarised in Table 2.15 and indicate little change since 1992. They do, however, indicate a contrast between strategy formulation and strategy implementation as it applies to the P/HR function: it appears that while there is a heavy emphasis on strategy formulation this does not result in a commensurately heavy emphasis on strategy implementation as measured by the extent of translation of P/HR strategies into operational work programmes and guidelines for the P/HR function. This trend may reflect traditional difficulties in quantifying personnel objectives and strategies. For example, issues such as employee commitment and morale are clearly important areas of focus for the P/HR function, but are not easily translated into performance targets against which the function can be evaluated. This area raises a number of process issues related to the actual conduct of HRM within organisations which cannot be adequately addressed through a quantitative survey of this nature but, rather, require more detailed case-study-based investigation.

Table 2.15: Translation of P/HR Strategy into Work Programmes for the Personnel Function

	1992	1995
Yes	66% (107)	67% (119)
No	34% (56)	34% (60)
	n=163	n=179

Source: Cranfield/University of Limerick Survey, 1995.

Turning to possible explanatory factors, we find that organisation size seems to be a very strong defining factor in influencing the extent to which P/HR strategies are translated into work programmes and guidelines for the P/HR function (see Figure 2.8). Over 80 per cent of large organisations responded positively on this dimension, in comparison to 42 per cent of smaller organisations. It appears that larger organisations require more explicit accountability in the HRM sphere than their smaller counterparts.

Figure 2.8: Size as a Determinant of whether Strategy is Translated into Work Programmes

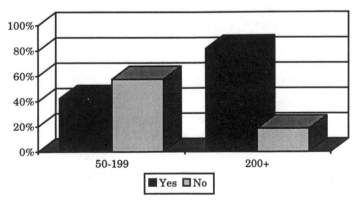

Source: Cranfield/University of Limerick Survey, 1995.

Systematic Evaluation of the P/HR Function

A related question is the extent of systematic evaluation of the role of the P/HR function in organisations in Ireland. Findings on this issue are outlined in Table 2.16 and indicate that less than half of the organisations studied evaluated their personnel department's performance on a systematic basis. This figure is quite low and indicative of the absence of a systematic, quantitative orientation towards evaluating the organisational contribution and role of the P/HR function. However, the figures indicate that the extent of systematic evaluation has increased since the last study in 1992.

Table 2.16: Performance of the P/HR Function Systematically Evaluated

	1992	1995
Yes	34% (63)	42% (91)
No	63% (117)	56% (121)
Don't know	4% (7)	2% (4)
	n=187	n=216

Source: Cranfield/University of Limerick Survey, 1995.

Again, organisation size emerges as an important explanatory variable. As indicated in Figure 2.9, a greater proportion of large organisations (50 per cent, compared with 28 per cent of small organisations) evaluate the performance of their P/HR function on a systematic basis.

Figure 2.9: Size as a Determinant of the Systematic Evaluation of the P/HR Function

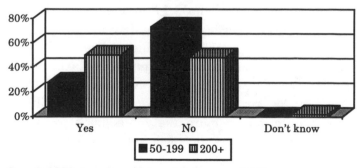

Source: Cranfield/University of Limerick Survey, 1995.

Looking at the impact of country of ownership, we find that Japanese/other-, Irish- and Continental European-owned organisations rate exceptionally poorly as regards the systematic evaluation of their personnel departments (see Figure 2.10). US-owned organisations have the highest level of systematic evaluation of the P/HR function (67 per cent), while some 56 per cent of UK-owned organisations engage in such evaluation.

Figure 2.10: Systematic Evaluation of the P/HR Function and Country of Ownership

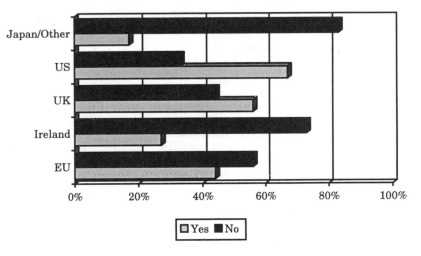

Source: Cranfield/University of Limerick Survey, 1995.

In considering those organisations which systematically assess their P/HR function, it is instructive to consider the criteria against which the work of the P/HR function is evaluated. These findings are outlined in Table 2.17 and indicate that the most popular criteria are (i) performance against objectives and (ii) performance against budget. This finding indicates the increasing importance of quantitative measurement methods among those organisations which systematically evaluate the work of their P/HR function. We also find that as organisation size increases, all methods of evaluation are more likely to be used, particularly performance against budget and objectives, and feedback from line management.

Table 2.17: Criteria on which P/HR Function is Evaluated

	1995	*1992*
No. of employees per personnel staff member	11% (28)	8% (17)
Cost of personnel function per employee	8% (21)	8% (17)
Numbers recruited	19% (49)	10% (23)
Numbers trained	20% (53)	15% (34)
Performance against budget	28% (72)	25% (56)
Performance against objectives	33% (87)	27% (61)
Feedback from line management	25% (64)	20% (46)
Other	6% (15)	5% (11)

Source: Cranfield/University of Limerick Survey, 1995.

To summarise, the findings on the role and profile of the specialist personnel function in Irish organisations are, in general, very positive. A greater number of organisations than in 1992 report having a personnel department and the findings also indicate quite a degree of specialisation within the function, an issue further discussed in the next section of this chapter. In addition, the profile of the personnel practitioner in Irish organisations is one of a highly educated and experienced individual. The findings also seem to indicate the development of a greater strategic focus within Irish organisations, particularly within large organisations and those with their headquarters in the US and the UK. A substantially higher number of respondents reported having a written mission statement and corporate strategy, with a slight (4 per cent) increase in the existence of written P/HR strategies. The presence of P/HR practitioners at board-level has also increased since 1992, with the extent of participation of the P/HR function in overall strategy formulation, particularly from the outset, increasing significantly. However, there has been little change in the area of strategy implementation in the past three years.

There does seem to be an increasing awareness of the importance of bottom-line indicators of the efficiency of the personnel department with an increase in the level of evaluation of the function. However, this figure is still quite low and may only be indicative of an emerging trend.

PERSONNEL POLICIES IN ORGANISATIONS AND THE ROLE OF LINE MANAGEMENT

To effectively gauge the nature of human resource management in organisations, it is of course necessary to look beyond the role of the specialist personnel function. Indeed many commentators suggest that the most important locus of HRM responsibilities are at top-management and line-management level (see, for example, Beer et al., 1984; Paauwe, 1996). This section initially considers the extent and nature of P/HR policy formulation in the organisations studied. It then looks at the role of line management in human resource management, paying particular attention to the division of HRM responsibilities between line management and the specialist P/HR function.

Formulation of Personnel/Human Resource Policy

An important indicator of P/HR policy sophistication in organisations is the incidence of policies covering the standard areas of HR activity such as pay, recruitment and training. Table 2.18 summarises the key findings in relation to the incidence of formal HRM policies in respondent organisations. These figures indicate that the great majority of organisations have either written or unwritten policies in most key activity areas of HRM. As might be expected, size emerges as an important explanatory factor with large organisations more likely to have written policies in all areas.

Table 2.18: P/HR Policy Formulation

	Written Policy	Unwritten Policy	No Policy	Don't know / Missing
Pay and benefits	63% (163)	28% (73)	8% (21)	1.5% (4)
Training and development	69% (179)	23% (61)	8% (20)	0.4% (1)
Recruitment and selection	55% (144)	33% (87)	11% (29)	0.4% (1)
Communications	42% (109)	34% (88)	22% (58)	2% (6)
Equal opportunity	48% (124)	30% (77)	22% (56)	1.5% (4)
People Management philosophy	32% (84)	30% (77)	34% (89)	4% (11)
High fliers	13% (34)	16% (42)	58% (151)	13% (34)

n=261

Source: Cranfield/University of Limerick Survey, 1995.

In addition to the extent of policy sophistication, a particularly interesting issue is the locus of policy determination. This is particularly significant in Ireland given the extensive presence of foreign-owned organisations. In this study respondents were asked to indicate whether their P/HR policies were developed at (i) International head-quarters (HQ); (ii) National HQ; (iii) Subsidiary; or (iv) Establishment level. The findings are presented in Table 2.19 and identify establishment level as the most important area of policy determination with national head office the second most important location. Since 1992, there has been a general increase in the international headquarters input into P/HR policy in all of the main areas. This may indicate that multi-national organisations wish to retain some control in ensuring that the overall corporate culture and philosophy is being maintained. The level of policy determination at national headquarters and subsidiary service departments have both decreased, while the level of policy determination at establishment level has increased.

Table 2.19: Location of Policy Determination

	Internat-ional HQ		National HQ		Subsidiary service dept.		Establishment local offices		N	
	1995	1992	1995	1992	1995	1992	1995	1992	'95	'92
Pay and benefits	22%	14%	39%	49%	10%	10%	29%	27%	165	148
Recruitment	7%	4%	39%	37%	10%	18%	44%	42%	165	148
Training	8%	4%	32%	32%	13%	22%	48%	42%	165	148
Industrial Relations	4%	3%	39%	41%	12%	14%	46%	42%	163	147
Health & Safety	13%	2%	33%	37%	13%	17%	41%	44%	165	148
Workforce adjustment	30%	16%	37%	38%	10%	13%	23%	32%	164	147

Source: Cranfield/University of Limerick Survey, 1995.

A general trend which emerges is that indigenous and European organisations (particularly UK organisations) are more likely to formulate policy areas at national level, whereas US organisations while retaining a certain amount of control at an international level, are more likely to delegate responsibility to the establishment level. The areas where US organisations are most likely to make decisions at international level are workforce adjustment, pay and health and safety. This is again indicative of the point mentioned earlier: that multinational organisations may modify policies and practices in order to conform with the culture and norms of the country in which they operate, but still seek to retain critical elements of their overall corporate culture/ philosophy.

Line Management Involvement in HRM

An important component of the HRM literature over the past decade is the devolution of greater HR responsibilities from the P/HR function to line management. This section considers the division of HR policy responsibilities between line management and the P/HR function.

The first issue which this study considered was the locus of responsibility for policy decisions in key areas of HRM. Specifically, respondents were asked to identify the division of responsibility between line management and the P/HR department. The findings are outlined in Table 2.20. Since the 1992 study, we find a slight movement towards greater line management responsibility

Table 2.20: Primary Responsibility for Major Policy Decisions

	Line mgt		Line mgt with P/HR Dept		P/HR Dept with line mgt		P/HR Dept		N	
	1995	1992	1995	1992	1995	1992	1995	1992	1995	1992
Pay and Benefits	18%	19%	12%	15%	38%	33%	32%	34%	235	209
Recruitment	18%	22%	26%	26%	41%	38%	14%	14%	251	212
Training	18%	18%	26%	21%	46%	49%	10%	12%	252	212
Industrial Relations	16%	18%	19%	20%	42%	39%	23%	23%	249	213
Health & Safety	24%	24%	24%	22%	37%	39%	16%	15%	249	215
Workforce adjustment	20%	24%	32%	28%	34%	36%	13%	13%	250	213

Source: Cranfield/University of Limerick Survey, 1995.

for policy decisions in areas of training and workforce adjustment. However, looking at the overall figures this trend is not significant. Only in the areas of pay and training has the specialist P/HR function reported a decrease in responsibility. The picture that emerges is, in effect, one of continuity rather than change: the specialist P/HR function *along with* line management has primary responsibility for policy decisions in most key areas of HR activity.

In considering the debate on the respective levels of involvement of line management and the specialist P/HR function in HRM, it is useful to consider whether respondents felt that line management's responsibility had increased or decreased in these areas over recent years. Findings on this dimension are outlined in Table 2.21. Again we see some shift in emphasis towards greater line management involvement. However, this is quite small and a high percentage of respondents indicated that levels of responsibility had remained the same (in some cases a greater number than in the last survey in 1992). Training, health and safety and recruitment are the main areas showing an increase.

Table 2.21: Changes in Line Management Responsibility

	Increased		*Same*		*Decreased*		*N*	
	1995	*1992*	*1995*	*1992*	*1995*	*1992*	*1995*	*1992*
Pay and Benefits	15%	14%	80%	81%	6%	5%	248	218
Recruitment	31%	27%	64%	67%	5%	6%	252	219
Training	44%	38%	51%	58%	4%	5%	252	221
Industrial Relations	24%	32%	70%	64%	6%	4%	248	216
Health & Safety	44%	53%	54%	43%	2%	4%	251	220
Workforce adjustment	23%	21%	73%	76%	5%	2%	247	217

Source: Cranfield/University of Limerick Survey, 1995.

Looking at potential explanatory factors, there appears to be a strong link between trade union recognition and the division of responsibilities between P/HR departments and line management. It seems that unionised organisations are giving more responsibility to line managers than has hitherto been the case, most particularly in the areas of industrial relations, workforce adjustment, training, and health and safety. While this is a clear trend among "unionised" organisations, the high percentage of respondents from non-union organisations who reported that there had been no change in line management responsibility may simply indicate that line management have always played a central role in personnel issues in those organisations. Of course, it may also be that line managers in such organisations play only a minor role in HRM matters.

A noteworthy issue emerging from Table 2.22 below is the change in line management responsibility for industrial relations. A considerable number of non-union organisations (12 per cent) reported that line management involvement in industrial relations had been reduced. On the other hand, the role of line

Table 2.22: Unionisation and Changes in Line Management Responsibility

	%	Union	Non-union	
Pay:	Increased	14	15	
	Same	81	76	
	Decreased	5	9	n=242
Recruitment:	Increased	31	31	
	Same	63	69	
	Decreased	6	–	n=246
Training:	Increased	46	36	
	Same	49	60	
	Decreased	5	4	n=246
Industrial Relations:	Increased	27	14	
	Same	68	74	
	Decreased	5	12	n=242
Health & Safety:	Increased	46	36	
	Same	52	62	
	Decreased	2	2	n=245
Workforce Adjustment:	Increased	25	14	
	Same	70	84	
	Decreased	5	2	n=241

Source: Cranfield/University of Limerick Survey, 1995.

managers in industrial relations in unionised organisations is becoming more important. This may be an indication that, in organisations which do not recognise trade unions, line managers
are concentrating on alternative personnel areas such as training.
In the unionised sector it may reflect a greater de-centralisation
of industrial relations responsibilities to the line, with line managers taking on more day-to-day industrial relations issues in an
effort to deal with them as close to the source as possible. It may
also reflect the capacity of union representatives to command
greater management attention to industrial relations issues.

There is a also a clear correlation between organisation size
and changes in the level of responsibility which line managers are
assuming in HRM, with larger organisations reporting extremely
high increases in line management responsibility (see Table 2.23).
This result corresponds very closely with the 1992 findings, which

Table 2.23: Organisation Size and Changes in Line Management Responsibility

	%	50–199	200+	
	Increased	10	19	
Pay:	Same	85	76	
	Decreased	5	6	n=241
	Increased	22	39	
Recruitment:	Same	74	57	
	Decreased	5	4	n=245
	Increased	35	52	
Training:	Same	60	44	
	Decreased	5	4	n=245
	Increased	15	32	
Industrial Relations:	Same	79	63	
	Decreased	6	6	n=241
	Increased	37	51	
Health & Safety:	Same	62	46	
	Decreased	1	3	n=244
	Increased	15	30	
Workforce Adjustment:	Same	81	66	
	Decreased	4	4	n=240

Source: Cranfield/University of Limerick Survey, 1995.

would indicate that larger organisations are placing much value on increasing line management participation. However, as mentioned previously in relation to trade union recognition, the fact that smaller organisations are not reporting such increases may be indicative of a generalist approach existing previously. Many smaller organisations do not have a specialist P/HR function, so line management may already have a high level of participation in HRM. This situation may explain the high percentage of respondents who report no change in the extent of line management responsibility.

In evaluating the impact of country of ownership, indigenous organisations do not seem to devolve HRM policy decisions to line management to the same extent as their foreign-owned counterparts (see Table 2.24). Indeed, Irish-owned organisations rate

Table 2.24: Country of Ownership and Changes in Line Management Responsibility

	%	EU	Ireland	US	UK	Japan/ Other	
Pay:	Increased	15	13	15	16	7	
	Same	78	80	79	84	93	
	Decreased	7	8	7	–	–	n=226
Recruitment:	Increased	52	23	34	37	27	
	Same	41	70	64	58	73	
	Decreased	7	7	2	5	–	n=229
Training:	Increased	63	41	41	47	47	
	Same	33	52	57	47	53	
	Decreased	4	7	2	5	–	n=229
Industrial Relations:	Increased	42	20	28	11	27	
	Same	46	75	69	83	60	
	Decreased	12	6	3	6	13	n=226
Health & Safety:	Increased	67	38	41	37	60	
	Same	33	59	56	63	40	
	Decreased	–	3	3	–	–	n=228
Workforce Adjustment:	Increased	30	24	22	21	13	
	Same	59	71	78	74	80	
	Decreased	11	5	–	5	7	n=224

Source: Cranfield/University of Limerick Survey, 1995.

poorly in delegating responsibility for HRM issues to line management, with training identified as the only area showing an increase comparable to foreign-owned organisations. This finding may partially reflect the impact of public sector organisations in Ireland which have traditionally been characterised by highly centralised decision-making structures. However, it also, most probably, reflects a highly centralised approach to management among Irish-owned organisations.

As clearly illustrated in Table 2.25, a greater proportion of public sector organisations report that there has been no change in line management responsibility in the areas of training, recruitment, pay and industrial relations. Health and safety is an area where both sectors report similarly high increases in line management responsibility, whereas in the area of workforce adjustment over 70 per cent of respondents from both sectors report no change.

Table 2.25: Sector and Changes in Line Management Responsibility

	%	Public	Private	
	Increased	11	16	
Pay:	Same	88	77	
	Decreased	2	7	n=246
	Increased	19	35	
Recruitment:	Same	76	61	
	Decreased	5	5	n=249
	Increased	36	47	
Training:	Same	62	48	
	Decreased	2	5	n=249
	Increased	21	25	
Industrial Relations:	Same	76	68	
	Decreased	3	7	n=245
	Increased	43	45	
Health & Safety:	Same	53	54	
	Decreased	3	2	n=248
Workforce Adjustment:	Increased	24	23	
	Same	71	73	
	Decreased	6	4	n=244

Source: Cranfield/University of Limerick Survey, 1995.

Overall, although there is evidence of greater line management involvement in HRM areas traditionally considered as the responsibility of the specialist P/HR function, the change that is taking place is not remarkable. While there are notable increases in line management responsibility in the areas of training, health and safety, and recruitment, respondents generally report high levels of stability. The picture which emerges is one where the specialist P/HR function, with line management, assumes responsibility for major policy decisions in the key HRM areas.

DATA COLLECTION IN PERSONNEL/HUMAN RESOURCE MANAGEMENT

Another useful indicator of the significance and nature of human resource management in organisations is the extent to which personnel/human resource data is systematically collected. For example, an increase in the number of organisations reporting systematic data collection particularly in the areas of absenteeism and staff turnover may be indicative of a greater preoccupation with determining the organisation's ability to successfully retain employees and is one of the principal elements of an effective human resource planning process (Bramham, 1989). Similarly, the collection of an extensive range of statistical data my indicate a strong quantitative, cost-measurement focus in HRM.

In this study participating organisations were asked to indicate the extent of systematic data collection in the following areas: (i) staff turnover; (ii) age profile; (iii) absenteeism. Some of the key findings on these aspects are outlined in Table 2.26. The findings indicate that absenteeism data is the most important area of focus among organisations. It is also the area of most change since our last study in 1992 with a major increase reported in the number of organisations collecting data on absenteeism (now 80 per cent of organisations). These findings indicate that absenteeism is a critical focus of attention in HRM in Ireland.

Looking at the extent of data collection on levels of staff turnover and age profiles, we find that the figures have more or less remained stable over recent years. However, the number of organisations who reported that they do not collect such data is quite high and has increased in some instances. This finding places a question mark over the capacity of many organisations to undertake "sophisticated" HR initiatives such as long term human resource and career planning.

As might be expected, larger organisations have a greater propensity to systematically collect data in these areas. This finding reflects the greater likelihood that, as organisations increase in size, they will adopt more formalised approaches to HRM and engage in formal human resource and succession planning.

Table 2.26: Data Collection on Staff Turnover, Age Structure and Absenteeism

	Yes		No		Don't know / missing		N	
	1995	1992	1995	1992	1995	1992	1995	1992
Staff turnover	62%	62%	31%	23%	7%	15%	261	228
Age structure	55%	52%	33%	29%	12%	19%	261	228
Absenteeism	80%	62%	17%	24%	4%	14%	261	228

Source: Cranfield/University of Limerick Survey, 1995.

To establish some insights into HRM practice this study also elicited information on actual levels of staff turnover and absenteeism as outlined in Tables 2.27a, b and c. Looking first at staff turnover we find a generally positive picture; some two-thirds of organisations report a staff turnover level of 5 per cent or less. The results

Table 2.27a: Staff Turnover in Irish Organisations

% Staff turnover	50–199	200+
2% or less	48%	37%
2.01–5%	13%	30%
5.01–10%	25%	22%
10.01–20%	13%	9%
20.01–30%	3%	0
>30%	0	2%

n=94

Source: Cranfield/University of Limerick Survey, 1995.

for absenteeism are even more positive, with over 80 per cent of organisations reporting absenteeism levels of 5 per cent or less. It appears that smaller organisations perform better in relation to turnover and (particularly) absenteeism: for example 57 per cent of smaller organisations have absenteeism rates of less than 3 per cent as compared with only 31 per cent of larger organisations.

Table 2.27b: Absenteeism in Irish Organisations

% Absenteeism	50–199	200+
2% or less	31%	9%
2.01–3%	27%	22%
3.01–4%	14%	37%
4.01–5%	10%	16%
5.01–10%	18%	15%
>10%	0	2%

n=117

Source: Cranfield/University of Limerick Survey, 1995.

Findings on the age profile of the organisations studied are outlined in Table 2.27c. While these figures are indicative of the relatively young age-profile of Irish organisations, the large number of missing organisations restricts our ability to generalise on the issue of age distribution. However, it again points to the widespread absence of an adequate statistical database to underpin comprehensive human resource management initiatives.

Table 2.27c: Age Profiles in Irish Organisations

Average age of organisation	
30 years or less	41% (38)
30–35 years	11% (10)
35–40 years	19% (17)
40–50 years	27% (25)
>50 years	2% (2)

n=92

Source: Cranfield/University of Limerick Survey, 1995.

In evaluating the findings in relation to data collection, the indications are that within a significant proportion of Irish organisations there is no systematic approach to the area. Although a relatively high number of organisations collect data on absenteeism, the situation in relation to age structure and staff turnover is not quite so positive. There seems to be no real change since 1992 in these areas, a factor which may arguably be seen as an indication of a lack of concern in relation to human resource, career and succession planning within Irish organisations. However, where data collection occurs there would seem to be very encouraging results with low levels of absenteeism and staff turnover.

CONCLUSION

The findings in this chapter on the presence of the P/HR function, the level at which it operates in the organisation, and it's main activity areas are generally very positive. The number of organisations with a specialist function have increased in the past three years, and although only 72 per cent of indigenous Irish organisations have a P/HR department this figure has increased from 59 per cent in 1992. There is a move towards greater line management involvement in personnel; however, this is most likely to be in conjunction with the specialist function. Despite this increased line management participation, the size of the P/HR function in respondent organisations is more likely to be expanding than contracting, with an average size of ten employees. Senior personnel practitioners are well-educated and highly experienced professionals, and over 50 per cent of respondents have a seat on the Board of Directors, indicating the high level at which the function operates. The overall trend is towards the greater strategic integration of personnel issues, with the P/HR practitioner operating in the higher echelons of the organisation, and increasingly involved in the formulation of strategy.

Chapter 3

RECRUITMENT AND SELECTION IN IRELAND

Noreen Heraty, Patrick Gunnigle & Noreen Clifford

INTRODUCTION

The way in which the employment relationship is structured and managed has been the focus of much of the recent literature on Human Resource Management (HRM). Plumbley (1985) suggests that the profitability and even the survival of an enterprise usually depends upon the calibre of the workforce, while Pettigrew et al. (1988) indicate that human resources represent a critical means of achieving competitiveness. Much of the recent literature on personnel management has emphasised the necessity for the recruitment and selection of employees who are committed to the goals of the organisation. Recent waves of organisational restructuring have dramatically changed and in many cases destroyed existing employment relationships. As traditional autocratic structures flatten and organisations utilise multi-disciplinary teams to remain competitive, the need for strategic and transparent systems becomes paramount. Today's organisation is being rapidly transformed from a structure built on functions and jobs, into a field of work where focused, self-directed work teams, made up of empowered individuals with diverse backgrounds, are replacing traditional specialised workers. Pfeffer (1994) argues that employees, and the way they work, comprise the crucial difference between successful and unsuccessful organisations and consequently firms need adaptable people who can adjust to rapidly changing customer needs and operational structures. He argues that as technology increases and product life-cycles shorten, the major source of competitive advantage will be the individual worker. Arguments such as these have led to Ripley and Ripley

(1994) suggesting that the critical organisational concern today is the hiring or promoting of the best qualified people while still meeting all regulatory requirements and the fairness and equality of opportunity to be selected.

The terms recruitment and selection refer to complimentary processes in employment. Recruitment is concerned with identifying requirements for new staff, and procuring a pool of appropriate applicants for these vacant job positions. The selection process is essentially concerned with assessing these applicants and engaging those that are deemed most suitable for employment. As such, the focus of recruitment and selection is on matching the capabilities and inclinations of prospective candidates against the demands and rewards inherent in a given job (Plumbley, 1985; Herriot, 1989). It has been argued that the recruitment and selection decisions are the most important of all decisions that managers have to make since they are a prerequisite to the development of an effective workforce, while the costs of ineffectual commercial viability can often be attributed to decades of ineffective recruitment and selection methods (McMahon, 1988; Plumbley, 1985; Smith and Robertson, 1993; Lewis, 1984). The costs of employing an individual can be examined from different perspectives. The first cost relates to the tangible costs of the process itself in terms of advertising, testing, interviewing and placement. The second cost is concerned with the employment contract itself and include such things as wages and attendant benefits, support services and training. The final cost is a potential cost and refers to the costs associated with making a poor selection decision in terms of poor productivity, low return on investment with a potential impact on general morale within the organisation.

In this chapter we reviews contemporary thinking on recruitment and selection and explore the nature of current recruitment and selection practices in Ireland.

THE PROCESS OF RECRUITMENT

Anderson and Shackleton (1986) indicate that the quality of new recruits depends upon an organisation's recruitment practices, and that the relative effectiveness of the selection phase is inherently dependent upon the calibre of candidates attracted. Indeed

Smith, Gregg and Andrews (1989) argue that the more effectively the recruitment stage is carried out the less important the actual selection process becomes. When an organisation makes the decision to fill an existing vacancy through recruitment, the first stage in the process involves conducting a comprehensive job analysis. This may already have been conducted through the human resource planning process, particularly where recruitment is a relatively frequent occurrence. Once a job analysis has been conducted, the organisation has a clear indication of the particular requirements of the job, where that job fits into the overall organisation structure, and can then begin the process of recruitment to attract suitable candidates for the particular vacancy.

Farnham and Pimlott (1995) suggest that one result of effective recruitment and selection is reduced labour turnover and good employee morale. Recruiting ineffectively is costly, since poor recruits may perform badly and/or leave their employment, thus requiring further recruitment. However, Wood (1985), in a cross-national study of recruitment practices, suggests that the reality of recruitment practices points to little or no attempt to validate practices. Personnel managers tend to rely on feedback from line managers and probationary periods and disciplinary procedures to weed out mistakes. Firms with high quit rates live with them and tend to build them into their recruitment practices — they do not analyse the constitution of their labour turnover.

A number of recent studies have suggested that some recruitment methods are more effective than others in terms of the value of the employees recruited. Cook (1993) indicates that while advertising is usual for job vacancies, applicants are sometimes recruited by word-of-mouth, through existing employees. Besides being cheaper, the "grapevine" finds employees who stay longer (low voluntary turnover) and who are less likely to be dismissed (low involuntary turnover) (Breaugh and Mann, 1984; Kirnan et al., 1989). People recruited by word-of-mouth stay longer because they have a clearer idea of what the job really involves. DeWitte (1989) reviewed five studies in which labour turnover of those recruited by advertising was 51 per cent. The labour turnover for spontaneous applicants was 37 per cent and turnover for applicants recommended by existing employees was 30 per cent. One hypothesis proposed to account for this was the "better information" hypothesis. It was argued that people who were suggested by other employees were better and more realistically informed about the job than those who applied through newspapers and agencies. Thus, they were in a better position to assess their own suitability. Better informed candidates are likely to have a more realistic view of the job, culture of the organisation and job prospects. In a survey by the Institute of Personnel Management (1980), 77 per cent of respondent companies recruited managers internally while the most common method of external recruitment was the local and national press. While internal recruitment can improve general morale and reduce training and associated costs, it may also deny the company access to new ideas and approaches and can allow complacency to set in.

RECRUITMENT PRACTICES IN IRELAND

The decision to expand the current workforce is inherently linked to the organisation's market performance. Of those organisations that responded to the Cranfield/University of Limerick Survey in 1995, 67 per cent indicated that demand for their products/ services had increased over the last three years. Furthermore, when asked to assess their overall performance in terms of gross revenue, 35 per cent indicated that performance was well in excess of costs, or sufficient to make a small profit (29 per cent). Taking these two results into account, it is not therefore unsurprising that organisations are more likely to have expanded their workforce, rather than reduced it, in the intervening time period (see Table 3.1).

Table 3.1: Change of more than 5 per cent in Workforce Size in past 3 years

Increased	Decreased	Same
50%	25%	25%

n=256

Source: Cranfield/University of Limerick Study, 1995.

While one quarter (25 per cent) of organisations surveyed indicated no change in organisation size, half of those surveyed indicated that they had, in fact, increased the size of their workforce over the past three years, which can, perhaps be attributed to the general upsurge being witnessed in the Irish economy over recent years. However, one-in-four of the organisations surveyed (24 per cent) reported that their workforce had decreased by more than 5 per cent in the same period suggesting perhaps that the general boom in the economy is not being experienced by all organisation types. Of those organisations that found it necessary to downsize their workforce, a variety of reduction methods were utilised (Table 3.2).

Table 3.2: Methods Used in Workforce Reduction

Recruitment freeze	13% (33)*
Natural wastage	16% (42)
Early retirement	15% (40)
Voluntary redundancy	19% (50)
Compulsory redundancy	7% (17)
Redeployment	5% (13)
Out placement	4% (10)
Other methods	2% (4)

*Actual numbers in parentheses

Source: Cranfield/University of Limerick Survey, 1995.

The data suggest that a combination of workforce reduction methods were utilised by organisations in an attempt to downsize their operations. It is interesting to note that just 7 per cent of such organisations found it necessary to introduce compulsory redundancy as a means of reducing their labour surplus. Voluntary redundancy policies were far more prevalent (19 per cent), while natural wastage (an expected level of labour turnover experienced by virtually all organisations), combined with a policy of non-recruitment and early retirement schemes appear to have worked for the greater proportion of the remaining organisations.

Policy Decisions on Recruitment and Selection

Increasingly, the management literature has suggested a growing tendency towards decentralisation and a concomitant shift towards greater devolvement of responsibility to line management. Nowhere has this been more evident than in the human resource literature (Lawler, 1986; Storey, 1992; Dobbs, 1993), which proposes that a transition is occurring where line managers are increasingly being awarded responsibility for policy decisions in a range of human resource activity areas. It has further been suggested that, as organisations become more strategic in the management of their human resources, we are likely to witness greater line involvement in a range of activities traditionally held to be the sole preserve of the specialist personnel/human resource function (Carroll, 1991; Kamoche, 1994; Storey, 1995). With this in mind, it becomes interesting to determine whether this theoretical imperative is being witnessed at the organisational level in the Irish context.

In order to understand the dynamics of the recruitment and selection process, respondents to the survey were first asked to indicate whether they had an explicit policy in relation to recruitment and selection. The results are quite positive since a total of 55 per cent of respondents reported that they had a written policy in relation to recruitment and selection, 33 per cent had an unwritten policy, and just 11 per cent had no policy at all. A further key area of interest here is a consideration of where decisions on such policy determination are taken. Table 3.3 presents some interesting comparisons (between the 1995 and 1992 data) on policy determination in the areas of recruitment and workforce adjustment generally.

Table 3.3: Location of Policy Determination

	Inter-national HQ		National HQ		Subsidiary		Establish-ment		N	
	1995	*1992*	*1995*	*1992*	*1995*	*1992*	*1995*	*1992*	*1995*	*1992*
Recruitment	7%	4%	39%	37%	10%	18%	44%	42%	165	148
Workforce Adjustment	30%	16%	37%	38%	10%	13%	23%	32%	164	147

Source: Cranfield/University of Limerick Surveys, 1992 and 1995.

The results above do not reveal any particular change since 1992 in the location of policy decisions on recruitment. Decision-making tends to be primarily centred at national HQ or establishment level, with some increase recorded at international HQ level. Interestingly, the only level that appears to have lost some responsibility for recruitment decisions appears to be that of the subsidiary. However, when one explores where policy decisions in relation to workforce adjustment are taken, a number of interesting changes can be detected. Here, international HQ appear to have considerably tightened their control over policies in this area over the three years — policy decisions in relation to adjustments to the workforce are now almost twice as likely to be taken at international HQ level than was the case in 1992 (30 per cent as against 16 per cent respectively). This increase in decision-making power at international HQ level appears to be to the cost of the establishment level which has suffered a decrease of 9 per cent in the same period. Taken together, the results on recruitment and workforce adjustment appear to suggest that, while organisations are largely free to establish specific policies in relation to their own recruitment needs, such decisions can be taken only within the broader ambit of policies relating to workforce adjustment, which are typically determined at either national or international HQ level.

If we take the decentralisation debate a step lower, it becomes necessary to look within the organisation to determine who has ultimate responsibility for developing policies in relation to recruitment and selection. Figure 3.1 outlines where primary responsibility for policy decisions on recruitment and selection lies.

The data here suggests that, for the most part, recruitment and selection is completed through a combination of the specialist personnel/human resource (P/HR) function and line management involvement. It is interesting to note, however, that just 18 per cent of respondents indicated that, in their organisation, line management is solely responsible for recruitment and selection policy decisions. This represents a decrease on the comparable figure for 1992, which was 25 per cent. However, the overall results do not indicate a general decrease in line involvement. When further comparisons are made with the 1992 results, one notes that there has been a concomitant increase in joint responsibility between P/HR and line management — an increase from 32 per cent in 1992 to 41 per cent in 1995.

Figure 3.1: Responsibility for Recruitment and Selection

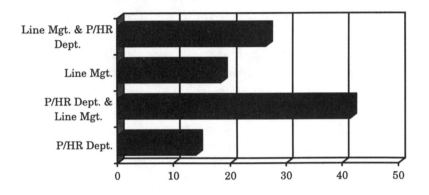

Source: Cranfield/University of Limerick Study, 1995

When the data is tested for variations linked with ownership, it would appear that, while the greater proportion of responding organisations report some increase in line responsibility for recruitment, Irish-owned organisations are the least likely to report such an increase. Thus while 23 per cent of Irish-owned organisations suggest that line management responsibility for recruitment has increased over the last three years, the comparable figures for EU-owned organisations is 52 per cent, for UK-owned organisations is 37 per cent and for US-owned organisations, 34 per cent. Furthermore, larger organisations are more likely to report increased line responsibility in this area (39 per cent) than are their smaller counterparts (22 per cent), while union status does not appear to have any impact on line involvement in recruitment decisions.

From the data presented here, it could be argued that line management responsibility in areas traditionally held to be the domain of P/HR specialists is becoming more pervasive than might traditionally have been the case. This is particularly true of larger, and non-Irish-owned organisations. However there is no evidence of complete devolvement to line managers and, given that the level of reported line management involvement, from an overall perspective, is not significantly different than it was three years ago, one can only suggest that the specialist HR function retains considerable input in, and responsibility for, recruitment and selection policy-making.

Recruitment Methods Utilised

Prior to a discussion of the various recruitment methods utilised by Irish-based organisations, it is useful to determine whether such organisations have actively introduced new strategies in relation to recruitment generally. In the survey respondents were asked to identify specific measures that had been introduced in order to aid them in the recruitment process, or in the retention of employees (see Table 3.4).

Table 3.4: Mechanisms Introduced for the Recruitment/ Retention of Employees

Relaxed qualification requirements	6%
Recruiting abroad	24%
Retraining	63%
Increased pay	35%
Relocation	3%
Marketing image	19%
Other	3%

n=261

Source: Cranfield/University of Limerick Survey, 1995.

While a variety of strategies are utilised by organisations to facilitate recruitment/retention, retraining is the most popular initiative (63 per cent). A total of 35 per cent of organisations felt it necessary to increase their pay/benefits package, while a further 24 per cent are actively seeking candidates from abroad. Relocation and relaxed qualifications have been introduced by very few organisations.

Various organisational characteristics are found to have some influence on the strategies employed by responding organisations. In terms of organisation size, larger organisations are more likely

to adopt a greater range of strategies than are their smaller counterparts. This is particularly so in terms of the use of those
strategies that require substantial resources, such as improving
the market image of the organisation, relocation, or increased pay
(Table 3.5).

**Table 3.5: Size as a Determinant of the Practices
Introduced to Aid Recruitment/Retention of Workers**

	Relaxed Qual.	*Recruit abroad*	*Re-training*	*Increase pay*	*Marketing image*
1–199	47%	29%	44%	38%	32%
>200	53%	71%	57%	62%	68%
	n=15	n=62	n=161	n=172	n=47

Source: Cranfield/University of Limerick Survey, 1995.

Organisation ownership is also found to have some influence on
the choice of strategy adopted, with US-owned organisations
emerging as the most likely to use increased pay or improve the
organisation's marketing image in order to aid in the recruit-
ment/retention of employees. Retraining appeared to be the strategy most favoured by Irish-owned organisations (57 per cent)
which may be linked to a general policy decision to build and
maintain a strong internal labour market.

Turning to the process of recruitment, the most immediate decision facing recruiters is whether to recruit internally from those
already employed by the organisation, or to source the external
labour market. The decision to access the internal labour market
brings with it a number of distinct advantages. It is cost-effective,
both in terms of eliminating the need for external advertising/
sourcing and also in terms of reducing the induction or settling in
period. It is also considered to be good personnel practice for, not
only may it be viewed as a positive motivator by current employees, but the quality of the internal labour market is continuously
upgraded and maintained through high quality recruitment, selection, promotion, career development and multiskilling. An examination of the data relating to recruitment practices indicates

that a broad spectrum of recruitment methods are being utilised to fill managerial vacancies (see Table 3.6).

Table 3.6: Usual Method of Filling Vacancies

	Senior Management	Middle Management	Junior Management
Internally	57%	75%	77%
Recruitment consultant	52%	38%	22%
National newspaper	47%	49%	37%
Professional magazine	12%	13%	5%
International newspaper	12%	7%	2%
Word-of-mouth	7%	10%	14%

n=261

Source: Cranfield/University of Limerick Study, 1995.

Here again the results point to a combination of recruitment methods being used by responding organisations to fill managerial positions. Utilising the internal labour market for recruitment purposes appears to be the most popular recruitment method at all managerial levels. However, some variation is evident between the different managerial levels where, for example, middle and junior management vacancies are more likely to be filled internally than are senior management positions. Furthermore, organisations report a greater tendency to utilise consultants for senior positions (52 per cent) than for middle management (38 per cent) or junior management (37 per cent) positions. These results are not unsurprising. Organisations have always displayed a preference for "growing" their own managerial expertise which is facilitated by an increased investment in management development programmes and management trainee schemes. However, the growing internationalisation of organisations and the heavy theoretical focus on top management team dynamics has focused increasing interest on the necessity for innovative, multi-experienced, dynamic senior management and so it is not altogether unexpected that organisations are unwilling to limit themselves to filling senior vacancies from within their organisation.

It is interesting here to note where the most senior P/HR manager is typically recruited from. In the present survey 36 per cent of respondents indicated that their most senior P/HR manager is a non-personnel specialist who has been recruited from within the organisation, while 34 per cent recruited their most senior personnel/HR manager as a specialist personnel practitioner from outside the organisation. Just 15 per cent of respondents indicated that their most senior P/HR manager was appointed from within their own personnel department. Interpretation of these results is necessarily cautious, because what is most interesting is the almost even breakdown between the recruitment of an external personnel specialist and the internal appointment of a non-specialist to what is considered a highly specialist senior position. However, if we are to adopt the top management thesis that calls for multi-disciplinary strategists at senior levels within the organisation, then the overall composition of the individual organisation's top management team might provide greater clarity in respect of these findings.

Perhaps the most commonly recognised recruitment method is the advertisement, at local or national level. Plumbley (1985) suggests that where advertising judgements are based on reliable and relevant factors, and where they are effectively communicated, external advertising serves as a powerful recruitment tool. In the current survey advertising at national level is common across all managerial grades, while targeted advertising at international level or in specialised magazines, although not that usual, is limited to more senior positions.

A positive correlation is found to exist between the frequency with which particular recruitment methods are used and the country of origin of the responding organisations. The most significant difference occurs between Irish-owned organisations and their US and EU counterparts, where, across managerial categories, Irish-owned organisations are seen to utilise their internal labour market to a lesser degree than do the foreign-owned companies surveyed (see Figure 3.2).

Figure 3.2: Ownership as a Determinant of the Use of Internal Labour Market Management Grades

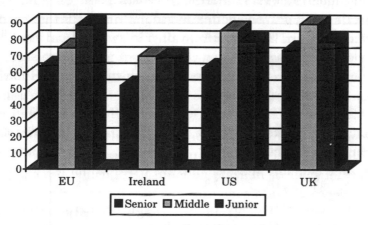

Source: Cranfield/University of Limerick Survey, 1995.

Data relating to the use of recruitment consultants reflect a similar trend (see Figure 3.3). US-owned organisations are more likely to use consultants in the recruitment process for all managerial grades, than are their European counterparts. Irish-owned

Figure 3.3: Ownership as a Determinant of the Use of a Recruitment Consultant

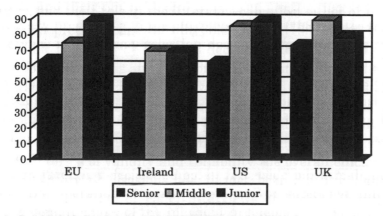

Source: Cranfield/University of Limerick Survey, 1995

companies, on the other hand, are the least likely to use a recruitment consultant, relying to a greater extent on external advertising, particularly in national newspapers. Higgins (1992) suggests that Irish-owned organisations discount the need for consultants except in cases where they wish to recruit from overseas or where they intend operating abroad.

These results are broadly consistent with the contention that multinational organisations operating in Ireland practice strong elements of HRM, one example of which is the development of internal labour markets through such techniques as progressive career planning, management development, and extensive communication and information sharing (see Gunnigle, 1992a and Murray, 1984).

When the data is analysed for organisation-size variations, a number of distinctions between the recruitment practices of larger and smaller organisations emerge. Table 3.7 provides a comparison of organisation size with three particular recruitment strategies.

Table 3.7: Size as a Determinant of Recruitment Method Utilised

	Internally			Recruitment consultant			National newspaper		
	Senior	Middle	Junior	Senior	Middle	Junior	Senior	Middle	Junior
50–199	54%	72%	70%	51%	33%	19%	42%	46%	30%
200+	60%	78%	82%	52%	43%	25%	53%	52%	42%

n=261

Source: Cranfield/University of Limerick Survey, 1995.

Larger organisations have a greater tendency to recruit internally, across all managerial grades, than do their smaller counterparts. This is not altogether unexpected since large organisations, by the fact of their size, have access to a larger pool of potentially suitable candidates. Smaller organisations utilise recruitment consultants to almost the same extent as larger organisations when recruiting for senior management posts, but marginally less so for lower managerial grades. Walton and Lawrence (1985) suggest that recruitment agencies are popular with smaller organisations, particularly where the personnel function is under-resourced and agencies are used to relieve the personnel department of an administrative burden. The picture in relation to national newspaper advertising suggests that both large and small organisations are more likely to advertise externally for more senior positions, than they are for junior management posts, but this trend is a little more evident is smaller concerns.

When the data is tested for variation associated with union presence, some differences again emerge (see Table 3.8).

Table 3.8: Unionisation as a Determinant of Recruitment Method Utilised

	Internally			Recruitment consultant			National newspaper		
	Senior	Middle	Junior	Senior	Middle	Junior	Senior	Middle	Junior
Union	56%	76%	79%	55%	38%	23%	50%	49%	38%
Non-union	64%	70%	64%	42%	40%	16%	36%	48%	30%

n=261

Source: Cranfield/University of Limerick Study, 1995.

In relation to internal recruitment, it appears that unionised organisations are typically more likely to recruit internally than are their non-union counterparts. Again, these results are not that unusual since union agreements often require that vacancies be advertised internally, while the existence of a structured internal labour market is also a particular feature of many unionised environments. What is interesting to note, however, is that, in a unionised environment, recruitment to senior management positions is less likely to be from within the organisation than is the case in non-unionised organisations (56 per cent as against 64 per cent respectively). Unionisation is clearly linked with the decision on whether to utilise the internal labour market with companies which recognise trade unions also more likely to recruit internally. The trend depicted in the 1995 data is inconsistent with results obtained in the 1992 survey when it was found that non-union respondents used current employees to fill vacancies at managerial and professional/technical levels to a greater degree than those that did recognise a trade union. It has often been recognised in recent employee relations literature that foreign-owned multinationals (which are increasingly non-unionised) are exerting considerable influence on the practices of more established firms (that are more likely to be unionised), and thus this strong focus on internal recruitment, by unionised organisations, might well be a reflection of this.

The survey data reveals a number of particular differences between the public and private sector with respect to their use of internal or external labour markets (see Table 3.9). Private sector respondents are far more likely to utilise the internal labour market for all managerial categories, than are their public sector counterparts. This is somewhat surprising since, traditionally, the public sector has been characterised by its heavy reliance on internal recruitment. In the current survey, just 39 per cent of respondents indicate that they recruit senior management posts internally — the corresponding figure for private sector organisations is 63 per cent. The use of recruitment consultants is significantly more likely in the private sector than in the public sector — across all managerial levels, private sector organisations are almost three times more likely than public sector organisations to employ the services of consultants. However, in relation to specific recruitment methods, it emerges that the use of recruitment agencies and search/selection consultants is more widespread in the private sector, across all categories of employees. These findings confirm those reported in the 1992 survey. When it comes to advertising at national level, it emerges that public sector organisations are the more frequent users of this particular recruitment strategy, across all managerial grades.

Table 3.9: Sector as a Determinant of Recruitment Method Utilised

	Internally			Recruitment consultant			National newspaper		
	Senior	*Middle*	*Junior*	*Senior*	*Middle*	*Junior*	*Senior*	*Middle*	*Junior*
Private	63%	79%	80%	61%	46%	26%	41%	48%	35%
Public	39%	63%	66%	22%	15%	9%	68%	54%	42%

n=261

Source: Cranfield/University of Limerick Survey, 1995.

From a broad perspective, then, it is suggested that, irrespective of particular organisation characteristics such as ownership, size, union status or sector, all organisations are making greater use of their internal labour markets when it comes to targeting prospective candidates to fill managerial vacancies. Higgins (1992) suggests that the filling of vacancies from current employees may increase employee commitment by giving staff an incentive to perform well and may serve to preserve the organisation culture where those recruited to new positions within the organisation are already familiar with the beliefs, attitudes and norms expected by the organisation. However, as indicated at the start of this chapter, recruitment is merely the first stage of a highly critical organisational process and the strategies employed by the organisation at the selection stage have a pivotal role to play in ensuring that the organisation remains competitive.

THE SELECTION DECISION

Smith and Robertson (1993) suggest that a company can be dragged to its knees by the weight of ineffective staff which decades of ineffectual selection methods have allowed to accumulate. While the calibre of candidate is determined by the value of the recruitment process, the selection decision remains a difficult one. Dale (1995) proposes that:

> most mistakes are caused by the fact that managers generally give little thought to the critical nature of the decisions. Employers are surprised and disappointed when an appointment fails, and often the person appointed is blamed rather than recognising the weaknesses in the process and methodology ... even the soundest of techniques and best practice (in selection) contain scope for error. Some of this is due to the methods themselves, but the main source is the frailty of the human decision-makers.

Selection tools available to organisations range from the more *traditional* methods of interviews, application forms and references, through to the more *sophisticated* techniques such as biographical data, aptitude tests, psychological testing and so forth. Each method of selection has its advantages and disadvantages and comparing their rival claims involves comparing each method's merit and psychometric properties. The degree to which a selection technique is perceived as effective is determined by its reliability and validity. Reliability is generally synonymous with consistency, while validity refers to what is being measured, and the extent to which those measurements are correct (Anastasi, 1982; Muchinsky, 1986). It is suggested that a good selection method should meet the following requirements: practical to utilise; sensitive in that it can distinguish between candidates; reliable in that it consistently comes up with the same answer; and valid, in that it measures what it is supposed to measure — the inferences that it makes about a person are correct.

Storey (1992) suggests that developments in the realm of selection lend some support to those who propound the HRM thesis, where a key feature has been the increase in testing designed explicitly to assess behavioural and attitudinal characteristics. He further indicates that the extent to which these more sophisticated and systematic approaches can be, and are, deployed, depends to a large degree on the sector circumstances and on the wider employment/management policies being pursued.

SELECTION PRACTICES IN IRELAND

The data generated by the Price Waterhouse Cranfield Project in 1992 indicated that relatively little use was being made, by Irish organisations, of what are considered the more "sophisticated" selection techniques. The picture emerging from the 1995 data confirms that finding, with the application form, the interview and reference checks continuing to remain the most commonly used selection methods in Ireland (see Table 3.10).

The *interview* continues to enjoy considerable popularity across all organisations; however, the data presented here might indicate a reduction in the traditional reliance on the interview. McMahon (1988), found that over 90 per cent of job categories in Ireland were filled with the assistance of an interview. In the present survey, however, just 41 per cent of respondents indicated that they make use of an interview panel for every position, while just 37 per cent suggested that a one-to-one interview was used for every appointment Over the years considerable research concerning

Table 3.10: Main Selection Methods Used

	Every appoint- ment	Most appoint- ments	Some appoint- ments	Few appoint- ments	Not used	
Interview panel	41%	28%	18%	6%	7%	n=235
One to one interview	37%	14%	23%	14%	12%	n=217
Application forms	59%	20%	12%	3%	6%	n=241
Aptitude tests	6%	13%	37%	15%	29%	n=201
Psychometric tests	4%	9%	27%	11%	49%	n=199
Assessment centre	2%	2%	9%	8%	79%	n=181
Graphology	0.6%	0.6%	4%	1%	94%	n=169
References	70%	22%	5%	1%	2%	n=230

Source: Cranfield/University of Limerick Survey, 1995.

both the validity and reliability of the selection interview have been undertaken, often with conflicting results (Anderson, 1992; Hunter and Hunter, 1984; Wiesner and Cronshaw, 1988). Any evaluation of the interview is complicated by the fact that it is a complex social event characterised by a dynamic relationship be-tween interviewer and interviewee where their perceptions of each other, and their role in the interview can affect either or both the interview processes and the outcomes. Rynes (1990) notes that the interview is a two-way selection decision where decisions are made by both candidates and their prospective employers and can thus be viewed as a recruitment device whereby expectations are set regarding the prospective future employment relationship (Herriot and Rothwell, 1981) and a psychological contract can be negotiated (Herriot, 1989). Anderson and Shackleton (1993) sug-gest that, in terms of validity and reliability, the overall efficiency of selection interview decisions has, in fact, been much maligned and that the operation of panel interviews or successive inter-views can obviate many of the inherent problems associated with interviewing and can facilitate greater validity and reliability in the final decision analysis. However rigorous the process, interviewing remains essentially a selective process and thus the interviewer needs to ensure, as far as possible, that errors or biases are eliminated from the process.

The reliability and validity of *application forms*, as a discrete selection tool have similarly been tested, and it is widely held that they are open to misinterpretation, particularly where applicants portray a false persona (Muchinsky, 1986). In the present survey, more than half of those who responded indicated that they utilise the application form for all appointments (59 per cent). Guest (1983) cautions that, in this age of increasing numbers of applicants per vacancy, pre-selection devices are becoming more and more of a necessity, hence the importance of designing application forms in an analytical manner.

References again feature as a popular tool in the selection process. Here 70 per cent of respondents make use of reference checks for all appointments which suggests continuing support for references as a key feature of the selection decision. In 1992, the PWCP found that 88 per cent of respondents used references as a selection device while Robertson and Makin (1986), in their UK study of best selection techniques, found that over 67 per cent of employers surveyed used references for all vacancies. As with many of the more popular and "traditional" selection tools, the validity and reliability of references has been questioned, particularly with respect to their unstructured and often ambivalent nature, and it has been shown that referees who "like" a candidate tend to write longer and more complimentary references (Reilly and Chao, 1982; Dobson, 1989).

Many commentators have supported the use of *assessment centres* and *psychometric testing* as consistently valid behaviour predictors which are ideally suited as a pre-selection device (see for example, Muchinsky, 1986; Hunter and Hunter, 1984; Smith, Gregg and Andrews, 1989). The use of these more sophisticated techniques is reported to be low both in Ireland (McMahon, 1988) and in the UK (Robertson and Makin, 1986). However, there is evidence to suggest that testing, in particular, is becoming more widespread in the US (Anderson and Shackleton, 1986), and therefore linked, perhaps, to the HRM thesis which is widely held to have originated in the US. Again, the figures presented in Table

3.10 above suggest that these more sophisticated techniques are not used to any great extent in Ireland at present.

Further analysis of the data reveals a number of interesting variances with respect to selection techniques used by particular organisation types. Thus, while *panel interviews* are popular across all organisations irrespective of ownership, unionised organisations are twice as likely to use panel interviews for all appointments than are non-union companies (45 per cent as against 21 per cent respectively). Larger organisations are also more likely to use panel interviews for all appointments (45 per cent) than are smaller concerns (35 per cent). More disparate results are evident when one analyses the use made of *one-to-one interviews*. Here, it appears that US-owned organisations are more than twice as likely to use this interview form than Irish-owned organisations. Thus 58 per cent of US-owned companies utilise the one-to-one interview for every appointment, while just 26 per cent of Irish-owned organisations use this interview type. The comparable figure for EU-owned organisations is 29 per cent. Again, as is the case with panel interview utilisation, unionised organisations indicate a far greater propensity to make use of the one-to-one interview than do non-unionised companies (61 per cent and 31 per cent respectively). However, smaller organisations record a slightly higher utilisation of this interview form than do their larger counterparts (41 per cent as against 34 per cent). Taken together, the data reported here suggests that the interview retains a central role in the selection decision. However, it is probable to suggest that organisations are, in fact, utilising both the panel interview and the one-to-one interview as a means of determining suitability, rather than relying solely on one meeting with job candidates. This can be seen to be a positive approach to selection since there is a greater likelihood that many of the inherent problems of interviewing will be obviated by having more individuals involved, and a greater number of stages in the process.

The use of *application forms* was earlier reported to be popular in Irish-based organisations. When their utilisation was analysed against various organisational characteristics, a number of pertinent differences emerge, particularly with respect to organisation ownership. The results revealed that Irish-owned organisations are,

in fact, the least likely of all organisations surveyed to use application forms for all appointments. Thus, while just 50 per cent of
Irish-owned organisations use application forms for all positions,
the corresponding utilisation for EU-owned companies is 60 per
cent, for US-owned organisations is 74 per cent and for non-EU responding organisations is highest at 80 per cent. Here again, the
data is suggesting some change has occurred since 1992 when the
use of application forms was found to be almost as high among
Irish-owned organisations as it was in foreign-owned companies. In
1992 87 per cent of Irish-owned respondents regularly utilised the
application form, 91 per cent of EU- and non-EU-owned companies
and 98 per cent of US-owned organisations did likewise. In the
1995 data, organisation size does not appear to have any impact on
level of usage, but unionised organisations are found to use application forms more frequently than do the non-unionised companies
surveyed (62 per cent as against 51 per cent respectively).

Turning to the use of *references* as a selection tool, one can
again detect a number of differences emerging with respect to
various organisation types. Here again one might be surprised to
note that Irish-owned organisations report the lowest frequency of
usage of the reference check than do any of their foreign-owned
counterparts. In fact, US-owned organisations indicate the highest level of usage (83 per cent) of the reference for all appointments, followed by other non-EU-owned companies (73 per cent),
and UK-owned concerns (73 per cent). The corresponding figure
for Irish-owned organisations is 59 per cent. Interestingly, just four
organisations indicated that they do not use reference checks at all
— all four are Irish-owned companies. When these results are compared with those reported in 1992, it would appear that Irish-
owned organisations are more likely to have reduced their reliance
on the reference check than are their counterparts (use of references in 1992 for Irish-owned companies was 88 per cent, for EU-
owned firms was 93 per cent, and for US-owned organisations was
98 per cent). In the present study the use of references is reported
to be marginally higher in larger organisations as compared with
smaller companies (76 per cent and 68 per cent respectively), but
union status does not appear to be a determining factor.

Turning to the use of what were described earlier as more "sophisticated" selection techniques it would appear that Irish-owned organisations display a lesser tendency to utilise such selection techniques than do non-Irish-owned organisations. A total of 36 per cent of Irish-owned companies do not utilise *aptitude tests* at all while the comparable figure for US-owned companies is 27 per cent, and for EU-owned companies is 22 per cent. When the data is compared with the 1992 survey results, however, it emerges that Irish-owned companies may, in fact, have increased their utilisation of aptitude tests since, in 1992, just 31 per cent of Irish-owned organisations reported that they used aptitude tests on a regular basis. As expected, larger-owned companies report a slightly greater propensity to use aptitude tests, while union status does not appear to have any discernible impact on aptitude testing.

The use of *psychometric testing* is reportedly low in most organisations surveyed, but again, it appears that Irish-owned organisations are the least likely to use this selection technique. Here, 58 per cent of Irish-owned organisations do not use psychometric tests while the comparator for US-owned organisations is 44 per cent, for EU firms is 43 per cent and for non-EU companies is 46 per cent. The data here supports the earlier findings in 1992 where Irish-owned organisations were far less likely to use psychometric testing than were their foreign-owned counterparts (just 14 per cent of Irish-owned companies used psychometric tests in 1992 compared with 37 per cent of US companies, 46 per cent of UK organisations and 46 per cent of non-EU-owned organisations). However, even though the use of psychometric testing is not that popular, the data here suggests that its use is becoming more widespread than was the case in 1992. While union status does not appear to affect the decision to utilise psychometric tests, their use tends to be more widespread in larger organisations (42 per cent of large organisations do not use such tests while the comparative figure for small organisations is 61 per cent).

The reported use of *assessment centres* as a selection device was reported low in the 1992 survey, and this appears to have continued in the intervening three years to 1995. Just 13 per cent of Irish-owned organisations report that they use assessment centres and, while this figure shows an increase on the 1992 figure of 4 per cent, assessment centres do not appear to be given serious consideration when making the selection decision. EU-owned organisations report a higher increased use of assessment centres than do any other ownership category which again is consistent with data reported in 1992, but this usage tends to be targeted at specific appointments rather than as a systematic assessment mechanism. This is not altogether unsurprising since the costs associated with assessment centres can often limit their application to certain job categories. No significant differences emerge with respect to union status or organisation size.

It would appear, then, that the traditional selection methods continue to be popular among most of the organisations surveyed but the data does suggest that organisations are slightly more disposed towards varying the selection techniques available to them, than was the case in 1992. For most organisations this is inherently linked to the job category involved and so it could be argued that sophisticated selection techniques are used on a piecemeal, incremental basis, rather than as the norm for all job vacancies.

MONITORING OF SPECIFIC GROUPS IN THE EMPLOYMENT RELATIONSHIP

The final section of this chapter focuses on whether organisations adopt any particular recruitment policies in relation to what are often termed "minority groups" within the labour market. In the survey, we were particularly concerned with policies targeted specifically at the employment of women, older workers and those with disabilities. Sparrow and Hiltrop (1994) argue that a series of social and demographic pressures, such as rising levels of unemployment (particularly of those in long-term unemployment), declining birth rates, ageing workforce and the increased propensity for female participation in the labour force, are combining to force organisations to rethink many of their HRM policies and strategies. While discrimination on the basis of gender is prohibited across the EU, recent studies by the International Labour Organisation (ILO) estimates that women will not reach equal representation in management jobs until the twenty-fifth century. Currently, the female participation rate for the EU stands at approximately 50 per cent (irrespective of the nature of this employment) although there is considerable variation on this figure across European countries (in Ireland, female participation rates are just under 40 per cent). Female participation rates in the US are estimated to be about 60 per cent. However, currently there is no explicit provision in relation to discrimination in employment on the basis of age in the EU but, given the likely demographic profile over the next number of years, it is expected that "ageism" is an issue that organisations will have to consider and make provision for sooner, if not later.

In the survey, organisations were asked whether they consciously monitored the proportion of women, people with disabilities, or ethnic minorities when it came to recruitment/ training/promotions (see Table 3.11).

Table 3.11: Monitoring of Specific Minority Groups in the Employment Relationship

	Recruitment		Training		Promotion		Don't know	
	1995	1992	1995	1992	1995	1992	1995	1992
Disabled	27%	21%	17%	9%	12%	6%	27%	23%
Women	36%	29%	26%	21%	34%	24%	21%	21%
Ethnic minorities	5%	2%	3%	1%	4%	0.4%	31%	27%

n=261

Source: Cranfield/University of Limerick Survey, 1992 and 1995.

The data suggests that, with respect to recruitment, women are the most likely employee category to be monitored by organisations (36 per cent), followed by those with disabilities (27 per cent). These figures indicate a small increase on 1992 data, but not significantly so. Given the national cultural profile, it is not surprising that ethnic minorities are monitored by just a small number of organisations. When the data is tested for variations according to organisation type, it emerges that some 18 per cent more of public than private sector organisations are likely to monitor women in relation to recruitment. The existence of a trade union also appears to be somewhat significant with unionised organisations more likely to monitor the number of women they employ.

Turning to the issue of targeted recruitment policies, respondents were asked to indicate, from a pre-determined list, those categories that they actively targeted in their recruitment process. Table 3.12 presents the results and compares them against data collected in 1992.

Table 3.12: Specific Sectors of the Workforce Targeted in Recruitment

	1995	1992
Long-term unemployed	9%	6%
People over 50	3%	9%
Disabled	11%	7%
Ethnic minorities	1%	0.4%
Women	21%	19%
School leavers	23%	31%
University graduates	51%	—
Women returners	12%	—
	n=261	n=228

Source: Cranfield/University of Limerick Survey, 1992 and 1995

Not unsurprisingly, university graduates are the most likely group to be targeted during recruitment. Over one-third of all school leavers in Ireland are likely to complete a third-level qualification and it is the existence of this highly qualified labour pool that has been instrumental in attracting so much foreign investment to Ireland in recent years. Given this continuing trend to acquire further qualifications, and the traditional high levels of unemployment, organisations may be moving from the traditional "milk rounds" in favour of university graduates, thus providing some explanation for the fall-off in school-leaver targeting (down 8 per cent since 1992). Women generally continue to be targeted by some 21 per cent of responding organisations, a marginal increase of 2 per cent on 1992 figures, while women who are returning to the workforce are also focused on by 12 per cent of organisations. This new focus on women returners may be linked to the New Opportunities for Women (NOW) initiative, launched in the early 1990s which was designed to promote and support the return, by women, to active participation in the labour force.

The long-term unemployed are only marginally more likely to be targeted now than was the case in 1992, while those over the age of 50 are now even less likely to be targeted for recruitment — suggesting that some form of "ageism" has indeed entered the equation in Ireland. When organisations were specifically asked whether there has been a change in the number of older recruits over the three-year period 1992–1995, the picture that emerges is one of considerable stability. Interestingly, however, 37 per cent of respondents indicated that they have an active policy of not recruiting individuals over the age of 50 years (see Table 3.13).

Table 3.13: Change in the Number of Older Recruits in the past 10 years

Increased	8%
Decreased	7%
Same	43%
Don't know	5%
Don't recruit over-50s	37%

n=247

Source: Cranfield/University of Limerick Survey, 1995

When the data is tested for variation in organisation size (Table 3.14), it would appear that smaller companies are, in fact, less likely than their larger counterparts to recruit individuals over the age of 50 years (44 per cent and 31 per cent respectively).

Table 3.14: Size as a Determinant of Changes in the Employment of Older Workers

Size	Increased	Decreased	Same	Don't know	Don't recruit over-50s	
50–199	7%	4%	40%	5%	44%	n=102
>200	9%	9%	46%	5%	31%	n=138

Source: Cranfield/University of Limerick Survey, 1995.

Few of the organisations surveyed recruit individuals who are past the state retirement age. However, those that are recruited are likely to be employed in manual positions. Similarly, few, if any organisations had introduced specific measures in order to aid the recruitment or retention of older workers. Where specific measures were introduced, they were most likely to include flexible working time or re-training programmes.

These results are not altogether unexpected. Ireland has a relatively young workforce at present which, when combined with high unemployment levels, provides a rich, well-educated labour pool for organisations to dip into. It will take some time for many of the demographic problems being experienced in other countries to affect the Irish labour market and so Irish based organisations continue to have considerable discretion over the types of individual they wish to target. Legislative provisions aimed at eliminating discrimination on the basis of age, if such are implemented, will, of course, require that organisations rethink their policies in this respect.

CONCLUSION

This chapter has sought to examine the nature of recruitment and selection practices in Ireland using data generated by the Cranfield/University of Limerick Study, 1995. Where possible, comparisons have been made with data collected by the PWCP in 1992 in an effort to explore possible changes in recruitment and selection practices in the intervening three-year period. Overall, the picture emerging with respect to the way in which organisations approach the recruitment and selection process is relatively unsurprising. Ireland has experienced an economic boom in the past few years and this upsurge in economic activity has resulted in more organisations expanding their workforce numbers to meet demands in their respective product/service markets. However, unemployment continues to be a pervasive characteristic of the Irish labour market, where a readily accessible pool of qualified young people available to fill vacant positions provides organisations with few difficulties in attracting job candidates.

A number of interesting findings emerged from the survey data that are worth summarising here. In general, policies in relation to recruitment and selection tend to be determined at either national HQ level or at the level of the establishment. However, it would appear that broader or more strategic policies concerned with workforce adjustment are more likely to be decided at either the international HQ or national HQ level, than at local level. This represents a significant change since 1992 when such policies were twice as likely to be determined at local rather than at international HQ level, suggesting, perhaps, that HQ are reclaiming more strategic policy decisions while concomitantly devolving responsibility for some of the more procedural personnel activities, such as recruitment and selection. At the organisational level, responsibility for policy decisions in relation to recruitment and selection continues to be shared jointly by the specialist HR function and line management. Here, most organisational types surveyed indicate some increase in line involvement, but this tends to be more prevalent in larger organisations, and in non-Irish-owned companies. However, the devolvement thesis that propounds the view that line management will become the primary "owners" of many personnel activities, including recruitment and selection, does not appear to be supported here.

A number of strategies have been adopted in an effort to facilitate the recruitment process. In particular, many organisations, particularly those that are Irish-owned, are investing heavily in retraining as a means of aiding their recruitment drive, while others have improved their pay/benefits package, targeted international recruits or sought to improve their corporate image. In terms of the recruitment process itself, a variety of internal and external recruitment methods continue to enjoy popularity. From an overall perspective, however, there is evidence to suggest that all organisations surveyed are making greater use of their internal labour markets for the purpose of filling managerial vacancies. This is particularly true for junior and middle management vacancies, whereas consultants are more likely to be utilised to fill senior management positions. Larger organisations continue to report a greater propensity to utilise their internal labour market, than do their smaller counterparts, while Irish-owned organisations are found to be less likely to make use of their internal markets than the foreign-owned organisations surveyed. This may be a reflection both of the loose nature of the external labour market where Irish companies have little difficulty finding suitable external candidates, and of the close association of HRM practices, particularly progressive internal career development, with foreign multinational organisations.

The results affirm the continuing popularity of the traditionally used selection techniques such as the interview, the application form and the reference, despite their reported unreliability and invalidity, while only a small number of organisations report their use of more sophisticated selection tools such as assessment centres and psychological testing. While this may again be attributable to an oversupply of potential candidates in the labour market, it needs to be carefully considered since, in times of recession, shrinking organisations have less capacity to deal with selection errors (Lewis, 1984). However, the data also indicates that organisations are demonstrating a greater propensity to vary the types of selection tools used depending on the vacancy being filled and so are likely to make greater use of some of the more "sophisticated" selection techniques for critical job positions. This does not, however, represent a deliberate, organisation-wide, strategic selection strategy.

Organisations are more likely to monitor the recruitment and promotion of women than any other employee category, while university graduates are the most likely targeted group for recruitment purposes. The age of a potential job candidate appears to be a prevalent determinant of the recruitment process with a number of respondents (37 per cent) indicating the existence of an active policy of not recruiting candidates over the age of 50 years.

Overall, the evidence presented in this chapter suggests that, while recruitment and selection practices remain largely unchanged since 1992, there is some evidence to suggest that organisations are gradually becoming more strategic in their approach to workforce management. The increasing importance being placed on having a well-developed, flexible workforce will create a need for mobile internal labour markets, which may result in increased internal recruitment in Irish organisations. Finally, it is proposed that some of the more sophisticated selection techniques may become increasingly utilised in the future, for as the number of school leavers begins to drop and the workforce ages, the external labour market will then begin to exhibit tighter properties. Some evidence of this tightening has already begun to appear, with skill shortages being experienced in the computer software and financial services sectors. As industries become more skill-intensive, it is estimated that the demand for knowledge based workers with the capacity to be creative and innovative will continue to escalate.

Chapter 4

FLEXIBLE WORKING PRACTICES

Noreen Clifford, Marian Crowley, Michael Morley &
Patrick Gunnigle

INTRODUCTION

A number of changes in employment practices have been taking
place in the labour market over the past decade, one being the
proliferation of non-standard employment forms (Atkinson, 1984;
Flood, 1990; Brewster et al., 1994a; Morley and Gunnigle, 1994).
The number of people employed on a part-time, temporary, and
short-term contract basis has increased in Ireland (and in many
countries across Europe), while the number of workers in secure,
full-time employment has declined (Rhodes, 1994: 125). Some
suggestions have been made regarding the contribution that various segregated employment strategies might make, both to organisational adaptability and performance, and different opportunities for employees (Marginson, 1991; Brewster et al., 1994a; Morley and Gunnigle, 1994). Sparrow and Hiltrop (1994) suggest that
organisations are pursuing two opposing strategies, either relying
heavily on the external labour market and low levels of employee
involvement, or favouring internal mobility and the development
of multiple skills among existing employees. Some aspects of this
debate are addressed in this chapter, with a detailed analysis of
the situation in Ireland regarding flexible employment practices.

Flexibility Forms

Atkinson (1984) propounded the emergence of the "flexible firm
scenario", an organisational model consisting of a core and periphery workforce, in response to external market changes and
threats. Here, the core is made up of full-time, permanent employ-

ees, who experience good working conditions and job security; whereas the periphery is composed of workers who enjoy fewer benefits, less security or training, etc. (Atkinson, 1984; Torrington et al., 1989; Armstrong, 1992). Atkinson (1984) identified three forms of flexibility: numerical, functional and financial flexibility. Numerical flexibility exists when the number of staff and the number of hours worked can be increased or decreased depending on the demand for labour. Such peripheral workers have become known as "atypical" employees,

> . . . defined as any form of employment which deviates from the traditional full-time, permanent format and this trend is one of the most visible in employment practices in Ireland (Morley and Gunnigle, 1994: 105).

It includes

> self-employment, . . . temporary work, part-time employment (casual or regular), home working, . . . and clandestine/black economy work (Flood, 1990: 16).

Functional flexibility refers to employment situations where employees are trained to perform a number of tasks and constantly learn new skills. Finally, financial flexibility occurs when the amount an employee is paid depends on the job done (contract work), hours worked (part-time or temporary) or the amount which the organisation can afford to pay at the time (more in boom periods and less in recessionary times) (Atkinson, 1984; Pollert, 1988b; Spellman, 1992; Nollen and Gannon, 1996).

Atkinson (1984) proposed that the implementation of each of these flexibility forms simultaneously within an organisation would allow that organisation to cater for and adapt to changeable economic circumstances. However, a number of weaknesses and limitations have been identified in relation to the "flexible firm scenario" (Pollert 1987, 1988a, 1988b; Elger, 1991; Burrows et al., 1992; Blyton and Morris, 1991; Brewster et al., 1994a; Morley and Gunnigle, 1994). The debate has centred on a number of key issues, not least of which is the extent to which organisations are pursuing a planned strategic approach to incorporating various forms of flexibility in order to improve organisational performance. Research evidence to date has not confirmed this argument. Rather it has held that:

> Despite the appeal of the flexible firm scenario in some quarters, the research evidence to date suggest that change in this area would appear to be more closely aligned with gradual incrementalism rather than with a radical post-industrial futurology (Morley and Gunnigle, 1994: 109).

Indeed Atkinson himself, in a later paper with Meager (1986), commented that:

> Although the observed changes were widespread, they did not cut very deeply in most firms, and therefore the outcome was more likely to be marginal, *ad hoc* and tentative, rather than a purposeful thrust to achieve flexibility (1986: 26).

This chapter examines whether the increase in the use of non standard forms of employment (numerical and functional flexibility) is a short-term, *ad hoc* reaction to wider economic circumstances, or alternatively, a planned, strategic approach to long-term workforce management with the aim of increasing flexibility and reducing labour costs. We review current data from the Cranfield/University of Limerick study, focusing specifically on changes in organisational usage of various forms of non-standard employment contracts and changes in the specification of jobs. Initially, it is useful to examine some of the contextual factors which have been identified as contributing to the increased utilisation of flexible working practices.

The Context For Change

A number of explanations concerning the increasing number of organisations utilising various flexible working practices have been suggested. Commentators have identified mass redundancies, economic uncertainty, rapid technological change, ongoing reductions in working time, market stagnation and world depression as being among the most important externalities which have resulted in organisations restructuring their workforce (Atkinson, 1984; Handy, 1984; Caudron, 1994; Barker, 1995). It is believed that the pressing economic circumstances which organisations experienced in the 1980s and 1990s have supported the adoption of different employment categories, besides the traditional permanent full-time employee (working eight hours a day, five days a week), which allow for a more efficient usage of labour:

> against a background of increasing competition, diminishing operating profits, redundancies and business closures, the call for structural changes in the labour market and in working conditions has become increasingly urgent (Van Hilst and Jansen, 1994: 5).

As Nollen and Gannon (1996: 284) noted:

> to succeed in this business environment, companies must be able to change rapidly, and they must continuously reduce costs.

Similarly, Sparrow (1994: 23) suggests that the increasingly evident drive towards productivity improvement and competitiveness has been the cause of "flexibility of function, numbers and time".

It is argued elsewhere that today's worker differs increasingly from any other workers in any other time, which is another factor that has led to the adoption of different work practices (Nollen and Gannon, 1996). Changing aspirations and demographic trends have resulted in younger people especially not prioritising work as highly as their forefathers may have done, but actually appreciating the freedom that is associated with other work options (Handy, 1989; Spellman, 1992).

In addition, the national employment rate is suggested as an economic factor which has lead to the proliferation of nonstandard employment, with members of the labour market working in an atypical capacity due to the looseness of the labour market and the lack of permanent employment available (Dineen, 1989, 1992; Morley et al., 1995). Increasing female participation rates in the labour force, and the need to balance work and domestic life have also had a role to play in promoting the changing employment practices prevalent today (Dineen, 1989; Brewster et al., 1994a; Gunnigle et al., 1994). Employers have moved to accommodate "the tremendous time constraints faced by the many employees with significant family responsibilities" (Rodgers, 1992: 183) by introducing a choice of employment forms.

Another suggestion put forward for the increasing breadth of employment options is that sectoral shifts — from traditional manufacturing (clothing, textiles, etc.) and agriculture to the services and more advanced engineering, chemicals, and electronics industries — have led to a need for greater flexibility and contributed to the increase in the numbers of workers who are part-time, temporary, sub-contracted, etc. (Pollert, 1988b; Dineen, 1989, 1992; Gunnigle et al., 1994; Morley et al., 1995). A significant proportion of the services sector, particularly the hotel and tourist industry, have traditionally used these forms of atypical employment due to the seasonal nature of their business.

However, the most widely accepted explanation for flexible working practices often appears under the rubric of "increased competitiveness" (Flood, 1990; Armstrong, 1992; Brewster et al., 1994a; Gunnigle et al., 1994; Nollen and Gannon, 1996). While this is a valid starting point, a problem relates to the sometimes generic nature of discussions on competitiveness. Consequently it is often difficult to precisely identify what is meant by "increased competitiveness", what are its sources and what are the implications for HRM. While this chapter does not seek to examine the competitiveness debate in detail, it is suggested that the main sources of change in organisational approaches to HRM have their roots in the following developments (Roche and Gunnigle, 1995):

- Globalisation of competition in product, service and (particularly) capital markets.

- Liberalisation of world trade.

- More intense price competition.

- Competitive strategies based on quality, product innovation *and* price.

- Diffusion of new production techniques to reduce cycle time, control costs and improve quality.

- Increased product and service customisation.

- Changes in the Public/Semi-State sector.

In effect, these environmental changes have forced employers to examine new ways of organising labour so that labour productivity and performance is improved, labour costs are reduced, and the labour supply is tailored to labour requirements (Nollen and Gannon, 1996). Speed of reaction is essential for organisational survival, and using a peripheral workforce to accommodate market demands has its advantages, as Atkinson (1984: 28) surmises:

> a workforce which can respond quickly, easily and cheaply to unforeseen changes, which may need to contract as smoothly as it expands, in which worked time precisely matches job requirements, and in which unit labour costs can be held down.

FLEXIBLE WORKING PRACTICES — NON-STANDARD CONTRACTS

Trends in the use of Non-Standard Contracts

In the Cranfield/University of Limerick (CUL) Survey (1995), respondents were asked to indicate whether their use of non-standard forms of employment had changed over the previous three years. It is important to note that the actual *extent* of any such changes in flexible work practices is not indicated in the study, so it may be inaccurate to draw too heavily on the findings in relation to this question. Nonetheless, for the purpose of comparative analyses, the results pertaining to changes in flexible working arrangements are useful. For the purpose of analyses in this section non-standard employment contracts are divided into three broad categories: a) those which are normally associated with the core workforce of the organisation, such as shift work, overtime, annual hours, job sharing, flexible working time and weekend work (time flexibility); b) those associated with the periphery workforce of the organisation, such as part-time work, temporary or casual work, fixed-term contracts and subcontracting (numerical flexibility); and c) newly emerging forms of flexibility which are not yet widely used in Ireland, such as tele-working and home-based work.

The CUL (1995) survey results showed a general increase in organisational usage of most forms of atypical employment in Ireland (see Tables 4.1a, 4.1b and 4.1c). Shift work and overtime appear to be the most stable forms of flexible work arrangements, with over 40 per cent of respondents reporting that there had been no change in the levels of either in the previous three years (see Table 4.1a). Annual hours contracts have not been widely adopted by Irish organisations, with 76 per cent of respondents reporting that they do not use such contracts, a notable increase since 1992 (64 per cent of respondents in 1992 did not use these contracts). It is also worth noting that when compared to 1992, a greater number of respondents in 1995 reported that they *did not use* weekend work, shift work and overtime. However, it should be mentioned that these forms of non-standard employment practices most often occur in the core workforce, and are seldom considered in discussions on atypical employment (Gunnigle et al., 1994).

Table 4.1a: Change in Organisational Use of Flexible Work Arrangements over the last 3 years — Core Workforce

	Increased		No Change		Decreased		Not used / Don't know		N	
	1995	1992	1995	1992	1995	1992	1995	1992	1995	1992
Weekend work	25%	21%	40%	47%	5%	15%	30%	17%	238	219
Shift work	24%	17%	44%	49%	2%	8%	30%	26%	240	215
Overtime	24%	24%	44%	40%	25%	33%	6%	4%	250	217
Annual Hours	5%	6%	15%	19%	4%	11%	76%	64%	222	191
Job sharing	29%	NA*	15%	NA	0	NA	56%	NA	233	NA
Flexible working time	25%	NA	31%	NA	1%	NA	43%	NA	225	NA

*NA: these figures are not available as the question was not asked in 1992.
Source: Cranfield/University of Limerick Survey, 1992 and 1995.

On the other hand, there seem to be substantial increases in the number of organisations reporting the use of forms of atypical employment which are associated with the peripheral workforce (see Table 4.1b). The most significant increase is in the tempo-rary/casual work category. This category also shows the greatest growth (10 percentage points) in the number of organisations re-porting an increase since 1992. An interesting finding from the data is that only 10 per cent of respondent organisations do not use temporary contracts, a significantly smaller number than for any other category of atypical employment in the peripheral workforce. It is also worth noting that there have been no major changes in the percentage of respondent organisations reporting non-utilisation of these flexible work arrangements since 1992. Thus, while quite a high percentage of organisations already utilising sub-contracting, part-time, temporary and fixed-term work arrangements have increased their use of such contracts, presumably in an attempt to create a more flexible workforce easily adjusted to cope with market fluctuations, the number of organisations adopting these flexible work methods has not changed to a large degree since 1992.

Table 4.1b: Change in Organisational Use of Flexible Work Arrangements over the last 3 years — Peripheral Workforce

	Increased		No Change		Decreased		Not used		N	
	1995	*1992*	*1995*	*1992*	*1995*	*1992*	*1995*	*1992*	*1995*	*1992*
Part-time work	40%	36%	29%	27%	6%	8%	25%	29%	240	204
Temporary/ casual	49%	39%	35%	36%	6%	16%	10%	8%	244	209
Fixed-term contract	47%	38%	29%	30%	2%	4%	23%	28%	234	204
Sub-contracting	41%	35%	23%	30%	2%	5%	34%	30%	237	207

Source: Cranfield/University of Limerick Survey, 1992 and 1995.

Tele-working and home-based work are the least popular forms of non-standard contract (see Table 4.1c), with 89 per cent and 91 per cent of organisations, respectively, reporting that they do not use these flexibility types. In a European context, Brewster et al.

(1994a: 190) suggest that the low levels of usage here may be accounted for by:

> ... the social elements involved in work: the value of face-to-face meetings and the psychological benefits of interactions with colleagues which are largely lost in home working.

Table 4.1c: Change in Organisational Use of Flexible Work Arrangements over the last 3 years

	Increased	No Change	Decreased	Not used	N
Home-based work	6%	5%	0.5%	89%	218
Tele-working	6%	3%	0	91%	220

Source: Cranfield/University of Limerick Survey, 1995.

On further analysis of the CUL (1995) data, organisational size appears to be an influential factor in determining the forms of non-standard contract that are adopted (see Tables 4.2a & 4.2b). The data suggest that a greater proportion of small organisations (organisations employing less than 200 employees) reported an increase in the adoption of flexibility in certain areas which are generally associated with the core workforce, such as overtime and weekend work (see Table 4.2a). This may be indicative of an emerging trend, where smaller organisations are adopting flexible working practices which enable them to utilise their current workforce more effectively, rather than increasing the size of the workforce. However, although small organisations are reporting increases in those flexible work practices associated with core employment, it is important to note that a greater number of large organisations (organisations employing more than 200 employees) are still more likely to employ *all* forms of flexibility. Organisation size was found to have no significant bearing on organisational use of annual hours contracts.

Table 4.2a: Organisation Size & Changes in the Use of Flexible Work Practices

	Inc.	No Change	Dec.	Not used	N
Weekend work:					
Small	29%	34%	6%	31%	
Large	23%	45%	5%	28%	232
Shift work:					
Small	24%	31%	1%	44%	
Large	24%	54%	3%	19%	234
Overtime:					
Small	30%	40%	19%	10%	
Large	19%	49%	28%	4%	243
Flexible working time:					
Small	18%	29%	1%	52%	
Large	30%	33%	1%	36%	219
Job Sharing:					
Small	18%	12%	0%	70%	
Large	37%	16%	0%	47%	227

Source: Cranfield/University of Limerick Survey, 1995.

With regard to atypical work practices in the peripheral work-force, a greater number of large organisations, particularly, report increases in the use of part-time contracts (see Table 4.2b). This represents an increase of 13 percentage points since 1992. On the other hand a greater number of small organisations in 1992 reported an increase in their use of part-time contracts (36 per cent in 1992, compared with 29 per cent in 1995). Therefore, the employment of part-timers in smaller organisations would seem to be remaining quite stable.

There is less variance concerning organisational use of temporary workers, with a very high percentage of both large and small organisations utilising this form of flexible work contract. Fewer small organisations use fixed-term contract workers, and as with sub-contracting, don't seem to be increasing their usage to the same extent as their larger counterparts. There are no substantial

differences between large and small organisations relating to the
use of home-based work or tele-working.

**Table 4.2b: Organisation Size & Changes in the Use of
Flexible Work Practices**

	Inc.	No Change	Dec.	Not used	N
Part-time work:					
Small	29%	31%	8%	31%	
Large	49%	26%	5%	20%	234
Temporary / Casual:					
Small	43%	38%	8%	11%	
Large	55%	32%	5%	8%	238
Fixed Term:					
Small	38%	25%	3%	34%	
Large	54%	31%	2%	13%	228
Sub-contracting:					
Small	37%	22%	0%	42%	
Large	45%	23%	4%	28%	231

Source: Cranfield/University of Limerick Survey, 1995.

Analysing the CUL (1995) data to determine if there is a correlation between unionisation and changes in the use of flexible work
practices, it was found that organisations that do not negotiate
with a trade union were more likely to have increased their use of
all of the forms of flexibility associated with the core workforce in
the organisation (see Table 4.3a). However, there are a relatively
high percentage of unionised organisations reporting *"no change"*
in the use of most of these non-standard contracts, which could be
an indication that they are already employing these forms of
flexibility.

Although unionised organisations are less likely to use weekend work, where weekend work is evident in unionised organisations, the levels of such have tended to remain the same (see Table 4.3a). Non-union organisations have, on the other hand, increased their use of weekend work more than unionised organisations (37 per cent and 23 per cent respectively). Similarly, al-

though the CUL data found that organisations that do not recognise a trade union are more likely to have increased their use of shift work, this could be explained by the high level of shift work already existing in unionised organisations. Table 4.3a illustrates that unionised organisations in Ireland use shift work to a greater extent than their non-union counterparts. The data on flexible working time and overtime reflect the findings relating to shift work.

The overall findings suggest high levels of stability in those organisations which recognise trade unions, while non-union organisations appear to be adopting some of the flexible work practices more often associated with the core workforce of Atkinson's flexible firm.

Table 4.3a: Unionisation & Changes in the Use of Flexible Work Practices

	Inc.	*No Change*	*Dec.*	*Not used*	*N*
Weekend work:					
Union	23%	41%	5%	31%	
Non-union	37%	33%	7%	24%	232
Shift work:					
Union	24%	48%	3%	25%	
Non-union	27%	27%	0%	47%	234
Overtime:					
Union	20%	47%	28%	6%	
Non-union	42%	31%	17%	10%	244
Flexible working time:					
Union	22%	34%	0	44%	
Non-union	39%	12%	5%	44%	219
Job Sharing:					
Union	28%	17%	0	55%	
Non-union	32%	5%	0	64%	227

Source: Cranfield/University of Limerick Survey, 1995.

Another significant finding was that a greater number of organisations which do not recognise trade unions reported increases in the use of temporary workers and fixed term contracts (see Table 4.3b). Again the findings here reflect a higher level of stability in unionised organisations. The only area in which a marginally higher number of unionised organisations reported an increase was in part-time work, whereas more non-union organisations reported a decrease in their usage of this employment form.

Importantly, a far greater number of non-union organisations are adopting flexible work practices associated with numerical flexibility and the peripheral workforce than in 1992: for example, 56 per cent of non-union respondents used part-time contracts in 1992, 73 per cent in 1995 (this compares with 74 per cent of unionised companies in 1992, 76 per cent in 1995).

The main finding thus pertaining to unionisation as a determinant of changes in the use of non-standard contracts in the past three years is that non-union organisations, in particular, have significantly increased their utilisation of most atypical forms of employment, principally overtime, shift work, weekend work, fixed-term contracts and sub-contracting.

Table 4.3b: Unionisation & Changes in the Use of Flexible Work Practices

	Inc.	No Change	Dec.	Not used	N
Part-time work:					
Union	41%	30%	5%	24%	
Non-union	40%	20%	13%	27%	234
Temporary / casual:					
Union	47%	36%	6%	11%	
Non-union	62%	27%	7%	4%	238
Fixed-term:					
Union	46%	29%	2%	23%	
Non-union	55%	21%	3%	23%	228

Source: Cranfield/University of Limerick Survey, 1995.

A further organisational characteristic, sector, was also analysed to determine its effect on the usage of flexible working practices. When comparing the private and public sectors, the data indicated very little change since the 1992 study. There were small increases in the number of public sector organisations that reported an increase in their use of weekend work, shift work and overtime, but it was the private sector which showed far higher results (see Table 4.4a). Public sector organisations are less likely to use these forms of flexibility, particularly shift work. Overtime is the only form of flexibility where there was notable decreases in organisational usage in both sectors, which may imply that organisations from both the public and private sectors are seeking alternative, perhaps less expensive, forms of flexibility. Public sector organisations also employ flexible working time and job sharing work options to a far greater degree than their private sector counterparts.

Table 4.4a: Sector & Changes in the Use of Flexible Work Practices

	Inc.	*No Change*	*Dec.*	*Not used*	*N*
Weekend work:					
Public	14%	46%	4%	37%	
Private	29%	38%	6%	28%	235
Shift work:					
Public	8%	51%	2%	40%	
Private	29%	42%	2%	28%	238
Overtime:					
Public	13%	54%	21%	13%	
Private	27%	42%	26%	5%	247
Flexible working time:					
Public	31%	44%	2%	24%	
Private	23%	26%	1%	50%	223
Job Sharing:					
Public	50%	41%	0	9%	
Private	22%	6%	0	72%	231

Source: Cranfield/University of Limerick Survey, 1995.

Increases in the use of part-time work were practically the same for both sectors (see Table 4.4b). However, 28 per cent of private sector organisations are non-users of part-time workers, compared to 15 per cent of public sector organisations. The private sector showed a substantial increase (53 per cent of organisations reporting an increase) in the use of temporary workers, and also greater increases in fixed term contracts, homebased working, and sub-contracting (see Table 4.4b). This represents a turnaround since 1992, where increases in part-time, temporary and fixed-term contracts were greater in the public sector, and may be the result of private sector organisations utilising peripheral workers to a greater extent to cater for market uncertainties and changes in demand.

Table 4.4b: Sector & Changes in the Use of Flexible Work Practices

	Inc.	*No Change*	*Dec.*	*Not used*	*N*
Part-time work:					
Public	40%	42%	4%	15%	
Private	41%	24%	7%	28%	238
Temporary / casual:					
Public	35%	46%	6%	15%	
Private	53%	31%	7%	9%	241
Fixed-term:					
Public	43%	41%	0	17%	
Private	48%	25%	3%	24%	231
Sub-contracting:					
Public	32%	26%	4%	39%	
Private	44%	22%	2%	32%	234

Source: Cranfield/University of Limerick Survey, 1995.

The breakdown of private sector organisations into manufacturing and services throws further light on the previous findings. The principal areas where differences emerge is in the use of shift work, flexible working time and job sharing (see Table 4.4c). It is not surprising that private sector manufacturing organisations are considerably more likely to operate a shift working arrangement. Private sector services organisations on the other hand, are more likely to use flexible working time and job sharing.

Table 4.4c: Private Sector Manufacturing & Services Organisations & Changes in the Use of Flexible Work Practices

	Inc.	No Change	Dec.	Not used	N
Shift work:					
Private Manufacturing	33%	47%	4%	17%	
Private Services	19%	31%	2%	48%	181
Flexible working time:					
Private Manufacturing	18%	19%	0	62%	
Private Services	30%	36%	3%	31%	164
Job Sharing:					
Private Manufacturing	20%	5%	0	76%	
Private Services	33%	9%	0	58%	171

Source: Cranfield/University of Limerick Survey, 1995.

Gunnigle et al. (1994) argue that a trend has been identified by many commentators towards greater flexibility, particularly numerical flexibility, in the services sector. The findings in relation to private services sector organisations in this study would support such a situation. Table 4.4d illustrates that organisations in this sector are more likely to use all forms of numerical flexibility (see Table 4.4d), particularly part-timers. A greater number of services sector organisations also report increases in the use of all of these work contracts with the exception of sub-contracting.

Differences between organisations of different national origins were also analysed. A greater proportion of organisations originating in the US reported increases in shift work, overtime and weekend work. Conversely, organisations originating within the EU were most likely to have reported a decrease in their use of these forms of employment. The only form of flexibility which shows a significant decrease across the board was overtime (20 per cent or more of organisations originating in each geographical area reported a decrease in its use).

Table 4.4d: Private Sector Manufacturing & Services Organisations & Changes in the Use of Flexible Work Practices

	Inc.	No Change	Dec.	Not used	N
Part-time Work:					
Private Manufacturing	35%	25%	7%	32%	
Private Services	49%	24%	8%	19%	178
Temporary / Casual:					
Private Manufacturing	51%	29%	7%	13%	
Private Services	53%	39%	6%	2%	182
Fixed-Term:					
Private Manufacturing	48%	22%	3%	29%	
Private Services	49%	29%	3%	20%	171
Sub-contracting:					
Private Manufacturing	45%	20%	2%	33%	
Private Services	42%	29%	2%	28%	171

Source: Cranfield/University of Limerick Survey, 1995.

A very high proportion of indigenous Irish and UK-owned organisations reported increases in the use of part-time work (over 47 per cent), while a high percentage of US- and EU-owned organisations reported increases in temporary/casual work, 56 per cent and 54 per cent respectively (see Figures 4.1 & 4.2). There is a

Figure 4.1: Ownership & Changes in the Use of Part-Time Contracts

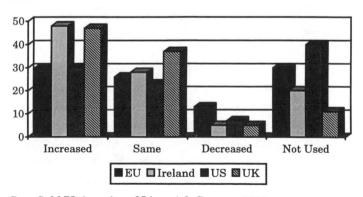

Source: Cranfield/University of Limerick Survey, 1995.

Figure 4.2: Ownership & Changes in the Use of Temporary/ Casual Contracts

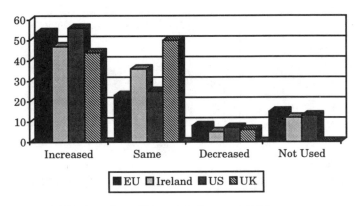

Source: Cranfield/University of Limerick Survey, 1995.

rise in the number of organisations reporting increases in fixed-term and temporary employment across the board and there are also significant increases in the number of organisations using sub-contracting, particularly in EU- and US-owned organisations.

Organisations with their headquarters in the UK and US are less likely to use job sharing or flexible working time than their Irish- and EU-owned counterparts whereas those organisations originating in both Ireland and the US were the only organisations to record increases in home-based working and tele-working.

Proportion of the Workforce on Non-Standard Contracts

As mentioned earlier in the chapter, it is difficult to draw definitive conclusions in relation to reported changes in work arrangements when there is no indication of the *extent* of those changes within organisations. The results are useful though, in illustrating an overall trend and, when taken in conjunction with the following results, portray quite clearly the situation which is emerging in Ireland with regard to flexible working practices.

Respondents to the CUL (1995) were asked what *proportion*, if any, of their workforce was working on a non-standard contract. The results which emerged were quite surprising in the context of previous findings which indicated increases in flexible working practices across Europe.

While 75 per cent of organisations that responded to the CUL (1995) survey use part-time employees, 49 per cent have less than 1 per cent of their workforce on such contracts (see Table 4.5). However, since 1992 the number of organisations reporting between 1–10 per cent of the workforce on part-time contract has increased slightly. The same trend can be identified in the use of temporary and fixed-term contracts. Annual hours contracts, while accepted as a cost-effective way of dealing with excessive amounts of overtime and having taken a firm foothold in countries such as Germany, Finland, The Netherlands and the UK, are not popular methods of flexible working in Ireland.

In the previous section of this chapter, findings in relation to changes in the use of non-standard contracts indicated a general increase in the use of such contracts. However, differences in the levels of utilisation of such contracts between 1992 and 1995 are marginal, with small decreases in the number of organisations reporting more than 20 per cent of their workforce on part-time, temporary and fixed-term contracts since 1992.

Table 4.5: Proportion of the Workforce on Non-standard Contracts

	<1%		1–10%		11–20%		>20%		N	
	1995	1992	1995	1992	1995	1992	1995	1992	1995	1992
Part-time	49%	51%	43%	37%	3%	6%	5%	6%	242	186
Temporary	28%	29%	55%	54%	14%	11%	3%	6%	243	197
Fixed-term	51%	52%	33%	27%	4%	5%	12%	16%	237	181
Home-based	98%	99%	0.5%	1%	0.5%	0	1%	0	206	106
Tele-working	95%	NA*	4%	NA	1%	NA	0	NA	208	NA
Shift working	42%	NA	18%	NA	10%	NA	31%	NA	220	NA
Annual hours	90%	NA	4%	NA	1%	NA	5%	NA	209	NA

*NA: these figures are not available as the question was not asked in 1992.
Source: Cranfield/University of Limerick Survey, 1992 and 1995.

On analysing these results with regard to organisational size, it was found that larger organisations are considerably more likely to utilise a higher proportion of part-time and temporary employees, fixed-term contracts and shift working (see Table 4.6). More than 50 per cent of smaller organisations have less than 1 per cent of their workforce employed under a part-time or fixed-term contract, while more than one-third have less than 1 per cent of their workforce employed on a temporary contract.

Table 4.6: Organisation Size & Proportion of the Workforce on Non-standard Contracts

	<1%	1–10%	11–20%	>20%	N
Part-time Workers:					
Small	53%	42%	1%	4%	
Large	46%	44%	5%	5%	236
Temporary Workers:					
Small	36%	52%	11%	1%	
Large	22%	57%	16%	5%	237
Fixed-Term Workers:					
Small	55%	28%	3%	14%	
Large	49%	39%	6%	7%	232
Shift Working:					
Small	51%	16%	9%	24%	
Large	33%	20%	11%	36%	214

Source: Cranfield/University of Limerick Survey, 1995.

Similar to the findings in 1992, the 1995 data reported that there is a greater proportion of the workforce in the public sector covered by part-time contracts (see Table 4.7). 39 per cent of private sector organisations have between 1 and 10 per cent of the workforce on part-time contracts; the corresponding figure for public sector respondents is 60 per cent. The results are not quite as clear-cut in the case of temporary/casual contracts. While 74 per cent of public sector and 68 per cent of private sector organisations have up to 10 per cent of their workforce on temporary contracts, significantly more private sector organisations have 11 per cent or more of their employees working temporarily. Likewise, the private sector engages in shift work to a far greater extent than public sector organisations (see Table 4.7).

Table 4.7: Sector as a Determinant of the Proportion of the Workforce on Non-standard Contracts

	<1%	*1–10%*	*11–20%*	*>20%*	*N*
Part-time Workers:					
Public	32%	60%	6%	2%	
Private	54%	39%	3%	5%	239
Temporary Workers:					
Public	33%	60%	8%	0	
Private	27%	53%	15%	4%	240
Fixed-Term Workers:					
Public	52%	31%	4%	14%	
Private	52%	34%	4%	10%	234
Shift Working:					
Public	65%	17%	6%	13%	
Private	36%	18%	11%	35%	218

Source: Cranfield/University of Limerick Survey, 1995.

Table 4.8 considers private sector organisations in both manufacturing and services. Some interesting findings emerge in this analysis. As would be expected, shift work is far more pervasive in manufacturing, while the same can be said of part-time work in

Table 4.8: Private Manufacturing and Services Sector Organisations and the Proportion of the Workforce on Non-standard Contracts

	<1%	1–10%	11–20%	>20%	N
Part-time workers:					
Private Manufacturing	62%	34%	3%	2%	
Private Services	37%	51%	3%	9%	184
Temporary Workers:					
Private Manufacturing	29%	46%	20%	5%	
Private Services	23%	70%	5%	2%	183
Fixed Term Workers:					
Private Manufacturing	51%	36%	6%	7%	
Private Services	63%	25%	2%	11%	177
Shift working:					
Private Manufacturing	23%	17%	13%	47%	
Private Services	58%	21%	10%	11%	170

Source: Cranfield/University of Limerick Survey, 1995.

the services sector. Temporary workers are used by a high percentage of both private manufacturing and services organisations, with 70 per cent of services organisations reporting between 1 and 10 per cent of their workforce covered by such contracts, and one-in-four manufacturing organisations employing more than 11 per cent of their workforce on a temporary basis. The findings in relation to fixed-term contracts would seem to point to a marginally higher utilisation in private manufacturing organisations.

Both indigenous Irish organisations and those with UK headquarters reported a high proportion of their workforce on part-time contracts compared to other countries (see Figure 4.3). 59 per cent of indigenous and 58 per cent of UK-owned organisations reported between 1 and 20 per cent of their workforce employed on a part-time basis. Conversely, 43 per cent of EU- and 44 per cent of US-owned organisations do not utilise part-time employees at all. This compares with 18 per cent of Irish- and 11 per cent of UK-owned organisations not using part-time employees (see Figure 4.3).

Figure 4.3: Ownership & the Proportion of the Workforce on Part-Time Contracts

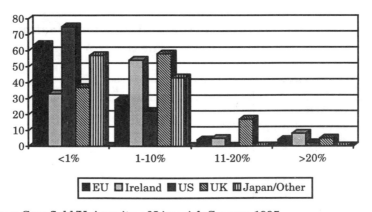

Source: Cranfield/University of Limerick Survey, 1995.

A large proportion of organisations, regardless of country of origin, reported using temporary/casual labour, whereas US-, Japanese-, and other non-European-owned organisations are more likely to have more than 1 per cent of their workforce employed on fixed-term contracts (see Figure 4.4 and 4.5).

Figure 4.4: Ownership & the Proportion of the Workforce on Temporary/Casual Contracts

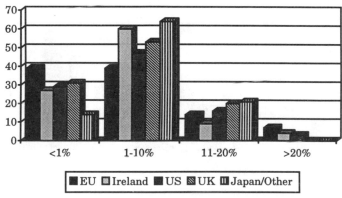

Source: Cranfield/University of Limerick Survey, 1995.

Figure 4.5: Ownership & the Proportion of the Workforce on Fixed-Term Contracts

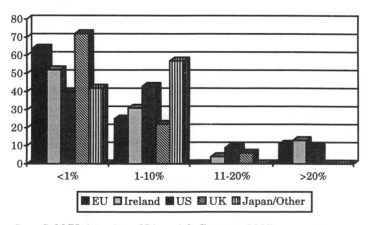

Source: Cranfield/University of Limerick Survey, 1995.

The CUL data suggest that there is a strong correlation between the proportion of the workforce on shift work and the ownership of the organisation. As Figure 4.6 illustrates, organisations with their headquarters in the US and the EU are far more likely to have a large proportion of the workforce operating under a shift arrangement. Indigenous organisations do not utilise this form of flexibility to the same extent.

Figure 4.6: Ownership & the Proportion of the Workforce Shift Working

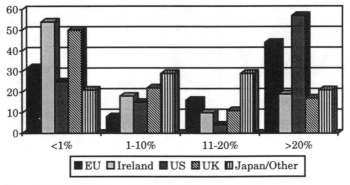

Source: Cranfield/University of Limerick Survey, 1995.

In examining the impact of union recognition on usage of non-standard contracts, no significant difference was found between unionised and non-unionised organisations regarding the use of part-time and/or temporary contracts. However, a significantly greater number of unionised organisations used shift work (see Figure 4.7).

Figure 4.7: Unionisation & the Proportion of the Workforce on Shift Contracts

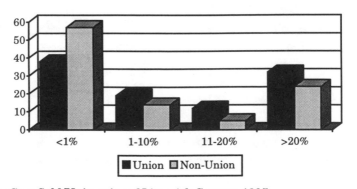

Source: Cranfield/University of Limerick Survey, 1995.

These are interesting findings, particularly when we consider the data in the previous section, where it was found that a greater percentage of non-union organisations reported increases in *all* forms of flexibility, with the exception of part-time work. Those findings may have been taken as an indication that organisations which do not recognise trade unions in Ireland are adopting a variation of the flexible firm scenario, and seem to be more intent upon developing a workforce that will adapt to changing economic circumstances. However, further analysis on the *proportion* of the workforce on non-standard contracts in union and non-union organisations seems to indicate no major differences between the two. The most likely scenario then is that unionised organisations were already utilising non-standard contracts, and therefore did not experience increases to the same extent as their non-union counterparts.

The principal reasons given by respondents to the CUL survey regarding increases in non-standard work arrangements were *fixed-term projects* and efforts to *reduce staff costs* (see Figure 4.8). This suggests that flexibility and efficiency are priorities in the organisation and management of human resources. Smaller organisations identified reducing staff costs as the chief incentive for the introduction of flexible work methods, with large organisations and those from the private sector identifying fixed-term contracts as their main motivation. Responding to a recruitment freeze was the principal rationale for public sector organisations in employing flexible work practices.

Figure 4.8: Principal Reason for Increases in Non-standard Contracts

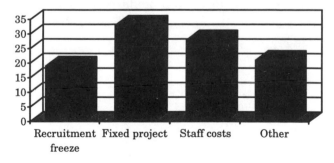

Source: Cranfield/University of Limerick Survey, 1995.

SUMMARY

It is apparent from the CUL (1995) survey that various flexible forms of employment are being adopted by different organisations. However, it is argued that the adoption of flexible work practices is occurring at a gradual, incremental pace (Morley and Gunnigle, 1994). Indeed, it is suggested that the managerial motives for using flexible workers include reduced costs, speed with which they can be recruited, administrative ease, and as a buffer to cope with market uncertainty (Pfeffer, 1994). Thus, flexibility could be considered as an on-going strategy to deal with environmental uncertainty, rather than a long-term strategic approach to manpower planning. It seems that different organisations are utilising different employment types (e.g. part-time, temporary workers) and practices (e.g. shift work, weekend work), and that such uses of flexible work practices appear to be more in response to cost and competitive strategies than deliberate flexibility strategies.

Flexible Working Practices — Functional Flexibility

Functional flexibility, often referred to as multi-skilling, has been defined by Gunnigle et al. (1994: 108) as "the expansion of skills within a workforce, or the ability of firms to reorganise the competencies associated with jobs so that the job holder is willing and able to deploy such competencies across a broader range of tasks". In the area of functional flexibility the CUL study examines the changing structure of jobs in Irish organisations. In analysing the changes which have occurred in this area over the past three years, a clear trend towards wider, more flexible jobs is apparent. Although the broad picture is still quite stable, a greater percentage of jobs in all categories, particularly for clerical employees, have been made wider to encompass broader duties and responsibilities (see Figure 4.9).

Figure 4.9: Changes in the Specification of Jobs

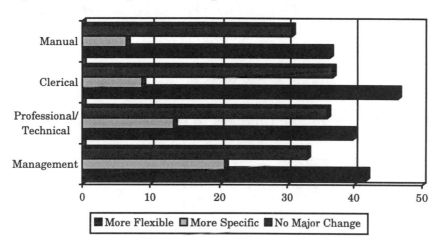

Source: Cranfield/University of Limerick Survey, 1995.

When compared to the results of the 1992 survey, it is clear that a significantly greater number of respondents in 1995 feel that jobs have become more flexible for all categories of workers in their organisations (see Table 4.9), with the greatest increases occurring in the manual and clerical categories of employees.

Table 4.9: Changes in Job Specification (1992–1995)

	Management		Prof/technical		Clerical		Manual	
	1995	1992	1995	1992	1995	1992	1995	1992
More specific	22%	24%	15%	17%	10%	12%	9%	12%
No major change	35%	38%	40%	49%	40%	52%	42%	56%
Made wider	44%	38%	45%	34%	50%	36%	49%	32%
	n=249	n=226	n=233	n=207	n=240	n=214	n=192	n=191

Source: Cranfield/University of Limerick Survey, 1992 and 1995.

However, when the figures are disaggregated to determine the effect of ownership on the degree of functional flexibility, it was found that indigenous Irish organisations were more likely to have made no changes whatsoever to the specification of jobs for all employee categories. Conversely, UK- and US-owned organisations tend to

have expanded job specifications for almost all levels of the hierarchy. Change was less likely to take place in public sector organisations across all job categories. A greater proportion of jobs have
been made more flexible in the private sector. The overall picture
that emerges from the data is one of change in the private sector
and relative stability in the public sector (see Table 4.10).

Table 4.10: Sector and Changes to the Specification of Jobs

	Private				Public			
	Mgmt.	Prof.	Cler-ical	Man-ual	Mgmt.	Prof.	Cler-ical	Man-ual
More Specific	22%	16%	12%	10%	20%	12%	2%	5%
No change	29%	36%	33%	35%	48%	54%	60%	62%
More flexible	47%	48%	55%	54%	29%	31%	34%	26%
Don't know	1%	0.5%	0	1%	3%	3%	4%	7%

Source: Cranfield/University of Limerick Survey, 1995.

Considering organisational size as an influencing factor, the CUL
(1995) found that change in the specification of jobs is less likely
to occur in smaller organisations. This may be due to the fact that
jobs in smaller organisations tend traditionally to be less specific
and therefore, as a result, required no change. In larger organisations, a greater percentage of jobs in all staff categories have become more flexible (see Table 4.11).

Table 4.11: Size and Changes to the Specification of Jobs

	50–199				200+			
	Mgmt.	Prof.	Cler-ical	Man-ual	Mgmt.	Prof.	Cler-ical	Man-ual
More Specific	21%	15%	11%	10%	23%	16%	9%	8%
No change	36%	42%	43%	48%	33%	38%	36%	36%
More flexible	41%	41%	45%	37%	48%	46%	54%	56%
Don't know	2%	2%	1%	5%	1%	1%	1%	1%

Source: Cranfield/University of Limerick Survey, 1995.

CUL (1995) results pertaining to job specification and unionisation were interesting. It has been argued that the existence of
trade unions can inhibit flexibility and change, a factor often considered to be the rationale behind an organisation's decision to
have non-union status. However, the actual survey results revealed that change is more likely in unionised organisations.
Similarly, a greater percentage of jobs for all categories, particularly manual and clerical, have become wider/more flexible in
unionised organisations. Conversely, a greater number of jobs
have become more specific in organisations that do not recognise
trade unions (see Table 4.12).

**Table 4.12: Unionisation and Changes in the Specification
of Jobs**

	Union				Non-union			
	Mgmt.	Prof.	Cler-ical	Man-ual	Mgmt.	Prof.	Cler-ical	Man-ual
More Specific	20%	14%	7%	7%	28%	20%	20%	18%
No change	34%	41%	40%	40%	34%	37%	41%	46%
More flexible	45%	44%	52%	51%	36%	43%	39%	29%
Don't know	1.5%	2%	1%	2%	2%	0	0	7%

Source: Cranfield/University of Limerick Survey, 1995.

CONCLUSIONS

The CUL survey (1995) represents broad trends in organisational
usage of different flexible work practices. There is no evidence to
support the propositions that the use of workforce flexibility today
is of any notable difference to its use in the past. Any proliferation
in the use of certain labour categories and work practices appears
to be less of a deliberate organisational strategy to adopt the
flexible firm model, and more an emerging, incremental strategy,
which can be accounted for by organisational, sectoral, and structural changes.

Overall, the CUL (1995) survey results show that although non-standard employment practices are being adopted on a piecemeal basis by some organisations more than others, there has not been a radical movement toward the adoption of the flexible firm model of employment practices since 1992. Similar to the results of the 1992 Price Waterhouse Cranfield Project (see Brewster et al., 1994a; Morley and Gunnigle, 1994), there is still a substantial proportion of organisations not adopting specific flexible work practices. Nonetheless, the CUL data also illustrated the importance of the flexibility phenomenon in modern organisations, with flexibility playing an increasing role in manpower and cost-reduction strategies. As Nollen and Gannon (1996: 296) noted:

> companies must accept continuous readjustment as turbulent product markets, rapid changes in technology, and global competition force them to accept flexible workforce arrangements. . . . The cost of production must be continuously reduced even as quality must be increased.

Chapter 5

TRAINING AND DEVELOPMENT

Noreen Heraty & Michael Morley

INTRODUCTION

A cursory examination of the history of training and development
in Ireland highlights a consistent focus on apprenticeship training, youth employment schemes and training for the unemployed.
However, little attention was given to management training and
development at organisational level and it was not until 1986 and
the launch of the white paper on manpower policy that explicit
reference was made to the importance of management development. In its recommendations, the advisory committee highlighted the strategic importance of management training and development and stressed the necessity for such training and development to be closely integrated with the strategic business objectives of the organisation. While the report was criticised on the
basis that it was overly prescriptive and that its case analysis was
highly selective, it is recognised that its proposals represent a
progressive development in highlighting the need for investment
in training and development at all levels of the organisation.

An organisation's employees are increasingly being viewed as
critical competitive resources which, if developed effectively, are
seen to contribute significantly to the attainment of strategic
business goals. Traditionally, competitiveness was gained through
either financial efficiency, marketing capability or technological
innovation. However, heightened global competition and rapid
technological development is leading to the realisation that the
primary source of competitive advantage in the future is sharply
focused on creating new knowledge which is disseminated
through the company and which, in turn, leads to continuous in-

novation (West, 1994). According to Iles (1994), the importance of people to organisational success is often acknowledged in rhetoric, at least in company reports and media statements, if not a belief much manifested in practice. It is increasingly recognised that the future cannot merely be an extrapolation of the past, and thus attention is focusing on various means of utilising human resources to create and sustain competitiveness. Reflecting this refocusing of training and development practices and specialists, in his Foreword to *Training & Development in Ireland: Context, Policy and Practice* (Garavan, Costine and Heraty, 1995: *xxiii*), the then National President of the Irish Institute of Training and Development Chris Taylor, writes that:

> training and development in Ireland is in a state of flux with the role of the Training Specialist undergoing major change, both in the depth of skills required and status within the organisation. The Training Specialist must become an agent of change . . . they must be aware of the best theory and practice available to meet demands for customer satisfaction, for innovation, and for new work structures and organisational redesign.

Donnelly (1987) cautions that the traditional model of training and development is insufficient to meet the changing needs of the new organisation, and that there is now, more than ever, a critical need to move from the provision of a narrow technical skills base to a situation where individuals are supplied with competencies in an ever-expanding range of skills. The emergence of the view which highlights the supremacy of the organisation that can learn faster than its competitor as the only sustainable competitive advantage (see for example Senge, 1990; Stata, 1989) has led to a burgeoning interest in continuous development as an organisational concern which in turn has resulted in a body of literature on the notion of a "learning organisation" and on the process of organisational learning. While there is no complete agreement on a definition of the learning organisation, the principles upon which the concept is founded represent a set of ideals to which most organisations would aspire, namely: the creation of an organisational climate that facilitates continuous development; a system that rewards continuous improvement; and a structural design that promotes on-going learning.

In view of the growing recognition of the value and economic necessity of training and development by all partners at the macro level, it remains to investigate training and development at the micro or organisational level. The data collected by the Price Waterhouse Cranfield Survey in 1992 suggested that training and development was receiving considerable focus at the organisational level. This was evidenced in increased expenditure on employee development; some attempt to develop a coherent approach to training needs identification and evaluation; and a clear recognition of the economic necessity for strengthened management development initiatives. This chapter builds upon the 1992 analysis in its investigation of the nature of current employee development practices in Ireland. In particular, we examine where responsibility for training and development policies lies, levels of training expenditure, the nature and extent of training needs analysis, the training methods employed, where the emphasis on training lies, number of days training given, and training evaluation. We also provide a picture in relation to longer-term developmental needs by highlighting the major employee development strategies currently in use.

Responsibility for Training and Development Policy Decisions

A training policy reflects the organisation's philosophy towards employee development and governs the priorities, standards and scope of its training activities. As such it provides the framework within which all planned interventions take place. An organisation's philosophy on employee development can be expressed along a continuum where, at the one extreme, training is viewed as an expense and only occurs as the need for it arises, and, at the other, employees are seen as a potential source of competitive advantage and so training and development is a central organisational concern (Gunnigle, Heraty and Morley, 1997). In this respect, all organisations have a training policy whether explicit or implicit, positive or negative. The extent to which organisations develop positive training policies is contextually bound and is influenced by factors such as prevailing employment legislation (i.e. equality, health and safety), state of the labour market (whether skilled labour is readily available, or can be contracted in/out), available resources that can be allocated to training, prevailing views on the value of training (particularly at senior and strategic levels), nature of the product/service market and, in some cases, the expectations of employees themselves. Furthermore, organisations can differentiate themselves as "desirable" employers by providing a range of employee and career development opportunities that are designed to attract and retain the required calibre of employee. Such an approach requires a high level of co-ordination between employee development and the range of other personnel policy choices such as recruitment and selection, performance appraisal, reward systems and employee relations. Clutterbuck (1989) argues that corporate strategies must be conceptualised and formulated within an employee development framework and, in order to ensure implementation, must be translated into actionable training and development policies. In the current survey, a total of 92.3 per cent of respondents suggest that they have a policy on training and development. However, 23.5 per cent continue to operate with an unwritten policy.

Many commentators have identified a shift in emphasis from the personnel function to line management in conducting tasks which traditionally were considered the responsibility of personnel, especially in the human resource development arena (see Heraty and Morley, 1995; Brewster and Soderstrom, 1994; Holden and Livian, 1992). There is widespread agreement that line managers have an active role to play in employee development generally, and that strategically focused training and development functions typically devolve responsibility for employee development to the line (Zenger, 1988; Schuler and Walker, 1990). An issues-orientation is advocated whereby human resource and line managers jointly identify issues critical to the function's effectiveness, thereby ensuring that human resource concerns are not ignored. Webster (1990) further suggests that, unless the line owns it, training and development will always be seen as something that occurs outside the mainstream.

Traditionally, training and development was taken to be the responsibility of the dedicated specialist function, however, this perception is being challenged as organisations identify and appreciate the key role that line managers play in employee development. Anderson (1993) proposes a role allocation which gives line managers a central role in the training and development process. The line manager, he suggests, must be highly regarded and should share many of the duties with the specialist. The sharing is seen to allow for the development of a "learning partnership".

In the current survey, respondents were asked to indicate where primary responsibility for training and development policy decisions lay in their organisation (see Figure 5.1).

Figure 5.1: Responsibility for Training and Development Policies

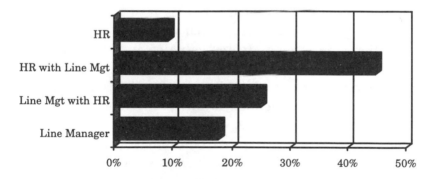

Source: Cranfield/University of Limerick Survey, 1995.

The data demonstrate that training and development policy decisions are most likely to be jointly shared between the personnel/human resource department and line managers. However, if it is not a shared responsibility then it is more likely that line management will determine the nature of such policy decisions rather than the HR function.

There appears to be a strong correlation between organisation size and changes in the level of responsibility which line managers are assuming in what were traditionally perceived to be the domain of the personnel department. When our data is tested for organisation size, it appears that larger companies are far more likely to report an increase in line management responsibility for training and development (see Table 5.1).

Table 5.1: Organisation Size as a Determinant of Changes in Line Management Responsibility for Training

	%	*50–199*	*200+*
	Increased	36	52
Training and Development	Same	61	44
	Decreased	5	4

n=245

Source: Cranfield/University of Limerick Survey, 1995.

Thus more than half (52 per cent) of those organisations which employ more than 200 employees report that line managers have increased their responsibility for developing major policy decisions on training and development. This result corresponds very closely with the 1992 findings, which would indicate that larger organisations are placing greater value on increasing line management participation. There is some evidence to suggest that smaller organisations are following this trend, where 36 per cent suggest that line participation is increasing. The corresponding figure for 1992 was 28 per cent.

When the data is tested for variance linked with organisation ownership, it emerges that, while increased responsibility is evident across all ownership categories, indigenous Irish companies are among the least likely to have increased line responsibility for training and development policy decision-making (see Table 5.2).

Table 5.2: Ownership as a Determinant of Changes in Line Management Responsibility for Training and Development

	%	*EU*	*Ireland*	*US*	*UK*	*Other*
Training and	Increased	63	41	41	47	60
Development	Same	33	52	57	47	40
	Decreased	4	7	2	5	—

n=229

Source: Cranfield/University of Limerick Survey, 1995.

The data suggests that EU-owned organisations are the most likely to have substantially increased line involvement for training and development (63 per cent), followed closely by non-EU-owned companies (60 per cent). The experience of Irish-owned companies tends to broadly mirror that of the US-owned organisations surveyed, which may be somewhat surprising given that the devolvement thesis is largely accredited with emerging with the practice of strategic HRM. In their European comparison of line responsibility for training and development, Mayne and Brewster (1995), reporting from data collected by the 1992 Cranfield Survey, suggested that the evidence relating to the devolvement of policies on training and development shows clear country distinctions. In relation to line management having sole responsibility for major policy decisions on training and development, they found that France, the UK, the Netherlands and Ireland emerged as the least devolved of the countries surveyed, while Turkey, Denmark and Portugal were found to be the most devolved.

In general and, despite the insistence of many commentators on the need for line managers to take responsibility for training and development activities, the process of devolvement is not unproblematic. Tsui (1987) argues that operating line managers are concerned with the production of goods or the delivery of services in the relatively short term, and they must respond to the concerns or needs of the present workforce, indicating perhaps that their perspective may focus more on short-term problem-solving activities rather than on long-term human resource strategies. Furthermore, Harrison (1992) suggests that line management is so often under pressure to achieve short-term objectives to do with profitability or reduction of costs that real support for human resource development — other than the most basic forms of training — is fairly rare.

As Holden and Livian (1992: 18) put it:

> First, there is often a dichotomy between the decentralised role and increasing responsibility of line managers, and the centralised role of the personnel/human resource function which must act as an interpreter of organisation-wide information and as a creator of human resource strategies. Sec-

ondly, the desire to empower the line manager may lead to sacrifices by the central personnel function in ensuring the relevant information is being relayed back.

Ashton (1984) highlights four problems when delegating to the line, namely: ownership of the training and development process; language relating to the problem of cognition outside the specialist area; role clarification in terms of the degree of line involvement in varying training and development activities; and the competence of line managers to undertake such specialist activities. Following a similar argument, Brewster and Soderstrom (1994: 144) highlight:

> Tasks are being taken away from specialists, with usually appropriate training in skills and, crucially, with a concentration in this one area. They are being passed to managers who may well have little training or skill in the area and who are often uncomfortable with or lack confidence in it, and who have myriad other responsibilities. . . . Risks also occur if HR tasks are transferred to (managerial) employees who already have a full or more than full workload. In such a case the new tasks get a low priority from those who are now responsible; in effect this may imply that devolvement equals a liquidation of tasks or, again, at least a serious loss in the quality of performance.

Training and Development Expenditure

Unlike many of their continental counterparts, Irish companies are not legally required to invest a minimum proportion of annual turnover or its equivalent in updating the skills and knowledge of their employees, nor are they obliged to make known the amount they spend annually on training and development (Heraty and Morley, 1994). Respondents to the survey were asked to indicate the proportion of their company's annual salaries and wages budget that was being spent on training. As with the 1992 survey, the respondents were asked to give an approximate figure. According to Fox (1987), however, when analysing approximations, problems continually arise in drawing up statistics on training and development, since different organisations have different perceptions of what training actually is, and since often organisations rely on informal methods of training, it becomes difficult to quantify the costs of same.

Expenditure on training and development varied considerably across the organisations surveyed with approximately 55 per cent of those who gave an estimate indicating that they spend 1 per cent or more of their salaries budget on training and development. The average proportion of annual salaries being spent on training for all respondent organisations in 1995 is approximately 3.59 per cent. The comparable figure in 1992 was 2.42 per cent.

Figure 5.2: Proportion of Annual Salaries/Wages Bill being Spent on Training and Development

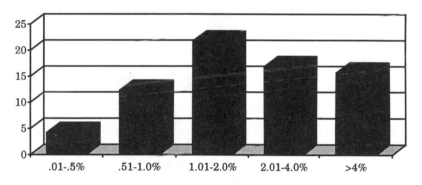

Source: Cranfield/University of Limerick Survey, 1995.

Testing the data for critical explanatory factors reveals a number of significant differences. Private sector organisations tend to spend a greater proportion on training than their counterparts in the public sector, with 82 per cent of private sector organisations spending more than 1 per cent, compared with 59 per cent of public sector companies.

It emerges that organisation size is not a significant variable in explaining variations in the amount spent on training in the 1995 data set. This is at variance with our 1992 findings which revealed that there was a significant correlation between the amount spent on training and the size of the organisation. While the presence or otherwise of a trade union (Figure 5.3) does not appear to have a significant impact on the proportion of the salaries/wages bill spent on training, those that spend in excess of 4 per cent are more than twice as likely to be non-union.

Figure 5.3: Proportion of Wages Bill Spent on Training and Development by Union Recognition

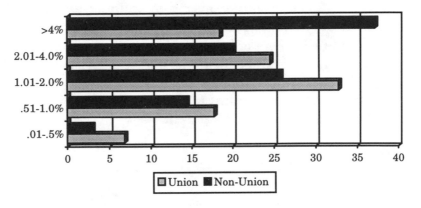

Source: Cranfield/University of Limerick Survey, 1995.

Indigenous Irish organisations do not compare favourably with organisations originating elsewhere, when the amount spent on training is examined (Table 5.3). While indigenous Irish organisations are two to three times more likely to spend less than 1 per cent of their wages bill on training activities, they are also 9 per cent less likely to spend more that 4 per cent.

Table 5.3: Proportion of Wages Bill Spent on Training by Ownership

	Other EU	*Ireland*	*US*	*UK*
0.01–0.51	4.3%	10.5%	0	0
0.51–1.0	8.7%	23.7%	15.6%	6.7%
1.01–2.0	39.1%	27.6%	28.9%	40.0%
2.01–4.0	21.7%	21.1%	28.9%	26.7%
>4	26.1%	17.1%	26.7%	26.7%

n=172

Source: Cranfield/University of Limerick Survey, 1995.

Analysis of, and Approaches to the Identification of Training Needs

Training needs analysis can be viewed as a systematic process of determining and ordering training goals, measuring training needs and deciding on priorities for training action. Such a needs analysis is a central component of the training process as it ensures that training and development occurs only where there is a valid need for it. Many organisations invest considerable resources in training but often fail to examine how effectively training can meet the business objectives. Training needs can be either current or future, or both. Current needs arise where inconsistencies emerge in the present training system and organisations must act to remedy the situation. Garavan, Costine and Heraty (1995) view this as a reactive needs analysis which usually provides a short-term solution. Future needs, on the other hand, arise from organisational changes and are usually diagnosed by proactive needs identification. They are prompted by internal and external factors such as strategy change, work restructuring, product/service diversification, introduction of new technology, skills inventories matched against future requirements, and so forth. Such needs are usually more developmental in nature, and there can be a temptation to dismiss them and deal only with immediate needs.

In an attempt to determine whether an underlying strategic imperative governs employee development activities, respondents to the survey were asked whether they systematically analysed employee training needs. A total of 75 per cent of respondents suggest that they do. This represents an increase of almost 6 per cent since 1992. However, one-in-four respondents still fail to carry out systematic training needs analysis and in such circumstances, it is difficult to envisage how employee development can make a strategic contribution to effective organisational functioning.

As with our 1992 results, the data here suggest that organisational size is a key determinant of whether respondents analyse their training needs. Larger organisations are substantially more likely to analyse their training needs than are their smaller counterparts (82 per cent as against 68.5 per cent respectively). Understandably, while time and resource constraints will impact more adversely on the smaller organisation in their training needs analysis effort, the necessity for such an analysis remains critical, regardless of size, and indeed arguably could be more critical in smaller concerns.

Sector also emerges as a critical determinant of the likelihood of a training needs analysis taking place. Almost 20 per cent more private sector organisations analyse training needs. It is interesting that almost 40 per cent of public sector organisations do not consider it necessary to conduct training needs analysis as a basis for effective training. This is again consistent with results from 1992 which revealed a broadly similar pattern.

Figure 5.4: Analysis of Training Needs by Sector

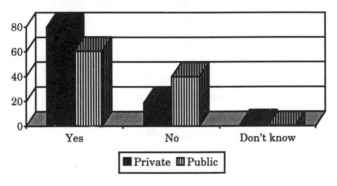

n=253

Source: Cranfield/University of Limerick Survey, 1995.

The existence or otherwise of a trade union appears to have a more marginal effect with approximately 76 per cent of unionised respondents and 70 per cent of non-union respondents reporting that they conduct a systematic training needs analysis. It would appear that some equalisation has taken place here since the comparable figures for 1992 were 68.1 per cent and 52 per cent respectively.

When compared with their foreign-owned counterparts, indigenous Irish organisations appear far less likely to conduct a systematic training needs analysis (61 per cent compared with more that 85 per cent). This seems to follow through from the 1992 findings which revealed that while 62 per cent of Irish-owned organisations conducted training needs analysis, some 73 per cent of UK-owned and 85 per cent of US-owned organisations systematically analysed training requirements.

Figure 5.5: Analysis of Training Needs by Country of Origin

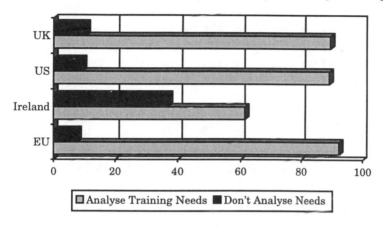

Source: Cranfield/University of Limerick Survey, 1995.

Where respondents indicated that they systematically analysed employee training needs, they were further asked to identify the actual methodologies employed and give an indication of the frequency with which they were drawn upon. Table 5.4 details the main findings, using 1992 as a comparator. Overall, we find stability in the results. The methodologies employed appear twofold i.e. highly formalised mechanisms (analysis of projected plans, training audits and performance appraisal) and less structured, more informal arrangements such as line management requests and employee requests, both types being relatively frequently drawn upon. Predictably, a greater proportion of respondents continue to rely on line management requests and/or the performance appraisal system to identify training needs. However, while there has been an increase in the use of training audits and analysis of projected plans since 1992, indicating perhaps some moves towards greater formality in this area, these methods remain largely under-utilised, thus militating against the strategic integration and functioning of employee development.

Table 5.4: Methods for Determining Training Needs

	Always		Often		Sometimes		Never		N	
	1995	*1992*	*1995*	*1992*	*1995*	*1992*	*1995*	*1992*	*1995*	*1992*
Analysis Projected plans	29	24	31	23	35	27	5	13	178	119
Training audits	22	21	30	28	34	28	15	16	173	115
Line mgt requests	31	28	44	55	24	17	0.5	0.7	189	145
Performance appraisal	37	35	28	38	29	22	5	6	187	149
Employee requests	15	9	42	48	42	40	1	4	184	141

Source: Cranfield/University of Limerick Survey, 1992 & 1995.

When the figures are disaggregated in order to determine the effect of the origin of the organisation, it emerges that indigenous Irish companies are less likely to use training audits, performance appraisal and employee requests than their EU- and US-owned counterparts. There are no real differences when organisation size is taken into account, with the exception that larger organisations are more likely to conduct training audits, and analyse needs against projected business plans. Union status and sector do not appear to have any discernible impact on the results.

Training Coverage

As indicated earlier, it is often difficult for respondents to estimate how much money is being spent on training. For this reason, it is useful to determine the extent of training coverage by exploring the level of training carried out at the organisational level. Respondents to the survey were asked to indicate the number of days' training per year that each staff category received (see Table 5.5).

Table 5.5: Number of Days' Training Received per Employee Category

Average number of training days per employee per year	Mgt 1995	Mgt 1992	Prof/technical 1995	Prof/technical 1992	Clerical 1995	Clerical 1992	Manual 1995	Manual 1992
0.01–1.0	4.6	3.5	3.1	2.2	19.5	11.4	11.9	8.3
1.01–3.0	24.9	17.5	25.3	19.7	27.6	26.8	20.7	14.9
3.01–5.0	26.4	26.8	22.2	21.1	15.7	15.4	10.7	11.8
5.01–10.0	10.3	15.8	12.3	16.7	5.7	7.9	4.6	11.8
>10 days	3.4	4.4	4.6	4.8	1.5	0.9	3.4	2.2
Don't know	30.3	32.0	32.6	35.5	29.9	37.7	48.7	50.9

Source: Cranfield/University of Limerick Survey, 1992 (n=228) and 1995 (n=261).

From the data reported here, the number of days' training received by employees tends to decrease as one descends the organisational hierarchy. It would appear that, on average, the greater proportion of management employees are likely to receive between three and five days' training per year (26.4 per cent), while the highest frequency for professional/technical staff (25.3 per cent) is recorded in the one-to-three days' training category. The highest frequencies for clerical and manual employees are also recorded in the one-to-three days' training category, but it is evident from the overall data distribution that such employee categories are typically less likely to receive as much training as either professional or managerial employees. These results are consistent with data recorded in 1992 and goes some way further towards disputing the view that management development is not given priority in Irish organisations. It is interesting to note however, that, across all employee categories, while there appears to be some increase in training provision, especially in the zero-to-one and one-to-three days' training categories, there is also a concomitant decrease in the provision of more than five days' training. Furthermore, there is a substantial reduction in the numbers of respondents that reported in 1992 that they were unaware of the amount of training employees in their organisations were receiving.

When the figures are disaggregated in order to examine sectoral differences and the impact of organisational size and union recognition, few significant findings are recorded. It would appear that clerical workers received marginally more training in smaller organisations, whereas in larger companies the manual employee category received slightly more training than is the case in smaller concerns.

Delivery of Training

The choice of training delivery method available to organisations is considerable and thus organisations, when deciding on the most appropriate method to use, must take cognisance of the principles of learning, the needs of the employees to be trained and the logistics of training that affect every organisation. All training delivery methods have their own particular strengths and can be modified to suit the organisation's requirements. The most important criteria in determining the choice of training delivery method is the extent to which it meets the particular objectives that have been established through the training needs analysis.

Respondents to the survey were asked to identify their choice of training delivery method and to indicate whether their use of such method(s) had changed over the previous three years (see Table 5.6).

Table 5.6: Changing Use of Training Delivery Methods

	Increased	*Same*	*Decreased*	*Not used*
Internal training staff	48.7	33.0	4.2	7.3
Line managers	34.9	41.8	3.4	8.8
External providers	54.8	31.4	5.7	3.1
On the job training	45.2	48.3	0.4	0.4
Internal courses	54.4	32.2	3.4	2.7
External courses	41.4	39.5	6.5	3.8
Coaching	23.8	32.2	1.5	27.2
Computer-based packages	44.1	24.1	0.8	20.7
Open learning	25.3	16.9	3.4	37.9
Mentoring	16.9	16.5	—	51.3

Source: Cranfield/University of Limerick Study, 1995.

It is evident that the responding organisations utilise a variety of delivery mechanisms in their training activities. Interestingly, it would appear that organisations are reluctant to rely solely on one training delivery strategy and appear to strike a balance between formal and informal delivery mechanisms in an effort to maximise efficiency returns. This is evident in the reported increased usage of internal and external formal training programmes (54.4 per cent and 54.8 per cent respectively) and so training is delivered through a combination of external and internal service providers. On-the-job training retains its popularity with just 0.4 per cent of responding organisations indicating that this delivery mechanism is not used by them. Traditionally, on-the-job training strategies were perceived as ineffective since they were usually unplanned, unsystematic, informal and difficult to evaluate. However, the advantages of on-the-job training delivery are recognised in terms of providing a natural learning environment and thereby facilitating the transfer of knowledge on the job situation. The use of computer-based packages as a delivery mechanism has increased substantially since 1992 (44.1 per cent), and, while particularly useful to develop specific skills, does require that the individual employee be capable of managing their own learning effort. The least popular training delivery mechanisms, among respondents, include mentoring and coaching. This may be due to the large commitment of time, and hence resources, required for coaching and mentoring, yet such delivery methods have consistently been lauded for their critical contribution to strategic employee development (see, for example, Wexley and Latham, 1991; Murray, 1991; Kram, 1985).

When the figures are disaggregated in order to consider size, the results show that large organisations have increased their use of all methods substantially more than small companies, particularly the use of line managers, external courses, open learning and mentoring. In relation to union status, we find that while there are no significant differences between unionised and non-unionised organisations, the non-union category do appear to have increased their reliance on internal training courses more than their unionised counterparts (69 per cent and 56 per cent respectively). In relation to sectoral explanations, four key areas of difference emerge. The increase in the use of external training providers is higher in the public sector than in the private sector (66 per cent versus 55 per cent). Conversely, on-the-job training is substantially more prevalent in the private sector. Approximately 53 per cent of private sector respondents report increased reliance on on-the-job training compared to 31 per cent in the public sector. Coaching, too, has increased more in the private sector, while the use of computer-based packages appears to be emerging at a faster pace in the public sector. A total of 59 per cent of public sector respondents report an increase in the use of such packages.

A central aspect of effective training practice concerns the identification and prioritisation of training requirements for the future. In an effort to determine training priorities, responding organisations were asked to identify those training areas they perceived to be important and to rate the relative importance of these training areas (see Table 5.7).

Table 5.7: Importance of Specific Training Areas over the next 3 years

	Very	*Quite*	*Average*	*Not very*	*Not at all*
People Mgt & Supervision	67.4	21.8	7.7	1.1	—
Computers/New technology	67.0	25.7	6.1	0.8	—
Business Admin.	17.2	39.5	31.0	7.3	0.8
Strategy Formulation	41.0	35.2	12.3	5.7	1.1
Marketing & Sales	36.0	23.8	11.9	10.7	11.1
Health and Safety	44.1	32.6	17.2	2.3	0.8
Customer Service Skills	57.5	18.8	12.3	4.6	3.4
Mgt. of Change	64.0	25.7	6.1	1.9	1.1
Quality Mgt	63.2	26.8	6.5	1.9	0.8

Source: Cranfield/University of Limerick Survey, 1995.

It is to be expected that training priorities will vary considerably across organisations depending on a whole range of internal and external considerations. While the results here reflect this variety in training priorities, they also point to particular emphasis being placed on developing skills in the areas of people management/supervision and computers/new technology. These results are not, perhaps, unsurprising. The pace of technological development and change poses considerable challenges for the nature and management of the work situation where, as Block (1990) indicates, the growing realisation that strict, tight controls, greater pressure, more clearly defined jobs and tighter supervision have, in the last 50 years, run their course in their ability to give organisations the productivity gains required to compete effectively in the marketplace. Given the pervasiveness of organisational change and the uncertainties of market forces, one would expect that skills in the areas of people management and new technology would represent key priority areas for organisations. Both the management of change and quality management further emerges as important training areas to be targeted in the future, while business administration and marketing appear to be of less concern to the respondents here.

Training Evaluation

Buckley and Caple (1990) describe evaluation as the process of attempting to assess the total value of training, that is, the cost benefit and general outcomes which benefit the organisation as well as the value of the improved performance of those who have undertaken training. Evaluation of training and development activities ensures that control is maintained over the training process and allows for assessment of the outcomes, methods and overall impact of any training and development programme. Easterby-Smith (1986) outlines three general purposes of training evaluation:

- Summative — testing to determine whether training and development was effective and achieved its objectives.

- Formative — qualitative analysis of training as it is occurring to determine whether improvements or adjustments are required.

- Learning — assessing the extent to which the trainee can transfer the learning acquired back to their job performance.

The systems approach to training evaluation, as proposed by, among others, Hamblin (1974) and Kirkpatrick (1967), delineates the contributions that training makes at different levels within the organisation and requires that data be quantifiable and based on pre-determined objectives. Such models propose a hierarchy of evaluation where each level requires a different evaluation strategy and is seen as a measure of the progressive transfer and application of training content.

Evaluation constitutes the final stage in the training and development process and, while difficult to measure, provides information that is critical to effective organisational functioning. Lack of training evaluation can result in inappropriate training which is wasteful of both financial and human resources. The difficulty for most organisations lies in identifying a set of measurable criteria that can facilitate the effective evaluation of employee development interventions. In particular, many of the perceived key benefits of employee development such as improved morale, increased job satisfaction and improved employee relations are, by their very nature, difficult to demonstrate in quantitative terms, and thus many organisations limit their activities to a level-one (reaction) evaluation.

Participants in the survey were asked to indicate whether they evaluate the effectiveness of their training activities. The results are presented in Table 5.8 and 1992 data is included for comparative purposes.

Table 5.8: Monitor the Effectiveness of Training

	1995	1992
Monitor effectiveness	74.3	71.9
Don't monitor effectiveness	20.7	21.9
Don't know	3.1	2.2

Source: Cranfield/University of Limerick Survey, 1995.

It would appear that almost three-quarters of those surveyed evaluate their training and development activities (74.3 per cent), which is broadly consistent with results obtained in 1992. However, some 20.7 per cent of respondents still fail to evaluate the effectiveness of their training. In a time of scarce resources and pressures of "bottom-line added value" the requirement for some evaluative process is increasingly evident if training is to continue to be considered a critical organisational activity. When these results are tested against various organisational characteristics, a number of pertinent findings emerge. Unlike the situation in 1992, here union recognition does not appear to have any significant impact on whether or not the organisation monitors the effectiveness of its training. However, organisation sector does appear to have some explanatory power where private sector companies are 18 per cent more likely to become involved in evaluating the effectiveness of their training activities than are organisations in the public sector.

A variety of techniques are employed by responding organisations to evaluate the effectiveness of their training output (see Table 5.9).

Table 5.9: Methods of Evaluating Training

How often are the following methods used?	Always	Often	Sometimes	Never
Tests	2.3	5.4	14.6	28.7
Formal evaluation immediately after training	30.3	14.6	15.3	5.7
Formal eval. some months later	3.8	10.7	27.6	13.8
Informal feedback from line managers	29.1	34.9	10.0	1.5
Informal feedback from trainees	33.0	28.4	12.3	1.1
Other	4.6	—	—	—

Source: Cranfield/University of Limerick Survey, 1995.

The findings indicate that responding organisations tend to place a large emphasis on informal mechanisms of evaluation, and are less likely to use more structured mechanisms such as formal evaluation or tests. Informal feedback from both line managers and trainees emerge as the most frequently utilised evaluation mechanisms, which is similar to the 1992 findings. However, the use of more structured and valid evaluation criteria which quantifiably measure learning and learning transfer, such as tests and formal evaluation some months after training, remains negligible in many organisations or, where utilised, is evidently on an *ad hoc* basis.

While organisation size has no discernible effect on the level of use of informal evaluation methods, larger organisations do appear more likely to use quantitative methods of evaluation, such as tests and formal evaluation directly after the training event and some time later (see Table 5.10).

Table 5.10: Methods of Training Evaluation by Organisation Size

	Tests	Formal eval. after event	Formal eval. later	Line mgt. feedback	Trainee feedback
50–199	33.4	85.3	68.5	98.8	97.4
>200	52.7	94.4	79.7	98.2	99.1

Source: Cranfield/University of Limerick Survey, 1995.

Informal evaluation is also common among both public and private sector organisations and, similar to results in 1992, private sector companies are more likely to use all methods of formal evaluation, particularly tests (see Table 5.11). No significant differences emerged with respect to organisations which recognise trade unions and those that maintain a non-union status and training evaluation mechanisms. In relation to organisational ownership, the data suggest that while informal evaluation mechanisms are common across all ownership categories, indigenous Irish companies are the least likely to draw upon formal mechanisms such as tests and formal evaluation immediately after training.

Table 5.11: Methods of Training Evaluation by Sector

	Tests	Formal eval. after event	Formal eval. later	Line mgt. feedback	Trainee feedback
Private	46.4	92.8	79.0	98.7	98.7
Public	30.0	84.8	57.7	94.7	97.7

Source: Cranfield/University of Limerick Survey, 1995.

Longer-Term Developmental Activities

Organisations are typically comprised of a range of different job types at various levels and so it is advisable to develop systems which ensure that the flow of personnel within the company hierarchy is managed well. London and Stumpf (1982) stress the importance of establishing career paths, keeping information complete and up-to-date, and ensuring that there is a system for matching people to jobs so that there is an improved pool of valuable skills and experience within the organisation. However, while both organisations and individuals are paying increasing attention to the planning and management of careers, the concept of career is becoming much more difficult to define. Accelerated economic change, organisational delayering and an increase in the use of outsourcing have combined to challenge the traditional perceptions of not only a job for life, but also of the existence of established, easily identifiable career paths and development initiatives. The concept of career is essentially perceptually based and there is no complete agreement about what it is. Greenhaus and Callanan (1994) describe the career as the pattern of work-related experiences that span the course of a person's life. From an employee's perspective this will encapsulate the sequence of jobs which individuals pursue throughout their working life. In organisational terms career development is a systematic process in which the organisation attempts to assist employees in the analysis of their abilities and interests and to guide their placement, progression and development while with the organisation (Gunnigle and Flood, 1990).

One key problem experienced by many organisations is the mismatch of employee expectations about the job and career prospects and the reality of the situation. This, in part, may explain the "induction crisis" experienced by many organisations, where several new employees leave the organisation within the first six weeks of starting employment. Organisations can reduce this crisis by developing a "realistic job preview" which attempts to describe the job and the company as seen by those who work there. In this way potential job applicants can self-match their skills, abilities and aspirations against the realistic job description provided.

Nicholson and Arnold (1989) identify four common shortcomings of organisational employee development systems:

- Restricted: while some restrictions are inevitable, organisations can often create unnecessary ones such as non-promotional transfers between functions;

- Political: where career opportunities can be blocked by managers who perhaps seek to advance their own interests at the expense of individual employees;

- Mechanistic: where career moves are controlled by rules and procedures that do not allow for exceptions and fail to take account of changing circumstances;

- Neglected: where possible career paths are simply not identified and no-one can see the way forward.

Gutteridge (1986) suggests that organisations can facilitate the long-term development of their human capital by providing a range of structures and systems that offer appropriate support and opportunities. Such supports might include:

- self-assessment tools such as career planning workshops;

- individual counselling services;

- information on the workings of the internal labour market;

- assessment of future potential through succession planning, testing, etc.;

- development programmes such as mentoring systems and/or job rotation.

In an attempt to gauge the extent to which organisations are concerned with the long-term strategic development of its employees, respondents to the survey were asked to indicate the type(s) of developmental strategies they employed in their organisation (see Table 5.12).

Table 5.12: Use of Longer-Term Developmental Strategies

Do you regularly use any of the following?	1995	1992
Formal career plans	23.0	15.8
Assessment centres	8.0	4.8
Succession plans	34.1	30.3
Planned job rotation	28.0	26.3
High-flier schemes	14.2	11.4
International experience schemes	19.2	19.3
	n=261	n=228

Source: Cranfield/University of Limerick Survey, 1995.

The results reveal that a variety of strategies are adopted by organisations in an attempt to develop a strategic orientation to their employee development initiatives. Again there is relative stability between the results presented here, and those recorded in 1992. In particular, succession plans, planned job rotations and formal career plans are favoured most by respondents, while assessment centres are utilised by only a very small minority of organisations. While it is recognised that assessment centres are costly, Arnold et al. (1995) suggest that, since they make use of a variety of behaviour predictors, they are particularly useful in taking decisions concerning promotion and career development in general.

There is a significant difference in the developmental strategies adopted by larger and smaller companies (see Table 5.13). International experience schemes, succession plans, high-flier schemes, formal career plans and planned job rotation are all put in practice by a substantially higher number of larger organisations. This may be as a consequence of the greater availability of resources, but may also be related to increased opportunities for promotion and career development among large organisations.

Table 5.13: Use of Developmental Strategies by Organisation Size

	50–199	*200+*
Formal career plans	16.4	29.2
Assessment centres	7.3	8.3
Succession plans	19.1	45.8
Planned job rotation	16.4	37.5
High-flier schemes	7.3	20.1
International experience schemes	10.9	25.0
	n=110	n=144

Source: Cranfield/University of Limerick Survey, 1995.

A substantially greater percentage of private sector respondents use career and succession plans, high-flier and international experience schemes, whereas 12 per cent more public sector organisations used planned job rotation. Planned job rotation and succession planning are more prevalent among unionised companies, while high-flier schemes and international experience schemes are more likely to feature in non-unionised organisations (see Figure 5.6).

Figure 5.6: Use of Various Employee Development Schemes by Union Recognition

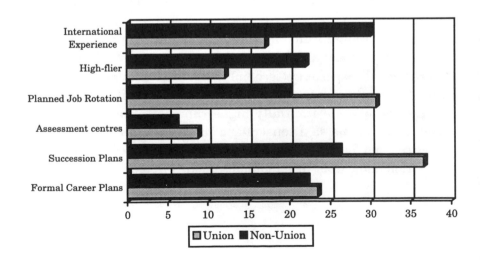

Source: Cranfield/University of Limerick Survey, 1995.

Organisation ownership appears to have some explanatory power in terms of the use of particular developmental strategies. In particular, we note that indigenous Irish companies are the least likely to adopt a range of developmental strategies, with the exception of planned job rotation which is used by about a quarter of the Irish-owned companies surveyed. US-owned organisations, on the other hand, appear the most likely to adopt a broader approach to employee development in the long term.

Table 5.14: Use of Developmental Strategies by Ownership

	EU	*Ireland*	*UK*	*US*
Formal Career Plans	21.4%	18.0%	34.4%	42.1%
Assessment Centres	10.7%	2.7%	7.8%	26.3%
Succession Plans	50.0%	20.7%	48.4%	57.9%
Planned Job Rotation	21.4%	25.2%	34.4%	21.1%
High Flier Schemes	17.9%	7.2%	29.7%	10.5%
International Experience Schemes	32.1%	10.8%	32.8%	15.8%
	n=28	n=111	n=19	n=64

Source: Cranfield/University of Limerick Survey, 1995.

CONCLUSION

The training and development function has experienced considerable change in recent years. While often viewed as an elusive activity, lacking any real strategic focus, there is evidence that this is changing. There is a growing body of literature on the emergence and growth of human resource development with some contributors highlighting the development of a strategic orientation. At minimum there appears to be a greater degree of consistency in decision-making in this area which is evidenced through the development and implementation of written employee development policies, the systematic identification of training needs, the utilisation of longer-term developmental strategies and the formal evaluation of training events. Arguably, however, there remains a multiplicity of values, priorities, strategies and orientations.

Specifically, there is evidence from both the contemporary literature and the data presented here of at least some devolvement of training and development responsibilities to line managers.

However, this devolvement would appear to be occurring in a less exaggerated fashion than one might anticipate. Thus, as demonstrated from this Europe-wide project, while devolvement is extensive in some countries, it is a rarity in others, with Ireland, along with France, the UK and the Netherlands emerging as the least devolved. Key factors inhibiting complete devolvement to the line include the importance of the activity from a strategic perspective, the issue of ownership, differing perspectives between line managers and specialists and the organisational support for line managers to conduct training and development activities in a competent fashion. Until these issues are addressed, the likely pattern of responsibility for training and development will at best be a joint one between the specialist and the line.

There is evidence of an increase in training and development expenditure over the last three years. The average proportion of annual salaries being spent on training in 1995 is approximately 3.6 per cent. The comparable figure in 1992 was 2.4 per cent. The majority of this increase is accounted for in the private, foreign-owned subsidiaries sector.

The ability to accurately identify and prioritise training needs to the maximum benefit of the organisation's goals remains the cornerstone of organisational training and development. Our data suggest that approximately 7 out of every 10 respondent organisations conduct a systematic needs analysis largely through either line management requests and/or the performance appraisal system. Size, sector and ownership act as critical explanatory factors here. Predictably, larger organisations are more likely to analyse their training needs than are smaller organisations, while private sector companies similarly record greater levels of training needs analysis than do public sector concerns. When compared to their foreign-owned counterparts, indigenous Irish companies appear far less likely to systematically analyse the training needs of their employees. There has been no improvement here since 1992, yet it is precisely activity of this kind which gives the necessary macro and micro perspectives to best diagnose skill deficiencies at the organisational level. In terms of actual delivery, our data once again highlight that organisations are reluctant to rely solely on one training delivery strategy and appear to strike a balance between formal and informal delivery mechanisms in an effort to maximise efficiency returns.

The level of complexity involved in training evaluation can vary, depending on the commitment given to it and the number of stakeholders involved in the process. Our data suggest that the number of organisations that evaluate training effectiveness has increased since 1992. However, their remains a tendency to continually rely on informal evaluation mechanisms such as informal feedback from both line managers and trainees. More formal, structured, objective criteria remain under-utilised.

Strategically oriented training and development activities can make a significant contribution to the success of the organisation. This may manifest itself in the organisation's ability to innovate, in the quality of its strategic decision-making, in individual/group performance and productivity, and in how closely the skills of the organisation are aligned with its strategic mission and plans. The challenge facing practitioners is to ensure that all training and development activity meets the organisations requirements for strategic functioning in order to give it centrality in organisational life.

Chapter 6

COMPENSATION AND BENEFITS

Michael Morley & Patrick Gunnigle

INTRODUCTION

An organisation's approach to compensation may be determined by a number of variables, including the workforce itself — skill, education level — the organisation's culture and philosophy, and the economy as a whole. Most importantly the system of remuneration can be an important indication of the organisation's approach to employee relations and workforce management, and to this end Goss (1994) argues that a central and recurrent debate concerns the extent to which remuneration should be treated as an individual or collective phenomenon. Put succinctly, an organisation's reward system is a powerful indicator of its philosophy and approach to workforce management (Gunnigle et al., 1997) and has meaning to the employee precisely because it conveys information about important aspects of employment other than pay (Thierry, 1992). Yet, the implementation of effective reward systems has proven a difficult task for many organisations, reflected in the myriad of forms now in common use in Ireland. Beer et al., (1985) suggest that many employee grievances and criticisms of reward systems actually mask more fundamental employee relations problems. Because extrinsic rewards are a tangible outcome of an employee's relationship with an organisation, they are an obvious target for discontent with the employment relationship. Dissatisfaction with elements of this relationship, such as the supervisory style or opportunities for personal development, may manifest themselves in dissatisfaction with aspects of the reward system (Gunnigle et al., 1994). Consequently, the design of payment systems "can evoke behaviours which, although meaningful to the recipient, are quite different from those expected or desired by those designing or implementing the system" (Goss, 1994: 85).

Our 1992 data on compensation highlighted that while national/industry-wide collective bargaining represented the predominant mechanism by which pay was determined for professional/technical, clerical and manual employees, managerial employees in the main were subject to individual pay determination. We noted that variable pay packages had increased in popularity in almost a third of respondent organisations in both the public and private sectors. Similarly, non-monetary benefits had likewise seen an increase in popularity especially among private sector, non-unionised organisations. Merit/performance-related pay and individual bonus/commission represented the most commonly utilised incentives across all grades in respondent organisations. Again such schemes were most popular amongst non-union and private sector respondents. As appears to be the established pattern, private and foreign multinational respondents indicated a greater propensity to implement group bonus schemes than public and indigenous organisations although usage remained relatively low across all categories. Finally, our 1992 data revealed that profit-sharing and employee share ownership were confined to private sector respondents and were more frequently utilised amongst non-unionised foreign multinational companies.

Using the evidence from the Cranfield/University of Limerick Study (1995), here we examine three facets of reward practices in Ireland: the level at which pay is determined for different employee grades; the extent of variable pay and non-monetary benefits and the use of various incentives. Finally, we also examine the nature and extent of performance appraisal.

Wage Determination

Roche (1997: 145) notes that it is scarcely possible to describe or analyse pay determination in Ireland without reference to the role of the State in industrial relations, even during periods in which governments have opted to remain outside the direct process of negotiating. In the vein of neo-corporatism, we have, in recent years, witnessed a return to centralised bargaining in Ireland, with the emergence of the PNR, the PESP, the PCW and the most recent, Partnership 2000. All of these programmes have been developed and agreed by the three social partners — the Government, the Irish Congress of Trade Unions, and the Irish Business and Employers Confederation. Such public policy developments should be set within the overall European context. Although Ireland's voluntarist tradition in industrial relations set it apart from the broad sweep of European developments, in recent years successive Irish Governments have clearly been taking steps towards a more broadly European approach with the emphasis on the development of a strong national consensus involving all the main social partners.

Overall, in the Irish context, economic and managerial factors, coupled with the strength of the trade union movement have shaped the development of pay bargaining carried out at all levels. In the European context, there has been a trend towards national determination for manual categories, and as one moves up the hierarchy, pay determination tends to become more individualised (Gunnigle et al., 1994). This is reflected in the findings on pay determination from the 1995 survey which largely support the pattern highlighted in 1992 (see Table 6.1).

Table 6.1: Level of Basic Pay Determination

	Mgt		Prof/Technical		Clerical		Manual	
	1995	1992	1995	1992	1995	1992	1995	1992
National/ Industry-wide	34.5	30.3	40.2	37.3	53.6	51.3	62.1	67.1
Regional	0	0	0.8	1.3	4.6	4.8	8.8	6.6
Company/division	31.4	28.9	26.4	25.4	23.8	26.8	11.9	18.9
Establishment	10.3	13.6	14.9	16.2	13.0	14.5	10.0	12.7
Individual	44.4	44.3	28.7	32.5	20.7	19.3	6.1	7.0

Source: Cranfield/University of Limerick Survey, 1992 and 1995.

Pay determination continues to be diverse with a range of mechanisms being pursued at various levels. For a majority of managerial employees, pay continues to be determined at either individual or company level. Conversely and predictably, for manual employees, pay is largely determined at national level. Gunnigle et al. (1994) rationalise this diversity in terms of the return to centralised bargaining in 1987, the breakdown of regional and industry bargaining and the ongoing change in the employer–employee relationship resulting in an increased emphasis on individualism.

Overall in the Irish context, economic and managerial factors, coupled with the resolve of the union movement, have shaped the face of pay bargaining carried out at all levels and resulted in a consensus on economic policy, which, according to Roche (1997) was not apparent in the earlier phase of sustained tripartism during the 1970s.

Companies recognising trade unions appear far more likely to determine pay at the national level for all categories of employees (see Figure 6.1) than is the case for non-union establishments. The integral role of the union movement in the development of tripartite agreements, coupled with the concentration of union membership among manual and clerical grades and the commitment of both employers and unions to pay norms negotiated under such agreements, has resulted in the dominance of national pay determination. Among the non-union group, individual pay determination dominates, in keeping with the European trend that denotes a growing shift in emphasis in the employment relationship in an effort to individualise the employment contract (see Figure 6.2).

Figure 6.1: Unionisation as a Determinant of Pay Determination at National Level

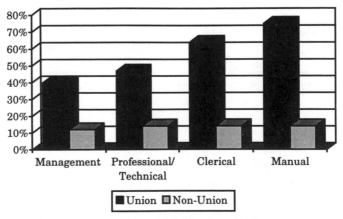

Source: Cranfield/University of Limerick Survey, 1995.

Figure 6.2: Unionisation as a Determinant of Pay Determination at Individual Level

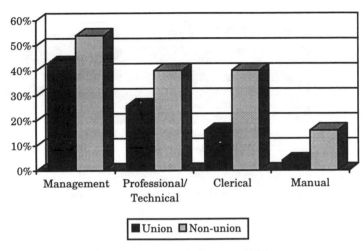

Source: Cranfield/University of Limerick Survey, 1995.

Across all employment categories, national pay determination represents the predominant mechanism by which pay is determined in Irish-owned organisations (see Figure 6.3). Predictably, however, national determination is most common among manual and clerical employees. Relative to the experience in the indigenous sector and to a lesser extent their European-owned counterparts, with the exception of manual grades, pay determination in US-owned organisations occurs at the level of the individual. Arguably, this emphasis on individualism may be understood by reference to historical developments in workforce practices in the US where the widespread growth in the non-union phenomenon, coupled with the growth of behavioural sciences initiated a fundamental refocusing on human resource policies emphasising individualism (Gunnigle et al., 1994).

Figure 6.3: Ownership as a Determinant of Pay Determination at National Level

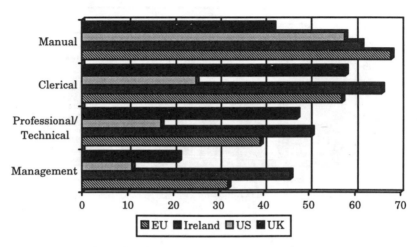

Source: Cranfield/University of Limerick Survey, 1995.

Variable Pay and Benefits

There has been an increase in variable pay in Ireland in recent years which is consistent with the European trend. This serves not only to allow employees enjoy periods of success, but also helps spread risk in times of difficulty. Zalusky (1991) suggests, however, that this growth in variable pay is limited as the banks that hold mortgages do not adjust monthly bills to fit changes in workers' income. This is particularly relevant in Ireland, given the open nature of the economy and the vulnerability of individuals to exchange rate volatility and resulting interest fluctuations (Foley et al., 1996).

Table 6.2: Change in the Total Reward Package

	Increased		Decreased		Same		Don't know	
	1995	*1992*	*1995*	*1992*	*1995*	*1992*	*1995*	*1992*
Variable	26.4	31.6	4.2	3.9	60.5	56.1	2.7	3.5
Non-monetary benefits	13.0	19.3	6.1	1.8	67.8	67.1	3.4	3.1

Source: Cranfield/University of Limerick Survey, 1992 and 1995.

Organisation size does not seem to have a significant impact on variable pay or non-monetary benefits. We also tested for the influence of country of origin and it was found to have no notable effect. However, sectoral differences and union recognition do have some explanatory power. Eleven percent more private sector organisations have increased levels of variable pay. Non-union companies are also more likely to have increased their use of variable pay. The picture emerging here is somewhat different to 1992. Then, our data revealed that the union/non-union split was not significant. Thus 33 per cent of unionised and 36 per cent of non-unionised respondents suggested that the use of variable pay had increased while 60 per cent and 57 per cent respectively noted that no major change had occurred in this area between 1989 and 1992.

Table 6.3: Unionisation as a Determinant of Changes in Variable Pay

	Increased	*Same*	*Decreased*
Union	26.0	67.7	4.7
Non-union	40.4	48.9	4.3

Source: Cranfield/University of Limerick Survey, 1995.

Turning to the issue of benefits, in general, they (both statutory and voluntary) are estimated to constitute an additional 25–30 per cent on top of basic weekly pay for manual grades. For clerical, administrative and managerial categories, a figure of 15–35 per cent should be added (Gunnigle et al., 1994). However, the percentage add-on is primarily related to the level of fringe benefits voluntarily agreed at company level, particularly items such as company cars, pensions, health/insurance cover, and sickness benefit and can, therefore, vary considerably between organisations. Perhaps the most widely applicable benefit available to employees under statute is an entitlement to a minimum of 16 days annual leave under the working time directive this will increase to 18 days in 1998, and to 20 days in 1999. Legislation has further increased this entitlement by providing for ten public holidays per annum. It must be realised however that the great majority of organisations provide entitlements greater than the statutory, varying from 18 to 23 days with the average being 20 days per annum. Female employees in the event of pregnancy are also protected by statute and are entitled to a minimum period of 14 weeks unpaid maternity leave in accordance with the terms of the Maternity Protection of Employees Act (1981 & 1984) and the Worker Protection (Regular Part-time Employees) Act (1991). Such employees are also entitled to paid time off for ante-natal and post-natal care. Employees on maternity leave are paid an allowance under the terms of the Social Welfare legislation. While there are no statutory requirements for the provision of canteen facilities, the Safety in Industry Act (1980) requires that "where more than five people are employed, there must be adequate provision for boiling water and taking meals". In practice, the majority of larger employers provide some form of canteen facilities. These may be subsidised by up to half the economic costs of meals, often with tea/coffee facilities also being provided at subsidised rates.

Voluntary fringe benefits refer to an ever-expanding group of facilities provided by an employer, the terms of which are set by unilateral decision or in negotiation with employees and their representatives. The most widely applicable schemes are pension plans and those schemes relating to employee health. Pension schemes in this context refer to those pensions provided by the organisation and governed by the Pensions Act (1990). Most larger organisations have such schemes. A 1988 survey of 579 organisations conducted by the Federation of Irish Employers found that 79 per cent of companies had a pension scheme for all or some employees. The majority of these schemes are contributory with the normal rate of employee contribution at 5 per cent of annual earnings. While there is no legal obligation on organisations to provide sick-pay or health insurance cover for employees, many organisations do undertake such schemes. A 1990 survey carried out by the Federation of Irish Employers found that of the 515 companies questioned, 351 (68 per cent) had sick-pay schemes for full-time manual workers, and 424 (82 per cent) had schemes for white collar grades. Also, over 75 per cent of private sector companies have VHI schemes in operation for employees. The FIE estimates that over half of the white collar schemes and one-third of the manual grade schemes incorporate an employer contribution to the cost of such schemes.

Table 6.4: Use of Benefits

Workplace child-care	1.9
Child-care allowances	0.4
Career break scheme	27.6
Paternity leave	10.3

Source: Cranfield/University of Limerick Survey, 1995.

Other widely used benefits include the provision of company cars for particular grades of employee, managerial incentive schemes and additional payments bonuses (e.g. Christmas Bonuses). In an effort to ensure that qualified and skilled individuals remain in the workforce, some organisations are adopting child-care facilities or allowances. However, such schemes are limited to a small number of Irish organisations (see Table 6.4).

Utilisation of Incentive Schemes

The use of incentives is not a new phenomenon with Pay-By-Results schemes having formed a significant part of the traditional remuneration package in many organisations. However, the applicability of pay-related incentive schemes across a wide range of organisational contexts is difficult to generalise on, largely because the empirical evidence to support the notion that money is a motivator is far from conclusive. Indeed, in some instances, failure of such schemes to fulfil their potential has been attributed to a flawed theoretical base (Pearse, 1987) which in many cases serves to undermine effectiveness by demotivating employees (Sargent, 1990). Notwithstanding these reservations incentive schemes seem to be becoming more popular in Irish organisations, but on a very incremental basis, and with limited applicability. There is remarkable consistency between our 1992 and 1995 results. Merit or performance-related pay does not seem to be applied to manual grades in the majority of organisations. However, the results would seem to confirm the fact that merit/PRP is the

most popular form of incentive used in Irish organisations, but
that it is not applied across all levels in the hierarchy (see Table
6.5).

Table 6.5: Use of Incentive Schemes

	Management		Prof/technical		Clerical		Manual	
	1995	*1992*	*1995*	*1992*	*1995*	*1992*	*1995*	*1992*
Share options	23.0	22.8	13.8	13.6	11.5	9.2	9.6	8.8
Profit sharing	19.2	15.8	13.4	12.3	12.6	10.5	10.0	10.1
Group bonus	21.1	14.9	15.7	12.7	16.1	11.0	15.3	14.0
Merit/PRP	51.3	49.1	44.8	42.5	36.8	29.4	15.3	13.2

Source: Cranfield/University of Limerick Survey, 1992 and 1995.

Organisation size has an influence on the decision to implement
profit sharing, group bonus and merit or performance-related pay.
Larger organisations are significantly more likely to use profit-
sharing for each employee category, and merit or performance-
related pay for managerial and professional employees (see Table
6.6).

**Table 6.6: Organisational Size as a Determinant of the Use
of Incentive Schemes**

	50–199				>200			
	Mgt.	Prof.	Cler-ical	Man-ual	Mgt.	Prof.	Cler-ical	Man-ual
Profit-share	13.6	7.3	7.3	4.5	22.9	17.4	16.0	13.2
Group bonus	20.9	13.6	12.7	12.7	22.2	18.1	19.4	18.1
Merit/PRP	43.6	38.2	32.7	15.5	57.6	50.7	38.9	15.3

Source: Cranfield/University of Limerick Survey, 1995.

Merit/PRP

Goss (1994) notes that while there are various systems that claim
to reward employees according to their performance, most of the
recent debate has centred on merit or performance-related pay.
McBeath and Rands (1989: 133) define Performance-Related Pay
(PRP) as "an intention to pay distinctly more to reward highly effective job performance than you are willing to pay for good solid

performance", the objective of which should be to develop a productive, efficient, effective organisation, while Goss (1994) notes that it reflects an attempt to define an explicit link between financial reward and individual, group or company performance. Kessler and Purcell (1992) argue that the very mechanics of PRP schemes involve a fundamental restructuring of the employment relationship which often results in greater managerial control over staff by isolating the individual from the work group and forcing the personalised design and evaluation of work. Ireland has, in recent years, seen a number of shifts in the application of financial incentives as a cure for low productivity. This change has been from a preoccupation with the productivity bargaining of the 1960s, measured day work in the 1970s (exorbitant levels of taxation in the 1970s, according to Clarke (1989), rendered bonuses and merit rewards ineffectual as a cure for low productivity), to PRP in the 1980s (Grafton, 1988). As the operating environment became ever more complex during the 1980s, organisations turned increasingly to performance appraisal and merit pay (Randell, 1994).

Support for contingent payment systems is based on the concept that it is fair and logical to reward individual employees differentially, based on some measure of performance. While this principle is rarely a source of contention, problems may arise in attempting to develop reliable and acceptable mechanisms for evaluating employee performance. These include the limited criteria used (e.g. work study), inconsistency of application (e.g. performance appraisal), or bias/inequity in employee evaluations. A more fundamental issue may be resentment towards the exercise of managerial control via performance measurement and reward distribution, which is inherent in many "reward-for-performance" approaches.

Our data reveal that private sector organisations are far more likely to have introduced incentive schemes for all grades (see Figure 6.4). Merit or performance-related pay is the most popular incentive used, with 59 per cent of private and 25 per cent of public sector companies implementing it at managerial level. As previously mentioned the figure declines rapidly as one moves further down the hierarchy, a factor that has not changed to any significant degree since 1992. Thus the established practice of differentiating between manual and managerial employees in the application of such schemes is still very much in evidence. Arguably, this may be rationalised in a number of ways; a traditional explanation for such treatment has been the difficulty of disaggregating the impact of the individual's effort and performance on effectiveness at the lower echelons of the organisation, and thus, Merit/PRP was generally considered to be applicable principally to managerial levels. This problem has been overcome in many organisations, in recent times, by assessing the individual within the confines of their particular task or job. A second and more compelling explanation is the opposition of trade unions which often prefer collective increases achieved through management–union negotiation.

Figure 6.4: Sector as a Determinant of the Use of Merit/PRP

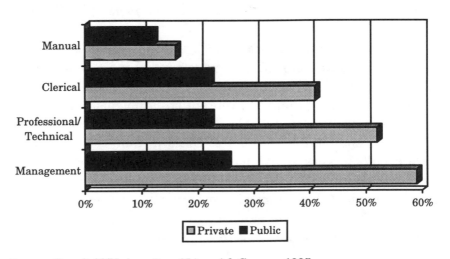

Source: Cranfield/University of Limerick Survey, 1995.

Figure 6.5 clearly shows the influence of trade unions on the incidence of individual performance-related pay. Trade unions have traditionally concentrated their presence in the manual and clerical grades, while higher level employees tended to have a more individual relationship with their employer, thus allowing for the introduction of PRP. At all levels, non-union organisations have a greater incidence of merit/PRP.

Figure 6.5: Unionisation as a Determinant of the Use of Merit/PRP

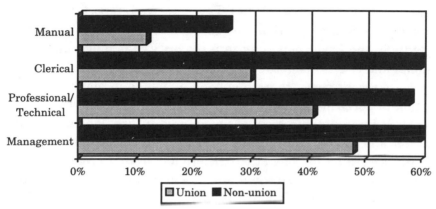

Source: Cranfield/University of Limerick Survey, 1995.

Overall, as Table 6.7 illustrates, the 1995 results show an increase in the number of companies in Ireland utilising merit/PRP, particularly in clerical and manual grades. There is however, a clear link between the ownership of the organisation and the implementation of merit or performance-related pay. As in 1992, companies originating in the US and UK have the highest incidence of PRP.

Table 6.7: Ownership as a Determinant of the Use of Merit/PRP

	EU	Ireland	US	UK
Managerial	46.4	38.7	75.0	63.0
Professional	35.7	28.8	73.4	68.4
Clerical	32.1	23.4	65.6	47.4
Manual	14.3	15.3	18.8	15.8

Source: Cranfield/University of Limerick Survey, 1995.

The penetration of foreign MNCs, particularly US-owned MNCs into Irish industrial structures is significant here. While McMahon et al. (1988) feel that MNCs have adapted to accommodate local practices, this need not necessarily result in an abandonment of foreign management philosophy, but rather, the pursuit of such within existing frameworks and customs. In the case of US multinationals, successive research has repeatedly emphasised the prevalence of linking pay to a measure of performance, often performance appraisal (Hay Associates, 1975; Locker and Teel, 1977; Eichel and Bender, 1984). The perceived importance of PRP amongst US organisations is maintained in their subsidiary plants in the Irish context, with a majority of managerial, professional and clerical employees qualifying for merit/PRP. In Britain, in more recent years, there has been a change in emphasis in relation to performance management techniques. Much of the effort was traditionally directed at assessing future labour requirements and labour training needs (Gill, 1977). However, more recently, according to Long (1986), there has been a greater emphasis on organisational survival and the assessment of current performance. Such emphasis has resulted in a large growth in PRP as a method of improving such performance.

It is interesting to note that 64 per cent of UK organisations introduced merit or performance-related pay between 1986 and 1990, while Irish organisations seem to be adopting such schemes in more recent years. Thus 45 per cent of Irish-owned respondents have introduced such schemes since 1991. US and EU companies have been utilising merit pay since the late 1960s and the numbers have been increasing on a more constant basis since then (see Table 6.8).

Table 6.8: Year of Introduction of Merit/PRP

1900–1965	1.9
1966–1975	4.6
1976–1985	15.7
1986–1990	14.9
1991–1993	8.8
1994–1995	6.9

Source: Cranfield/University of Limerick Survey, 1995.

Group Bonus Schemes

This type of incentive seeks to allocate rewards on the basis of group performance and, according to Goss (1994) represents an attempt to avoid the problem of divisiveness associated with individual PRP. It is highly visible because rewards are based on group performance and thus there is an explicit link between performance and reward. Such rewards are wide in applicability as they seek to determine the individual's incentive by reference to the performance of a group of individuals rather than linking them to individual effort and performance (Gunnigle et al., 1994). Ost (1990) feels that all incentives based on group or team work are subject to a number of guiding premises:

(a) They always have one or more explicitly stated unit or firm-level performance goal that can only be achieved through team work;

(b) A team-based incentive system always contains a reward component that is contingent on the successful achievement of those goals;

(c) The reward must be perceived by the employee as resulting from contributions that they have made;

(d) The reward must be perceived as a fair reward;

(c) The behaviours and the rewards offered must clearly signal what is meant by good performance.

The use of this incentive, while relatively limited amongst respondent organisations when compared with the use of merit/PRP, has increased slightly for managerial, professional/technical and clerical employees. While only 13 per cent of our 1992 respondents operated group bonus schemes for managerial employees, our 1995 data reveal that this has risen to 21 per cent. For clerical employees the increase is approximately 5 per cent (from 11 per cent to 16 per cent) and for professional/technical categories, the increase is a more marginal 4 per cent. As has previously been stated one of the key reasons cited for not extending individual incentive schemes is the difficulty in disaggregating the particular contribution of the individual. However, what is a little more surprising is the low level of group bonus schemes in place for manual employees. It has remained constant since 1992 at between 14 and 15 per cent.

Figure 6.6: Sector as a Determinant of the Use of Group Bonus Schemes

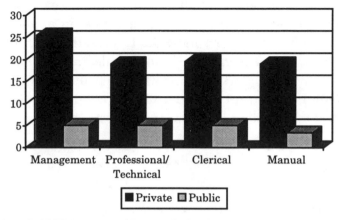

Source: Cranfield/University of Limerick Survey, 1995.

Private sector organisations are at least three times more likely to use group bonus schemes than their public sector counterparts while non-union firms reported a higher incidence of group bonus schemes for managerial, professional and clerical grades. However, a greater number of manual employees in unionised firms have group bonus schemes.

Figure 6.7: Unionisation as a Determinant of the Use of Group Bonus Schemes

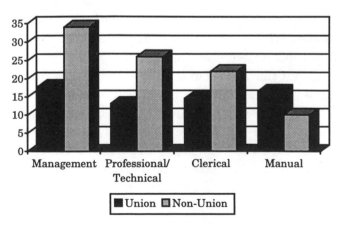

Source: Cranfield/University of Limerick Survey, 1995.

In terms of ownership, US-owned subsidiaries again reported a relatively high incidence of group bonus schemes. Other EU-owned organisations also indicated a preference for this type of incentive scheme, particularly for managerial and manual employees. When compared to 1992, all ownership categories, with the exception of the UK, have increased their use of group bonus schemes.

Table 6.9: Ownership as a Determinant of the Use of Group Bonus Schemes

	EU	*Ireland*	*US*	*UK*
Managerial	28.6	12.6	34.4	15.8
Professional	17.9	11.7	28.1	5.3
Clerical	17.9	11.7	25.0	10.5
Manual	21.4	10.8	23.4	10.5

Source: Cranfield/University of Limerick Survey, 1995.

Employee Share Options

Interest in Ireland in employee share ownership schemes has traditionally been relatively low (Long, 1988). The growth, small though it has been, is rooted in the Finance Acts of 1982–1984 which were driven by governmental commitment to "ensuring the success and efficiency of Irish industry and the prosperity and security of Irish workers for the future" by developing employee share-holding.

These Acts sought to provide tax relief for the adoption of share ownership schemes. However, employers and employees were under no obligation to adopt such schemes and tax concessions only applied to approved schemes. The Irish Productivity Centre (1986) felt that "the relevant Acts do not provide a rigid model for the advancement of employee share-holding, but rather a framework of corporate and individual incentives within required guidelines".

Despite government intervention in the shape of tax concessions, take-up of such schemes has remained relatively static. Prior to 1990, Ireland demonstrated relatively restricted interest in employee share participation schemes in terms of both numbers involved and the range of schemes offered. Of the small numbers of individuals who were covered, such participation was often confined to executive levels. There has been no change in this regard between the last round of our survey in 1992 and the data emerging from this 1995 round. Where share options are provided they are more likely to occur among managerial employees. However, companies which originate in the US and UK are far more likely to adopt share ownership schemes for all grades in the organisation and our evidence suggests that share ownership schemes are growing substantially in US- and UK-owned establishments, compared to their Irish- or EU-owned counterparts. Since 1992, growth in the former two has been between 10 and 15 per cent approximately, while in the latter two growth has been negligible.

Table 6.10: Ownership as a Determinant of the Use of Share Ownership Schemes

	EU	*Ireland*	*US*	*UK*
Managerial	7.1	14.4	46.9	42.1
Professional	3.6	5.4	32.8	26.3
Clerical	3.6	3.6	25.0	26.3
Manual	3.6	2.7	21.9	21.1

Source: Cranfield/University of Limerick Survey, 1995.

In the present data trade union recognition does not appear to have a statistically significant impact on whether or not the organisation chooses to implement such a scheme and arguably union opposition to such schemes may not be as universal as has been traditionally supposed. Our earlier 1992 data did reveal a difference here, with those organisations which do not formally recognise a collective presence more likely to have share option schemes. However, this divergence decreased substantially as one descended the hierarchy from managerial to manual employees and was much less significant at that level.

Profit-Sharing Schemes

Profit-sharing is a scheme under which employees, in addition to their normal remuneration, receive a proportion of the profits of the business. Profit-sharing may take a number of forms and it is largely at the discretion of the employer and employees to decide to what measure of profit the incentive should be tied, what percentage should be allocated and how it should be administered to employees. The take-up has traditionally been low in Ireland. In a study in 1988, Long found that organisations expressed little interest in profit-sharing, with only a minority of organisations having approved schemes. Our evidence also suggests that they are less common than other incentive schemes. Approximately 19 per cent of managerial employees, 13 per cent of both professional/technical and clerical employees and 10 per cent of manual workers are covered by such schemes. The results are entirely consistent with our earlier data.

Unionisation would seem to have an effect on the presence or otherwise of a profit-sharing scheme. A higher percentage of non-union firms for all levels in the hierarchy report the implementation of such a scheme, but the difference decreases as one descends from managerial to manual grades in the organisational hierarchy.

Table 6.11: Unionisation as a Determinant of the Use of Profit-Sharing Schemes

	Union	*Non-union*
Managerial	16.1	32.0
Professional	11.7	20.0
Clerical	11.2	18.0
Manual	9.3	14.0

Source: Cranfield/University of Limerick Survey, 1995.

The opposition of unions to profit-sharing schemes is understandable from an ideological/employee attachment perspective. However, Gunnigle et al. (1994) argue that union opposition to such schemes is not universal, largely because enhanced employee involvement in the productive effort which results from such schemes may be viewed as a step towards workplace democracy. Secondly, and perhaps more importantly, such schemes do represent an opportunity to increase wages. Consequently, as our data demonstrate, where one might expect highest union density (among manual grades) the divergence between unionised and non-unionised organisations is not particularly large.

As has been the established pattern in relation to other incentives, foreign MNCs appear to have a higher take-up rate. UK and US companies have a far higher percentage of profit-sharing for each employee grade. UK companies particularly, demonstrate a notable increase in the use of this form of incentive, particularly when one examines the 1992 results. In 1992 approximately 20 per cent of managerial employees working in UK-owned establishments in Ireland were covered by a profit-sharing scheme. This has risen to almost 37 per cent. The pattern for professional/technical and clerical employees in these organisations is similar, though less dramatic. Coverage has risen by approximately 7 per cent for both categories.

Table 6.12: Ownership as a Determinant of the Use of Profit-Sharing Schemes

	EU	*Ireland*	*US*	*UK*
Managerial	17.9	10.8	32.8	36.8
Professional	10.7	4.5	29.7	26.3
Clerical	7.1	3.6	28.1	26.3
Manual	7.1	2.7	23.4	15.8

Source: Cranfield/University of Limerick Survey, 1995.

Utilisation of Performance Appraisal Systems

The management of performance is a key variable in the effectiveness and growth of an organisation and, according to Randell (1994) an examination of a company's appraisal scheme can show a great deal about how the company views its staff and how they should be managed and developed. Sparrow and Hiltrop (1994) in their treatise of human resource management in Europe highlight a number of important organisational and social variables influencing the current emphasis on performance assessment and evaluation. The tendency towards de-layering, changing career and job expectations and the individualisation of the employment relationship through union avoidance and individualised pay systems are all, they argue, critical contributors to the new performance order being established at job and organisational level. In this vein, performance appraisal techniques, as systematic approaches to evaluating performance, have increased in popularity in recent years in Irish organisations.

Figure 6.8: Existence of Performance Appraisal Systems

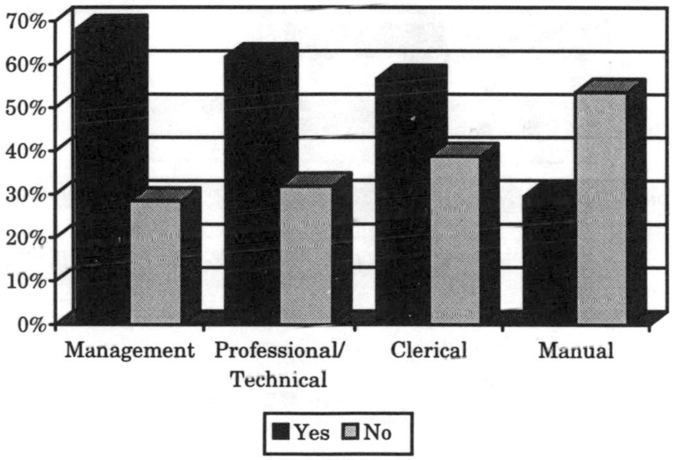

Source: Cranfield/University of Limerick Survey, 1995.

However, our data suggest that appraisal might not be as universal as previously thought. While approximately 70 per cent of managerial employees are subject to an appraisal system, only 30 per cent of manual employees are, the figures for professional/technical and clerical being in between (see Figure 6.8). Shivanath's (1987) earlier work on personnel management practices revealed that approximately 80 per cent of respondents operated an appraisal system. Our global result on appraisal from the 1992 data was approximately 65 per cent.

Large organisations are more likely to have performance appraisal systems for all grades, particularly senior management. Similarly, McMahon and Gunnigle's (1994) research revealed that while appraisal tends to be a regular feature in many organisa-

tions, there appeared to be a notable absence in smaller, indigenous organisations. The gap between large and small companies
decreases as we move down the organisational hierarchy (see
Figure 6.9). Fewer indigenous Irish organisations reported the
existence of performance appraisal systems in their organisations,
for all levels of the hierarchy, than respondent organisations with
EU or US headquarters.

**Figure 6.9: Organisation Size as a Determinant of the
Existence of Performance Appraisal Systems**

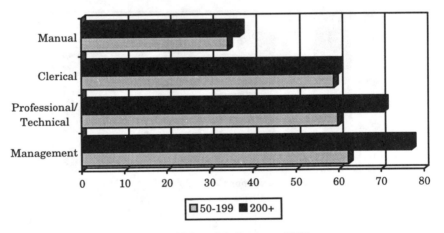

Source: Cranfield/University of Limerick Survey, 1995.

An extremely important defining variable is the sector in which
the organisation operates. As Figure 6.10 demonstrates, almost
twice as many private sector organisations, for each category of
employee, utilise performance appraisal, despite the fact that the
public sector is such a significant employer in the State. Similarly
McMahon and Gunnigle (1994) revealed that private sector multinationals of comparable size were more than twice as likely to
operate an appraisal system for all employee grades.

Figure 6.10: Sector as a Determinant of the Existence of Performance Appraisal Systems

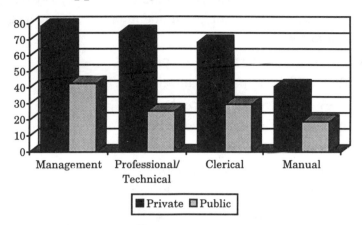

Source: Cranfield/University of Limerick Survey, 1995.

Union recognition is also seen to have critical explanatory power. It has been difficult to pinpoint particular policies and practices adopted by organisations which have opted to remain non-union, but it is clear here that there is a relationship between performance appraisal and union recognition. Non-union companies are far more likely to have systems in place, the difference being most pronounced for manual and to a lesser extent clerical employees (see Figure 6.11).

Figure 6.11: Unionisation as a Determinant of the Existence of Performance Appraisal Systems

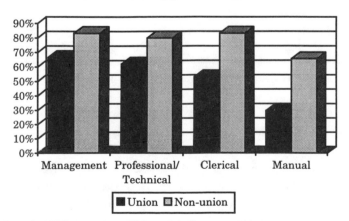

Source: Cranfield/University of Limerick Survey, 1995.

The Purpose and the Process of Performance Appraisal

McMahon and Gunnigle (1994) identified a range of key objectives associated with appraisal in Ireland. Among the most frequently cited objectives were to:

- improve future performance (98 per cent)
- provide feedback on performance (96 per cent)
- agree key objectives (95 per cent)
- identify training needs (95 per cent)
- strengthen employee commitment and motivation (89 per cent)
- improve communication (84 per cent) and
- assess promotion potential (82 per cent).

Our data, set out in Table 6.13, reveal that in the vast majority of cases performance appraisal is used to identify individual training needs. The identification of promotion potential and career development are also important outcomes of the appraisal process. Only 45 per cent of respondents reported using performance appraisal in order to determine pay increases. This may be due to a number of factors, not least of which is the difficulty in developing a system which is perceived as being fair by employees.

Table 6.13: Purpose of Performance Appraisal

Individual training needs	69.7%
Organisational needs	43.3%
Promotion potential	51.3%
Career development	51.7%
Individual PRP	44.8%
Organisation of work	35.2%

Source: Cranfield/University of Limerick Survey, 1995.

Large organisations are more likely to use performance appraisal for all of the purposes mentioned, with the exception of work organisation. Private sector organisations are also far more likely to use performance appraisal to determine each of the needs mentioned particularly performance-related pay, individual training needs and promotion potential, than the public sector (see Figure 6.12).

Figure 6.12: Sector as a Determinant of the Purpose of Performance Appraisal

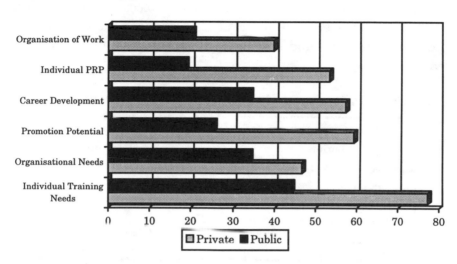

Source: Cranfield/University of Limerick Survey, 1995.

Ownership appears to influence the focus of the appraisal system. Of particular interest is the number of US organisations (73 per cent) that report using their appraisal system in order to establish pay increases. This contrasts significantly with Irish indigenous organisations. McMahon and Gunnigle also flag the variability among objectives in different countries. Of particular significance is the fact that, from a trawl of secondary research, they identify reward issues and employee development issues to be the most likely focus of the appraisal system in US-owned establishments.

Table 6.14: Ownership as a Determinant of the Purpose of Performance Appraisal

	EU	Ireland	US	UK
Individual training needs	71.4	55.9	89.1	94.7
Organisational needs	50.0	33.3	53.1	73.7
Promotion potential	64.3	41.4	62.5	73.7
Career development	57.1	42.3	62.5	78.9
Individual PRP	42.9	29.7	73.4	63.2
Organisation of work	32.1	31.5	39.1	52.6

Source: Cranfield/University of Limerick Survey, 1995.

In terms of how the actual process is conducted, predictably, the immediate superior and individual employees themselves are the most likely contributors to the appraisal process. The next-level superior is involved in 46 per cent of respondent companies, with peers, subordinates and customers featuring in only a minority of cases.

Table 6.15: Participants in the Appraisal Process

Immediate superior	72.0
Next-level superior	46.0
Employee	62.8
Subordinates	5.7
Peers	9.2
Customers	8.0
Others	1.5

Source: Cranfield/University of Limerick Survey, 1995.

CONCLUSION

The utility of using pay to promote performance has been a subject of debate for many years with empirical and theoretical support for both sides of the argument. Notwithstanding the reservations expressed, however, pay and benefits are increasingly becoming areas of extreme importance in determining the effectiveness of the organisation.

Our data point to a pattern of stability in the area of compensation since 1992. Pay determination for most non-managerial employees is conducted at national level. Rewards for managerial employees are predominantly, as has traditionally been the case, determined at the level of the individual, although almost 35 per cent of respondent organisations indicated that national determination is the method by which such categories had their pay determined. With the exception of manual employees, US-owned establishments demonstrate a preference for individual pay determination. In conjunction with the increased use of variable pay, particularly among private sector, non-unionised establishments, respondent organisations indicated an increased interest in the use of financial incentives. Such incentives varied not only on the criteria on which they were to base reward allocation, but also on the aims they were trying to fulfil. Merit/performance-related pay represented the most commonly used incentive amongst organisations in Ireland once again. While Merit/PRP has become quite popular in recent times other incentives have not witnessed anything like the resurgence witnessed in respect of this incentive. Consequently, the utilisation of other schemes remains rather lower.

While incentive use in Ireland is quite low this is subject to the qualification that take-up is correlated quite closely to ultimate ownership of the respondent organisation. US organisations on the whole are far more likely to utilise incentives than others, particularly Irish indigenous organisations which indicated low take-up across a wide range of incentives.

Performance appraisal schemes are now common for managerial employees (approximately 70 per cent said they had one), but much less so for manual categories. Sector is important here with private sector establishments being twice as likely to have some appraisal system. Where such schemes do exist the likelihood is that they have objectives relating to training, promotion and career development at their core, although this does vary with ownership.

Chapter 7

EMPLOYEE RELATIONS

Patrick Gunnigle, Noreen Clifford & Michael Morley

INTRODUCTION

As previously noted, *industrial relations* has traditionally been the most significant area of personnel activity (see, for example, Shivanath, 1987). This industrial relations focus reflected an essentially pluralist orientation whereby collective bargaining with trade unions was the primary means of handling management–labour relations. However, since the 1980s there is considerable evidence of a decreasing emphasis on collectivist industrial relations (McGovern, 1989; Gunnigle, 1992b, 1995a). Increasingly the term *employee relations* has been adopted to reflect a broader focus in management–labour relations which incorporates union and non-union approaches. This chapter considers contemporary trends in employee relations in Irish organisations. It considers both collectivist dimensions, such as trade union recognition and density, and more individualist aspects such as direct management–employee communications.

THE TRADE UNION DIMENSION

As we have seen, employee relations in Ireland has been synonymous with a strong pluralist approach, and an associated emphasis on collective bargaining as the principal mechanism for handling management–employee relations. This "traditional–pluralist" model is associated with high levels of union recognition and has been coupled with a reactive, "fire-fighting" approach to employee relations. The extent of trade union recognition and membership and the nature of management–union relations are seen as key indicators of management approaches to, and changes in, employee relations. This section considers degrees of trade union density and recognition at the level of the organisation. It also reviews perceived changes in the extent of trade union influence at organisation level.

Trade Union Density: An Overview

Trade union density refers to the actual level of trade union membership expressed as a percentage of the potential membership. It is normally based on either of two measures: (i) *employment density* (actual number of trade union members expressed as a percentage of all employees) or (ii) *workforce density* (actual number of trade union members expressed as a percentage of the total workforce, incorporating employees and the unemployed). As mentioned earlier, the Republic of Ireland has traditionally been characterised by relatively high levels of trade union density. In 1990 the number of trade unions in Ireland totalled some 65 unions catering for a total membership of over 460,000. This figure represented an employment density of approximately 55 per cent and a workforce density of approximately 44 per cent (Roche, 1992) (see Table 7.1).

We have also seen that the 1980s has been identified as a decade of change in HRM and particularly, employee relations. This period witnessed the most serious decline in trade union density in the post war period. The decline in trade union density in the period 1980–1987 is principally attributed to macroeconomic factors, particularly economic depression, increased unemployment and changes in employment structure involving decline/ stagnation of employment in traditionally highly unionised sectors (traditional manufacturing and the public sector) and growth in sectors which have traditionally posed difficulties for union penetration (foreign manufacturing and, particularly, private services) (Roche, 1992, 1994). However, it is likely that developments at organisational level have also contributed in part to this decline. Of particular significance are changing management approaches to employee relations, particularly a growth in union avoidance "strategies" and an increased management emphasis

Table 7.1: Trade Union Membership 1945–1993

Year	Membership	Employment Density[1]	Workforce Density[2]
1945	172,300	27.7	25.4
1960	312,600	49.6	45.4
1975	448,800	59.3	52.3
1980	527,200	61.8	55.2
1981	524,400	61.5	53.5
1982	519,900	60.3	51.4
1983	513,300	61.1	49.7
1984	500,200	60.7	48.2
1985	483,300	59.9	46.6
1986	471,000	58.0	45
1987	457,300	56.2	43.1
1988[3]	470,644	57.1	44.2
1989[3]	458,690	55.6	43.4
1990[3]	462,451	54.6	43.2
1992	479,400		
1993	485,700		44.0

1. Employment Density = Trade union membership ÷ civilian employees at work x 100

2. Workforce Density = Trade union membership ÷ civilian employee workforce x 100

3. Figures for 1988–1990 are estimates and are derived from the annual affiliated membership of unions affiliated to the Irish Congress of Trade Unions

Source: DUES Project UCD (1992).

on individualist HRM approaches (see Roche and Larragy, 1989; Mc Govern, 1989; Gunnigle, 1995a and b). Despite the extensive decline in union density during the 1980s, the national figures indicate that union density is holding up quite well: figures from the Department of Enterprise and Employment based on returns from unions affiliated to the Irish Congress of Trade Unions suggest that figures for trade union membership rose from approximately 470,600 in 1988 to some 485,700 in 1993 (IIRR 1993). This increase in membership appears to reflect the fact that more people are now at work than ever before.

Trade Union Density at Organisation Level

While national statistics provide us with an aggregate picture of trade union density, it is necessary to look at union membership levels at organisation level to gain insights into the operational role and impact of trade unions. In this study, respondents were asked to indicate the proportion of the workforce in their organisation which was in membership of a trade union. These findings are summarised in Figure 7.1. As we can see, levels of trade union density in the organisations surveyed is very high with 64 per cent of organisations reporting that 50 per cent or more of their employees are members of a trade union. This represents a slight decrease since our last study (1992) when the corresponding figure was 66 per cent.

Figure 7.1: Proportion of Workforce Members of a Trade Union

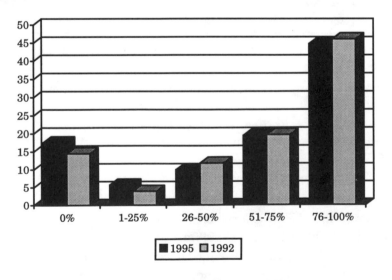

Source: Cranfield/University of Limerick Survey, 1995.

Looking at potential explanatory factors, we find that *organisation size* has a considerable influence (see Figure 7.2). It is far more likely that *a proportion* of the workforce will be unionised in larger organisations. It is also likely that a *greater proportion* of the workforce is unionised in larger organisations.

Figure 7.2: Organisation Size as a Determinant of Proportion of Workforce Unionised (1995)

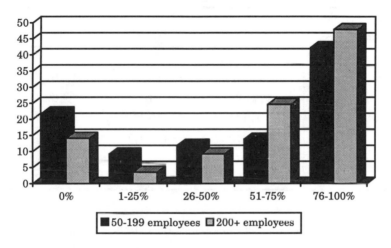

Source: Cranfield/University of Limerick Survey, 1995.

As previously mentioned, a large proportion of the sampled organisations report union membership levels in excess of 50 per cent of their workforce. The exclusion of non-union establishments reveals an even clearer picture: eight in every ten organisations which recognise a trade union have 50 per cent or more of the workforce unionised. Given an aggregate union density among the employed labour force of almost 56 per cent, it is not surprising to find a high level of union density in the *Top 2000* trading and non-trading organisations in the country. Levels of union density were particularly high in the public sector. While constituting just 23 per cent of the organisations studied, the public sector accounted for some 40 per cent of the most highly unionised establishments (i.e. 76–100 per cent of the workforce unionised) (see Table 7.2). This finding is in line with other studies: for example, Hourihan (1996) estimates that union density in the public service is approximately 80 per cent but only around 36 per cent in the private sector. Our analyses also considered comparative levels of union density in private sector services and manufacturing organisations. These findings are outlined in Figure 7.3 and indicate a higher level of unionisation in private manufacturing organisations.

Table 7.2: Level Of Union Membership by Sector

Level of Union Membership	% of Firms by Sector		
	Private	Public	Total
0%	21.5% (42)	7% (4)	18% (46)[*]
1–25%	8% (15)	0	6% (15)
26–50%	12% (24)	1.7% (1)	10% (25)
51–75%	22% (43)	12% (7)	20% (50)
76–100%	36% (70)	80% (47)	46% (117)
Don't know	0.5% (1)	0	0.3% (1)
TOTAL	100% (195)	100% (59)	100% (254)

*Actual numbers in parentheses.

Source: Cranfield/University of Limerick Survey, 1995.

Figure 7.3: The Proportion of the Workforce Unionised in Private Manufacturing and Services

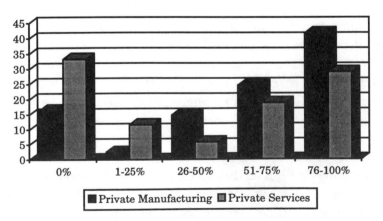

■ Private Manufacturing ▨ Private Services

Source: Cranfield/University of Limerick Survey, 1995.

A factor considered particularly influential in explaining variations in employee relations and, particularly, levels of union density is *country of ownership* (Beaumont, 1985). As indicated in

Figure 7.4, ownership has a clear influence on the proportion of the workforce unionised. Irish- and other European-owned organisations report the highest level of union density, while US-owned organisations have the lowest level. Over half the Irish-owned organisations report that more than 76 per cent of their workforce are members of a trade union. Similar figures may be found among European-owned organisations. However, US-owned organisations report the lowest levels of unionisation, with some 31 per cent reporting zero union membership in their organisations.

Figure 7.4: Ownership as a Determinant of Proportion of Workforce Unionised

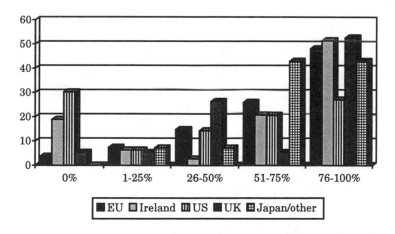

Source: Cranfield/University of Limerick Survey, 1995.

Trade Union Recognition

Despite the relatively high level of trade union density, there are no specific statutory provisions to govern the process of trade union recognition in the Republic of Ireland (see Gunnigle, McMahon and Fitzgerald, 1995). The Constitutional guarantee of freedom of association embodied in article 40.6.1 of the Constitution confers the right on workers to form or join associations or unions. This provision has also been interpreted to include an implied right not to join trade unions where individuals do not wish to do so. The extent of trade union recognition is therefore an important indicator of management approaches to employee relations since the granting of such recognition is largely an issue of management prerogative (see, for example, Gunnigle, Heraty and Morley, 1997).

Key findings on the extent of trade union recognition are outlined in Table 7.3. We find that 80 per cent of participating organisations recognise trade unions for collective bargaining purposes. While this figure is a little lower than in the 1992 study, it still presents a healthy picture of union recognition in Ireland. In relation to the incidence of non-union approaches, we find a total of 50 organisations reporting that they do not recognise trade unions for the purposes of collective bargaining. However, nine of these organisations acknowledged that a proportion of their workforce were members of a trade union.

Table 7.3: Trade Union Recognition

	1992	1995
Trade Union Recognition	83% (186)*	80% (205)
No Trade Union Recognition	17% (38)	20% (50)
	n=224	n=255

*Actual numbers in parentheses.

Source: Cranfield/University of Limerick Survey, 1995.

As union recognition is pervasive in public sector organisations, it is useful to focus on the extent of union recognition in the private sector as a means of assessing any changes that may be occurring. Of the 195 private sector organisations studied, some 23 per cent (45 organisations) did not recognise trade unions. In 1992 exactly the same percentage of private sector respondents reported that they did not recognise trade unions.

When organisation size is taken into consideration the result again bears out our previous findings on union density: larger organisations are considerably more likely to recognise trade unions (see Figure 7.5). This finding also reflects the likelihood that smaller organisations adopt a more unitarist perspective and more informal approaches to employee relations.

Figure 7.5: Organisation Size as a Determinant of Trade Union Recognition

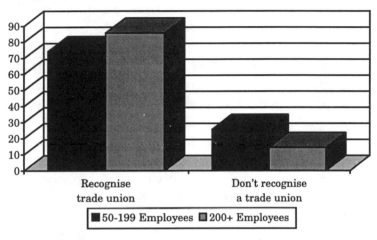

Source: Cranfield/University of Limerick Survey, 1995.

In evaluating trends in relation to union recognition, it is clear that private service organisations are less likely to recognise trade unions than private manufacturing organisations (see Figure 7.6).

Figure 7.6: Trade Union Recognition in Private Manufacturing and Services

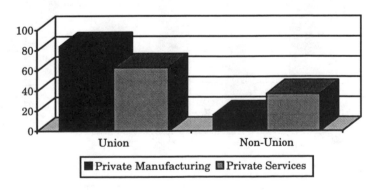

Source: Cranfield/University of Limerick Survey, 1995.

An issue mentioned above in our evaluation of trade union density was the important influence of *country of ownership*. The study findings on the impact of ownership on the extent of trade union recognition are outlined in Figure 7.7. This illustrates a clear variance between different countries, with US-owned organisations less likely to recognise trade unions: some 69 per cent of US-owned organisations recognise trade unions, while more than 80 per cent of indigenous Irish, UK, EU, Japanese and "other" organisations reported that they recognised trade unions for collective bargaining purposes. In this analysis country of ownership may be used as a proxy variable to indicate the impact of managerial values on variations in the extent of trade union recognition. This approach is based on the assumption that decisions on trade union recognition will closely reflect underlying managerial values associated with country of ownership (Poole, 1986; Guest and Rosenthal, 1992). These findings bear out the suggestion that US-owned organisations are more likely to pursue a strategy of union avoidance (see Beaumont, 1985; Kochan et al., 1986). The findings also seem to confirm the willingness of European employers to recognise and bargain with trade unions (Poole, 1986).

Figure 7.7: Ownership as a Determinant of Trade Union Recognition

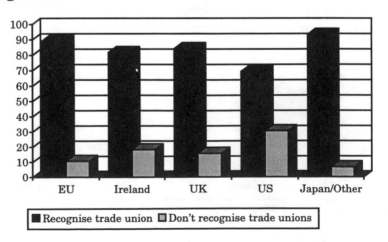

Source: Cranfield/University of Limerick Survey, 1995.

The Changing Influence of Trade Unions

In contrast to "hard" indicators of role and penetration of trade unions, such as density and recognition, it is also interesting to explore management perceptions of the influence of trade unions. In this study respondents were asked to indicate whether they felt the influence of trade unions had increased, decreased or remained the same over the past three years. The results, outlined in Figure 7.8, present a picture of relative stability in relation to perceived union influence. Some 71 per cent of respondents report that the influence of trade unions in their organisation has remained the same over the past three years (compared with 66 per cent in 1992).

Figure 7.8: Changes in Trade Union Influence in the past 3 years

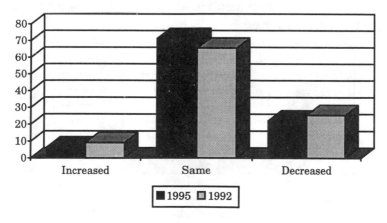

Source: Cranfield/University of Limerick Survey, 1995.

Turning to potential explanatory factors, it is significant that it is *larger organisations* which report the greatest decrease in trade union influence. This is interesting, as numerous studies point to the comparatively greater levels of union penetration in larger organisations than in smaller organisations (see, for example, Thomason, 1984). It may be that unions are seeing some dimunition of their influence in larger organisations where they have traditionally been at their strongest (see Table 7.4).

Table 7.4: Organisation Size as a Determinant of Changes in Trade Union Influence

	Increased	*Same*	*Decreased*
50–199	7%	76%	18%
200+	6%	69%	26%

n=243
Source: Cranfield/University of Limerick Survey, 1995.

Looking at the impact of other factors on union influence, we find that *private sector* organisations were more likely to report a reduction in trade union influence than their public sector counterparts. In relation to country of ownership, the findings indicate that European-owned organisations report the greatest decrease in union influence (see Figure 7.9).

Figure 7.9: Ownership as a Determinant of Changes in Trade Union Influence

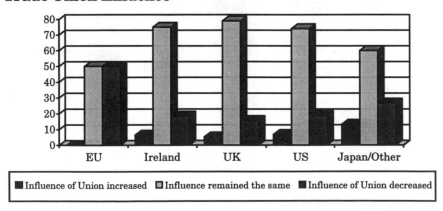

Source: Cranfield/University of Limerick Survey, 1995.

Overall, there is a strong sense of continuity, with many of the findings relating to trade unions from our 1995 study corroborating those which emerged from the 1992 data set. While trade union density at organisation level is holding up, predictably, organisation size, the industrial sector in which the organisation operates and the country from which it originates are critical explanatory factors. Trade union recognition for collective bargaining purposes remains largely unchanged at 80 per cent. Union influence remains strong.

Where there has been a diminution in influence, it seems most likely to have occurred in larger organisations.

MANAGEMENT–EMPLOYEE COMMUNICATIONS

One of the most significant themes identified in the contemporary literature on developments in employee relations is the suggestion that managements have shifted the focus of their communications with employees away from trade unions and towards direct communications with individual employees (see, for example, Salaman, 1992; McLoughlin and Gourlay, 1992; Beacon and Storey, 1993). In some quarters, this shift has been seen as part of a managerial strategy to adopt a more individualist employee relations orientation which may concurrently involve attempts to bypass or marginalise trade unions in the communications process (Kochan et al., 1986; Blyton and Turnbull, 1994). Differences in organisational approaches to communications with employees tend to focus on the nature and content of management–employee communications and the range of mechanisms used to facilitate such communications. This study focused on two key aspects of the debate on management–employee communications: (i) the communications forums used by management in communicating with employees; and (ii) the type of information communicated to employees using such forums.

Communications Forums

In relation to communications forums, this study sought to examine trends in the modes used in the communication of major issues to employees. A particular area of interest here is the relative emphasis on collectivist and individualist forums in the communications process (McLoughlin and Gourlay, 1992; Blyton and Turnbull, 1994). This study examined trends in the pattern of utilisation of particular communications modes, namely; (i) direct verbal communications; (ii) direct written communications; (iii) representative staff bodies, including trade unions; (iv) team briefings; (v) videos; and (vi) computer/e-mail. Management representatives were asked to indicate whether the pattern of utilisation of each of these communications modes was increasing, decreasing or constant. The summary findings are shown in Table 7.5 together with comparisons to the 1992 findings.

Table 7.5: Changes in Management–Employee Communications

	Increased		Same		Decreased		Not used/ missing		N	
	1995	1992	1995	1992	1995	1992	1995	1992	1995	1992
Verbal direct	51%	55%	42%	34%	2%	1%	5%	11%	261	228
Written direct	46%	39%	43%	42%	1%	4%	11%	16%	261	228
Rep. staff bodies	13%	16%	51%	48%	7%	12%	29%	24%	261	228
Team briefings	49%	–	24%	–	2%	–	26%	–	261	228
Videos	18%	–	14%	–	2%	–	66%	–	261	228
Electronic mail	31%	–	14%	–	0%	–	55%	–	261	228

Source: Cranfield/University of Limerick Survey, 1995.

These findings indicate a substantial increase in direct written and verbal communications with employees, a pattern which is more or less a repeat of the 1992 findings. Looking at the findings on the use of representative staff bodies, what emerges is a relatively stable picture with over half the respondent organisations reporting no change in their level of utilisation as a communications device. Among those organisations reporting change in usage levels, a greater number reported that the use of representative bodies had increased rather than had decreased. Thus the aggregate data suggests an increased level of utilisation of direct communications with employees. As in 1992, this is not occurring at the expense of traditional collective lines of communication as there would seem to be no major change in the amount of communication conducted through representative bodies (generally trade unions). So, although other forms of direct communication are being used to an increasing extent, it appears this is occurring alongside existing collectivist approaches.

The use of team briefings, video and e-mail was not explored in the 1992 study and thus we cannot make any comparative observations. However, it was interesting that respondent organisations reported a considerable increase in the use of team briefings.

Explanatory Factors

A range of factors has been advanced to explain variations in employee relations and, particularly, management–employee communications. These factors include union recognition and sector (Beaumont, 1992; Beaumont and Harris, 1994; Roche and Turner, 1994; Storey and Sisson, 1994). However, while the literature identifies a range of factors which may explain variations in management styles in employee relations, there is no consensus on the relative importance of these factors, particularly in the Irish context. This section considers the impact of organisation size, sector (public or private), country of ownership and trade union recognition on variations in the level of utilisation of the communications forums identified in Table 7.5 above.

Looking firstly at the impact of *organisation size*, the key findings are illustrated in Table 7.6. It appears that larger organisations have placed a greater emphasis on increasing all forms of communications than smaller ones. This is particularly the case in relation to direct written and verbal communications, team briefings and video/e-mail. This may be related to the bureaucratic nature of larger organisations and related attempts to rationalise and de-layer their organisation structures through "formal" communications forums. It may also reflect higher levels of informality in smaller organisations, which serve to lessen the need for more formal communications forums. The greater use of videos and e-mail may reflect the greater resources and technological capacity of larger organisations. It is interesting that the area where differences between large and small organisations is least pronounced is in the use of trade unions/other representative staff bodies. This is also the only area where large organisations report a greater level of decrease in utilisation than their small firm counterparts. In general it appears that, while the use of representative staff bodies such as unions has remained stable, large organisations are placing significant emphasis on increasing the utilisation of most forms of direct communications with employees.

Table 7.6: Organisation Size and Change in Management–Employee Communications

Form of Commu-nication / Org. Size	Increased	Same	Decreased	Don't know / Missing	N
Direct Verbal					
50–199	47%	49%	3%	0.9%	
200+	59%	41%	0.7%	0%	243
Direct Written					
50–199	44%	51%	2%	3%	
200+	55%	43%	0.7%	0.7%	232
Representative Bodies					
50–199	15%	52%	6%	27%	
200+	15%	67%	8%	10%	218
Team Briefings					
50–199	47%	30%	4%	19%	
200+	62%	24%	0.8%	13%	224
Videos					
50–199	21%	15%	2%	62%	
200+	28%	23%	2%	47%	185
Electronic Mail					
50–199	36%	13%	0%	51%	
200+	42%	22%	0%	36%	202

Source: Cranfield/University of Limerick Survey, 1995.

Turning to the impact of *sector*, we find that private sector organisations are more likely to have increased direct verbal communications with the workforce: 57 per cent reported an increase compared with 42 per cent of public sector organisations (see Table 7.7). Private sector organisations also reported a 13 per cent greater increase in their use of team briefings when compared to the public sector, which is another indication of the greater importance attached to developing direct channels of communication in the private sector. Also, 10 per cent more public sector organisations reported that they did not use team briefings at all. An associated point is that 11 per cent of private sector organisations reported a decrease in communications through representative bodies (generally unions), whereas the corresponding figure for the public sector was zero. This finding suggests that the traditionally pivotal role which trade unions have played in the communications process is coming under greater pressure in the private sector, whereas in the public sector there is less evidence of a diminution of the trade union role.

Table 7.7: Industrial Sector and Change in Management–Employee Communications

Form of Commu-nication / Org. Size	Increased	Same	Decreased	Don't know / Missing	N
Direct Verbal					
Public	42%	55%	2%	2%	
Private	57%	41%	1.5%	0.5%	247
Direct Written					
Public	49%	49%	2%	0%	
Private	51%	46%	1%	2%	236
Representative Bodies					
Public	17%	76%	0%	7%	
Private	14%	54%	11%	21%	222
Team Briefings					
Public	45%	29%	2%	24%	
Private	58%	26%	2%	14%	229
Videos					
Public	24%	11%	0%	65%	
Private	25%	22%	3%	50%	189
Electronic Mail					
Public	39%	22%	0%	39%	
Private	40%	17%	0%	44%	205

Source: Cranfield/University of Limerick Survey, 1995.

The impact of *country of ownership* on variations in approaches to communications is illustrated in Figures 7.10a–7.10e. While these results indicate some minor differences, the overall picture in relation to direct verbal and written communications and team briefings is one of increased utilisation of all forms of direct communications with employees, regardless of the country of ownership. The situation in relation to utilisation of trade unions/other representative staff bodies is one of little change. Within this overall perspective there are some points of note. All organisations, regardless of origin, report large increases in the use of team briefings. However, indigenous organisations report the lowest level of take-up in this respect. Also a comparatively high number of Irish-owned organisations felt that communications through trade unions/other representative bodies had increased. The impact of ownership on the uptake of newer communications forms (video and e-mail) is summarised in Figure 7e. These findings suggest that indigenous organisations report lower utilisation levels of these newer methods of communications. Seventy-seven per cent of Irish organisations do not use video at all in the communications process, compared to 28 per cent of US and 40 per cent of UK and other EU organisations. Electronic mail is such a recent innovation that it would be difficult to envisage any organisation reporting decreased utilisation. However, it is clear from this study that US-owned organisations are leading the way in adopting it as a method of communication with employees.

Figure 7.10a: Country of Ownership and Changes in Direct Verbal Communication

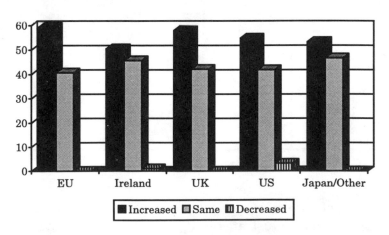

Source: Cranfield/University of Limerick Survey, 1995.

Figure 7.10b: Country of Ownership and Changes in Direct Written Communication

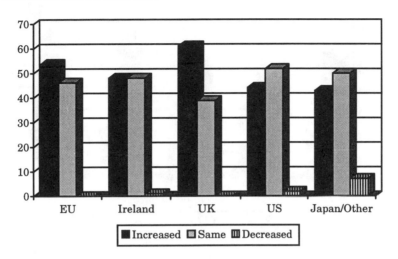

Source: Cranfield/University of Limerick Survey, 1995.

Figure 7.10c: Country of Ownership and Changes in the Use of Communications through Representative Bodies

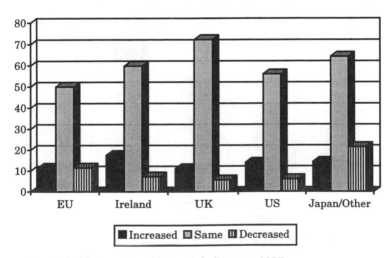

Source: Cranfield/University of Limerick Survey, 1995.

Figure 7.10d: Country of Ownership and Changes in the Use of Team Briefings

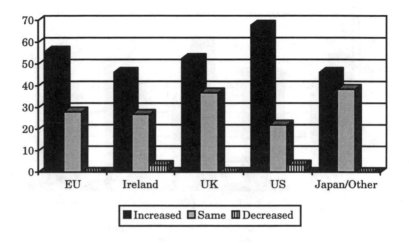

Source: Cranfield/University of Limerick Survey, 1995.

Figure 7.10e: Country of Ownership and Increases in Video Communication and Electronic Mail

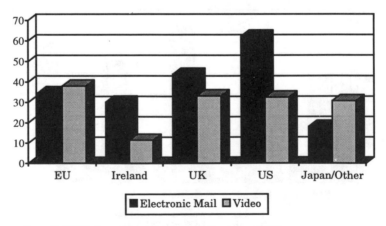

Source: Cranfield/University of Limerick Survey, 1995.

The study findings on the impact of *trade union recognition* on variations in the level of utilisation of direct written and verbal communications with employees are summarised in Figure 7.11.

These findings indicate that unionised organisations are increasing direct communications at a faster rate than non-union organisations. This may be due to the fact that organisations wishing to maintain a non-union status have traditionally emphasised direct communications, and it is more recently that unionised organisations have begun to adopt such practices. However, it is interesting to note that trade union density and influence seem not to have decreased significantly, so it is reasonable to assume that although there are substantial changes taking place in the communications process in Irish organisations, these are occurring in conjunction with traditional structures remaining in place. Communication through representative bodies in unionised organisations has remained stable, with only sixteen organisations (8.5 per cent) reporting a decrease.

Figure 7.11: Unionisation as a Determinant of Increases in Direct Written and Verbal Communication

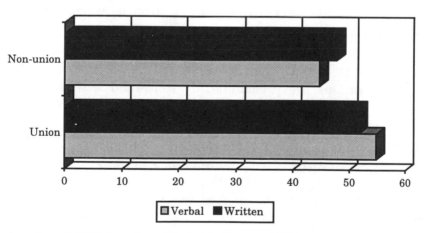

Source: Cranfield/University of Limerick Survey, 1995.

Overall, our data once again confirm the rise of direct verbal and written methods. Concomitantly, the use of representative staff bodies including trade unions has not decreased, pointing to the concurrent use of collectivist and individualist communications forums. While larger organisations were more likely to increase all mechanisms, private sector companies were more likely to have increased direct communications, when compared with their public sector counterparts. Furthermore, the increase in direct communication mechanisms appears to be occurring at a faster pace in the unionised organisations (outside the public sector).

Communications on Business Strategy and Financial Information

Turning to the actual content of management–employee communications, this study also explored the extent to which senior management communicated formally with employees on business strategy and financial performance. Summary data on this aspect is outlined in Table 7.8. Looking firstly at communications on *business strategy*, we find a high level of communications on strategy with management and professional/technical grades but a much lower level of communications with clerical and manual grades. Just 38 per cent of participating organisations reported that they communicate on strategy with manual grades. This result is surprisingly low even allowing for an expected differential in the level of communications on strategy between higher and lower ranking employees. It is all the more surprising given that, as we have seen above, most organisations are increasing direct communications with their workforce. It seems that such direct communications are predominantly concerned with operational matters and not strategic issues. Quite a similar picture emerges in relation to the extent of communications on *financial performance*. Again we find much lower levels of communications on financial issues with clerical and manual grades.

Table 7.8: Formal Communications on Business Strategy and Financial Performance

Employee Category	Formal Communications on:			
	Strategy		Financial performance	
	1995	1992	1995	1992
Management	95%	94%	94%	93%
Professional/Technical	72%	66%	64%	60%
Clerical	50%	42%	51%	41%
Manual	38%	39%	39%	36%

N=261

Source: Cranfield/University of Limerick Survey, 1995.

Turning to the impact of *trade union recognition* on the level of management–employee communications, some aggregate data is summarised in Table 7.9. Overall, it would seem that union recognition does not have a significant effect on whether or not employees are briefed on the organisation's strategy. This finding is interesting given the suggestion that non-union organisations communicate extensively on issues relating to organisation strategy (see, for example, Foulkes, 1980). The results show a similar trend when communication on the issue of financial performance is examined. Indeed these findings confirm the low level of communications on strategy and financial performance with lower ranking employees and indicate that the presence or absence of trade unions have little impact on this situation.

Table 7.9: Unionisation as a Determinant of the Information Distributed to Employees

	Non-Union		Union	
	Strategy	*Financial*	*Strategy*	*Financial*
Management	92% (46)	90% (45)	96% (197)	96% (196)
Professional	72% (36)	62% (31)	71% (146)	67% (133)
Clerical	56% (28)	58% (29)	48% (99)	48% (99)
Manual	32% (16)	34% (17)	40% (81)	41% (83)

n=50   n=205

Source: Cranfield/University of Limerick Survey, 1995.

Sector (public or private) does not seem to have a significant effect on the information provided to managerial grades (see Table 7.10). However, it does appear to have a significant impact on the extent of disclosure as one descends the organisational hierarchy: private sector organisations report that they provide more information to their manual and clerical grades, particularly in relation to financial matters.

Country of ownership also appears to impact on the extent of information provided to employees. US- and UK-owned organisations tend to give more information to all grades of employee below management level. UK organisations appear to provide most information on financial matters, whereas US organisations tend to give more information on strategy. More than 50 per cent of US organisations report giving information on both strategy and financial performance to manual employees, compared with less than 30 per cent of indigenous organisations.

Table 7.10: Sector as a Determinant of the Information Distributed to Employees

	Public Sector		Private Sector	
	Strategy	Financial	Strategy	Financial
Management	95% (56)	97% (57)	96% (190)	94% (187)
Professional	71% (42)	58% (34)	72% (143)	67% (133)
Clerical	42% (25)	39% (23)	53% (83)	55% (92)
Manual	25% (15)	17% (10)	42% (83)	46% (92)
	n=59		n=199	

Source: Cranfield/University of Limerick Survey, 1995.

In summarising on the actual content of management–employee communication, predictably the communication of strategic business/financial information, while high for managerial employees, remains low for manual and clerical grades. By extension, it is plausible to argue that much of the direct communication that appears to be occurring relates to operational matters and concerns. Union recognition or sectoral location do not have much explanatory power, while ownership, particularly US and UK ownership, correlate positively with the provision of more information on these matters.

EMPLOYEE PARTICIPATION

Employee participation has been broadly interpreted as incorporating any mechanisms designed to increase employee input into managerial decision-making (see, for example, Gunnigle, Heraty and Morley, 1997). Increasing the extent of employee participation is an important aspect of many recent change initiatives in HRM (Marchington and Parker, 1990; ICTU, 1993; Kochan et al., 1986). However, it is clear that employee participation may vary both in form (the types of mechanisms used to facilitate participation) and extent (the degree to which employees' viewpoints influence decision-making). It is also clear that employee involvement initiatives may range from the relatively superficial level of management informing employees of decisions which affect them, to that of consultation with employees on certain decisions or joint participation in the actual decision-making process (see, for example, Gunnigle, 1995b). Such initiatives may result in a variety of institutional arrangements to facilitate employee participation at workplace level, such as suggestion schemes, joint consultative committees/works councils, or quality circles.

In the current study, the nature of employee participation was explored through an investigation of (i) the incidence of joint consultative committees and works councils and (ii) the techniques used by management to facilitate upward communications by employees.

Joint Consultative Committees and Works Councils

Summary findings on the utilisation of joint consultative committees/works councils are outlined in Figure 7.12. These findings indicate that the extent to which organisations are facilitating increased employee participation through institutionalised arrangements in the form of joint consultative committees and work councils is quite modest. Just one-quarter of participating organisations reported the existence of joint consultative committees or works councils.

Figure 7.12: Existence of Joint Consultative Committees/Works Councils

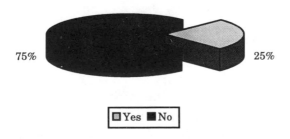

75%   25%

Yes ■ No

Source: Cranfield/University of Limerick Survey, 1995.

Participation is more widespread in the public sector with 38 per cent of organisations reporting the existence of some form of institutionalised participation, compared with 21 per cent of private sector organisations. This is probably due to legislation (The Worker Participation (State Enterprise) Acts, 1977 and 1988) introduced to provide for employee representation at board level and below in the semi-state sector. Hourihan (1994: 384) states that: "In Ireland, had it not been for legislative intervention, no significant advance in employee participation would have occurred". Participation may become more prevalent in the private sector in the light of a new European Works Council directive on information and consultation, although as Hourihan (1994) argues this is confined to a relatively small number of large employers. The vast majority of organisations that do have a works council or joint consultative committee, are also unionised (53 of the 63 organisations). The fact that many of these companies are located in the public sector is an important consideration in this respect.

Respondents were also asked to indicate when such committees/councils were established and their main areas of activity (such as quality, new product development, task flexibility, etc.). As Table 7.11 illustrates, the majority of these were established more than three years ago. 91 per cent of these committees in the public sector were established more than three years ago, compared with 65 per cent in the private sector.

Table 7.11: Establishment of Joint Consultative Committees/Works Councils

| Less than 3 years ago | 26% (16) |
| More than three years ago | 74% (46) |

Source: Cranfield/University of Limerick Survey, 1995.

The findings in relation to the areas of activity of these joint committees showed that the principal focus was quality enhancement (see Table 7.12). Looking at the impact of organisation size, it appears that quality issues are a more important area of focus for Joint Consultative Committees/Works Councils in smaller organisations, whereas task flexibility is slightly more significant in larger organisations (see Table 7.13). This finding may reflect the likelihood that levels of task flexibility are lower in larger than in smaller organisations, leading to a greater focus on increasing task flexibility in larger companies.

Table 7.12: Area of Activity of Joint Consultative Committees/Works Councils

Quality	56% (82)
New Product Development	14% (20)
Task Flexibility	30% (44)

n=146

Source: Cranfield/University of Limerick Survey, 1995.

Table 7.13: Organisation Size as a Determinant of Areas of Participation

	50–199	*>200*
Quality	60% (35)	53% (45)
New Product Development	12% (7)	15% (13)
Task Flexibility	28% (16)	32% (27)

n=143

Source: Cranfield/University of Limerick Survey, 1995.

Employee Participation and Employee–Management Communications

In examining the area of employee participation, it should be noted that this study does not attempt to analyse comprehensively the extent or nature of employee involvement and participation in Irish organisations. Rather, it focuses on the extent to which management adopt particular practices to facilitate greater participation by employees in management decision-making. To examine trends in this area, respondents were asked to indicate whether the level of employee utilisation of a range of employee–management communications mechanisms had changed in recent years. The major findings on this dimension are summarised in Table 7.14.

Table 7.14: Change in Utilisation of Various Channels of Communication

Means of Employee–Mgt. Communications:	Increased	Same	Decreased	Not used
Senior managers	36%	60%	2%	3%
Immediate supervisor	32%	65%	2%	1%
Trade union/ works council	14%	53%	14%	19%
Workforce meetings	35%	40%	3%	22%
Team briefings	45%	30%	2%	23%
Suggestion schemes	17%	27%	5%	52%
Attitude survey	28%	11%	0.5%	60%
Quality circles	15%	11%	2%	72%

Source: Cranfield/University of Limerick Survey, 1995.

The greatest increases in upward communications by employees were through team and work force briefings and via immediate supervisors and more senior management. The findings in relation to the increased utilisation of direct communications with managers is in line with our earlier findings on downward (management–employee) communications. It appears that Irish organisations are witnessing a significant increase in line management involvement in employee communications. The increase in workforce and team briefings is also significant. When taken in tandem with our earlier findings on the (low) level of management–employee communications on strategy and financial performance, an immediate question arises: what is the focus of these team and workforce briefings? While one cannot be definitive, the evidence points to higher levels of employee participation on immediate work-related issues. This trend may reflect a management perspective that employee involvement should be focused on immediate work-related issues rather than on broader employee involvement in higher-level management decision-making (such as strategy and financial performance). Another interesting finding outlined in Table 7.14 was that the only substantial decrease was in the reported utilisation of employee representative bodies, either trade unions or works councils.

Increases in employee communication through all of the mechanisms mentioned is more likely in larger organisations. Areas of particular interest were increases in the use of team briefings and attitude surveys, which showed a variance of 18 percentage points between large and small organisations. As mentioned previously, there were no significant decreases in employee communication, with the exception of the use of trade unions or work councils, and in that case smaller organisations were more likely to have reported a decrease (17 per cent compared with 12 per cent of larger organisations). However, when unionised organisations are examined (see Table 7.15) it emerges that although 15 per cent report a decrease in communication through representative bodies, there is a corresponding percentage (14 per cent) of organisations reporting an increase, with the overall picture being one of stability (63 per cent of organisations that recognise a trade union reporting no change).

Table 7.15: Unionisation as a Determinant of Employee–Management Communication

Form of Communication / Unionisation	Increased	Same	Decreased	Not Used	N
Direct: Senior Mgrs.					
Union	34%	61%	2%	3%	
Non-union	44%	54%	2%	0	n=236
Immediate Superior					
Union	34%	65%	2%	0	
Non-union	27%	64%	4%	4%	n=247
TU/Works Council					
Union	14%	63%	15%	8%	
Non-union	10%	10%	10%	69%	n=234
Team Briefings					
Union	44%	29%	1%	26%	
Non-union	49%	37%	2%	12%	n=221
Quality Circles					
Union	14%	10%	1%	75%	
Non-union	15%	21%	3%	62%	n=199

Source: Cranfield/University of Limerick Survey, 1995.

A greater number of unionised organisations report increases in communication via immediate supervisors. Not surprisingly, non-union organisations are more likely to utilise direct communication channels to senior management.

Private sector organisations are more likely to use and/or increase their use of all of the communications channels mentioned with two exceptions: (i) trade unions or works councils; and (ii) attitude surveys (which seem to be becoming more popular in the public sector).

In evaluating the overall findings on employee participation, it appears that the predominant focus is on facilitating the involvement of individual employees and small groups on issues of immediate work relevance. In the terminology of the Harvard Business School analysis, such initiatives seem to be predominantly concerned with encouraging greater employee "voice" on workplace issues rather than employee "influence" on higher-level management decision-making. More qualitative case study research is necessary to verify such a trend. Overall, the study findings do not point to a high level of employee participation in the more strategic areas of management decision-making. However, there is evidence of management initiatives to facilitate increased levels of employee participation on immediate work-related decisions. The study findings also point to a relatively low take-up of works councils/joint consultative committees among Ireland's leading organisations.

CONCLUSION

This chapter has focused on several critical aspects of employee relations. Many of the issues discussed relate to institutional arrangements governing the employment relationship, such as trade union recognition and employee participation. The evidence points to a strong sense of continuity in these matters. Where innovations are occurring, they appear to be occurring alongside/in conjunction with pre-existing arrangements and appear to be emerging in a rather incremental and piecemeal way.

Chapter 8

ANALYSIS AND REVIEW:
IMPLICATIONS FOR HUMAN RESOURCE
MANAGEMENT IN IRELAND

**Patrick Gunnigle, Michael Morley, Noreen Clifford &
Thomas Turner**

INTRODUCTION

In the concluding sections of our last book on the 1992/93 study
findings, we suggested that while the evidence pointed to a number of changes, there was also a strong sense of continuity in
HRM, particularly in employee relations practice in Ireland
(Gunnigle et al., 1994). Now some three years on, and with the
benefit of a second study of HRM in Irish organisations, what
additional perspectives can we provide on HRM in Ireland? This
final chapter attempts to synthesise the research findings presented in earlier chapters and review the implications for HRM in
Ireland.

CONTEXT

In the *Continuity and Change* text we noted that a key backdrop
to the analysis of developments in Ireland was the removal or dilution of trade barriers to facilitate greater trade liberalisation. In
evaluating the HRM implications one can point to a number of
factors. Firstly, the competitive threat to Irish organisations from
lower-cost economies and the related dangers of organisations re-
locating from Ireland to such lower cost regions. Secondly, increased trade liberalisation provides extensive opportunity to expand into new markets. To capitalise on such opportunity, how-

ever, it is likely that organisations will have to increase their HR capacities on dimensions such as speed to market, cycle time, etc.

Looking specifically at the European context, the prospect of Economic and Monetary Union (EMU) raises a number of issues. To satisfy the conditions for EMU, the Irish economy must meet the so-called convergence criteria in relation to inflation, interest rates, debt level and debt/GDP ratio, and exchange rate stability (see Burton et al., 1996). This will require a strict approach to budgetary policy and, particularly, public expenditure. Adhering to the Maastricht strictures will thus have important implications for HRM, particularly in the public sector. Related European Union initiatives designed to de-regulate state monopolies and increase competition in areas such as energy, air travel and telecommunications are likely to result in extensive rationalisation in these sectors as well as significant initiatives to enhance productivity and flexibility among remaining employees (see, for example, Hastings, 1994; Hourihan, 1994).

In addition to the globalisation of competition, we can also point to the greater intensification of international competition. Again, numerous sources may be identified: in addition to traditional sources of competition such as the US and Japan, we can point to the improved performance of Asian tigers such as Korea, Taiwan and Singapore who are combining a low-cost base with strong performance on dimensions such as productivity and labour skills. Nearer home, many of the countries of the former Soviet Union are also going through a period of re-structuring and are likely to provide considerable competition as a result of their low-cost base, industrial tradition and an educational system with a strong technical and scientific foundation. Other areas of the world, particularly in Mexico and a possibly resurgent South Africa, are also likely to emerge as significant competitors both in the production of goods and services and as alternative locations for direct foreign investment.

Finally, there is the changing nature of competitive strategies as a source of change in HRM. In particular, such changes as the increased customisation of products and services, and reduced cycle time as organisations strive to improve their speed to market, have implications for HRM. These changing competitive strategies require greater flexibility in employment patterns as organisations seek to align their need for workers with the level of business demand. Secondly, they require greater skill flexibility in terms of the variety of tasks which workers may be asked to perform. Finally, organisations have a requirement for greater pay flexibility as they seek to align pay levels both to market conditions and to the contribution of employees. A key aspect of the changing nature of competitive strategies has thus been to focus attention on both cost and quality as factors impacting on competitive positioning and to create a "flexibility imperative" whereby companies have to be responsive to consumer demand on dimensions such as customisation, delivery and support services. The implication of these developments seems to have significantly diluted the concept that companies compete on either a price (low cost) or a product differentiation (premium price) basis (see Marchington and Parker, 1990). Increasingly, it appears that all organisations, and not just the low-cost producers, must tightly control their cost structures, including their labour costs.

THE STATE OF HRM

These factors provide an important backdrop in evaluating developments in HRM in the mid-1990s. With this context in mind we can now turn to the study findings and consider what they tell us about the state of HRM in Irish organisations. In so-doing it may be useful to ask some questions about our findings:

- What does the data tell us about the role of the personnel/ human resource (P/HR) function in Irish organisations?

- What is the evidence of a strategic role for personnel/HRM?

- What is the evidence on the role of trade unions?

- What are the predominant types of pay systems?

- What do the findings tell us about employment flexibility and team working?

THE TRADITIONAL PERSPECTIVE:
"INDUSTRIAL RELATIONS ORTHODOXY"

A theme emerging from a historical review of the development of the P/HR function in Ireland is the predominance of industrial relations as the most significant area of personnel activity (see, for example, Shivanath, 1987; Gunnigle and Flood, 1990; Monks, 1992). The increasing influence of trade unions, particularly in the period from the early 1960s to the late 1970s, required a greater employer focus on industrial relations. This was largely achieved through multi-employer bargaining via employer associations and the employment of personnel practitioners whose primary role was to deal with industrial relations matters at enterprise level. The primacy of industrial relations within the personnel role reflected a widespread acceptance of the "pluralist model" incorporating a reliance on collective bargaining. This pluralist tradition was underpinned by public policy support and employer acceptance of trade union recognition and collective bargaining. For the personnel function, industrial relations became the priority with personnel practitioners taking primary responsibility for negotiations with trade unions, grievance and disciplinary issues and third-party referral. This industrial relations emphasis helped position the personnel function in a more central management role, albeit a largely reactive one.

In tracing the emergence of human resource management and the personnel function in Ireland one can therefore identify a relatively predictable pattern of development towards what might be termed "industrial relations orthodoxy" (Gunnigle, 1996). In this model the role of personnel practitioners was essentially that of "fire fighter", reacting to problems as they arose in a largely adversarial environment. While essentially reactive — rather than proactive or strategic — this industrial relations role was significant in both defining the objectives of the personnel role and establishing the personnel department as an important aspect of organisational management (see, for example, Keating, 1987; Shivanath, 1987; Monks, 1992; Gunnigle et al., 1994).

In assessing contemporary developments, the last decade may be typified as a period of both "continuity and change" for HRM and the specialist P/HR function (see Monks, 1992; Foley and

Gunnigle, 1994, 1995). The continuity dimension is manifested in the widespread presence of a specialist personnel function in Irish organisations and a continuing emphasis on industrial/employee relations as a significant aspect of the personnel role. However, we can also point to some evidence of important changes such as a movement away from traditional industrial relations to more individualist approaches, a greater focus on training and development and an increase in atypical employment forms. We have also witnessed the fashioning of a debate on the strategic role of the P/HR function (Monks, 1992; Gunnigle and Morley, 1997). Given such debates it is useful to consider evidence from the Cranfield/University of Limerick (CUL) study on the current role of the P/HR function in organisations operating in Ireland.

THE PERSONNEL/HUMAN RESOURCE FUNCTION TODAY

This section examines the traditional role of the P/HR function in Ireland and then evaluates what the study findings tell us about its current role in organisations. In Chapter 2 we considered a number of aspects of the role of the specialist personnel function in organisations, notably functional presence, scale, activity areas and reporting level. Some of the key findings are summarised in Table 8.1.

These findings indicate a high level of functional presence with over three-quarters of respondent organisations reporting the existence of a P/HR function. It also appears that where there is a change in the scale of the P/HR function this is over twice as likely to be an expansion rather than a contraction. The study findings point to a clear link between country of ownership and the existence or otherwise of a personnel function. Functional presence was greatest among US-owned organisations (86 per cent) while the corresponding figure for indigenous organisations was 72 per cent. However, it appears that functional presence is increasing in Irish organisations: in 1992 only 59 per cent of indigenous organisations reported the presence of a P/HR function. Looking more closely at the scale of the P/HR function, we find the average size of the personnel function — ten people — is quite large and indicative of quite a degree of specialisation within the personnel function itself. On the issue of gender balance, while there is a greater number of females employed in personnel (average of 6.5 compared to 4.43 males), there is an equal number of males and females employed at a professional level. This male–female imbalance is most pronounced in the most senior personnel position: over three-quarters of senior P/HR practitioners were male.

Table 8.1: The P/HR Function in Irish Organisations: Summary Overview

Presence of a P/HR function	Yes		No	
	76%		22%	
Changing size of P/HR function	**Expanding**	**Contracting**	**Stable**	
	26%	12%	38%	
Number of Individuals employed in P/HR	**1–5**	**6–10**	**11–25**	**26+**
	43%	18%	8%	8%
No. of years experience of P/HR practitioner	**1–5**	**6–10**	**11–20**	**20+**
	15%	15%	27%	8%
Where P/HR manager was recruited	**Externally** Non-specialist	**Externally** Specialist	**Internally** Non-specialist	**Internally** Specialist
	6%	31%	34%	15%
P/HR manager holds a degree	**Yes**		**No**	
	62%		38%	

Note: Figures do not add up to 100 per cent as missing/don't know categories are excluded in this table: see tables in Chapter 2 for greater detail.
Source: Cranfield/University of Limerick Survey, 1995.

Generally, it appears that Irish personnel practitioners have considerable previous experience (the average length of experience was 13 years). There was a clear link with organisation size, with notable increases in levels of experience as organisations become larger. Most senior P/HR managers were recruited either from another functional area within the organisation, or had been a personnel specialist in another company. Looking at the educational level of personnel practitioners we find quite a positive picture with some 61 per cent of practitioners holding a primary degree, usually in a business discipline.

Looking at the aggregate findings, this study provides evidence of the continuing importance of a specialist P/HR function in Irish organisations. On dimensions such as functional presence and scale, personnel departments are clearly a well-established feature in the management structure of organisations.

STRATEGIC ROLE OF THE PERSONNEL/HUMAN RESOURCE FUNCTION

As noted earlier, while measures such as presence and scale represent the most obvious indicators of the role of the P/HR function, they are also the crudest, relying on the assumption that presence indicates an organisational concern with HR issues. To establish a more accurate picture it is useful to evaluate the findings on the level of strategic involvement of the P/HR function.

Sparrow and Hiltrop (1994), identify three proxy measures which may be used to evaluate the strategic role of the P/HR function: (i) an organisational structure which provides for the head of the HRM function to be present at the key policy forum; (ii) perceived involvement in developing corporate strategy; and (iii) the existence of a written personnel/human resource management strategy. The study findings on these measures of the strategic role of the P/HR function in Irish organisations are outlined in Figure 8.1.

Figure 8.1: Indicators of Strategic Role of the P/HR Function

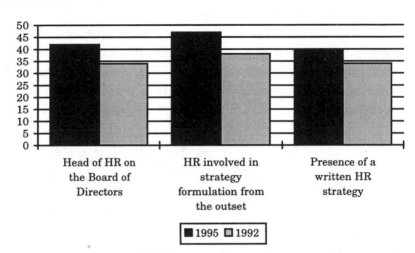

Source: Cranfield/University of Limerick Survey, 1992 and 1995

A traditional indicator of the status of the P/HR function in organisations is board-level participation. In this study some 42 per cent of senior P/HR practitioners were members of their organisation's Board of Directors or equivalent. This figure represents an increase since our last study in 1992. Turning to the role of the P/HR function in strategy development we find that almost half (47 per cent) the respondents report that they are involved in strategy formulation from the outset. This figure again represents an increase since the 1992 study. The final measure of strategic involvement outlined in Figure 8.1 relates to the existence of a written P/HR strategy. Here we find that 40 per cent of respondent organisations reported having such a written strategy, an increase of some 6 per cent since 1992. Overall, these findings indicate a general trend towards greater P/HR involvement in strategy formulation among organisations in Ireland.

The P/HR Function and Line Management

Many authors have identified a shift in emphasis from the personnel function to line management, with line managers having greater involvement in conducting tasks which traditionally might have fallen within the remit of the specialist personnel function (see, for example, Beer et al., 1984). This espoused development is often linked to the suggestion that the P/HR function is adopting more of a consultancy orientation and generalist focus, with line management taking more responsibility for day-to-day human resource management. Such a development may have positive or negative implications for the specialist P/HR function. For example, it could be seen as dilution or "stripping" away of responsibilities traditionally seen as the work of the personnel function. Equally, this trend may be seen as a kind of emancipation, freeing the personnel function from operational personnel activities and providing an opportunity to develop a more strategic, proactive role in organisations. An analysis of the results of this study can provide some pointers on the extent and nature of change which has taken place.

Looking at the key findings, although there is some evidence of an increase in line management involvement in HRM, this trend is limited in its extent. The two areas where there is most evidence of a transfer of responsibilities from the P/HR function to line management are pay and training. This trend is likely to reflect: (i) the greater uptake of performance-related pay systems based on appraisals of employee performance (a necessary element of such appraisals and related PRP decisions is the input of line managers); (ii) a greater internal focus on training and retraining of workers to meet changing job and organisational needs. However, the more general picture is one of joint HR/line management involvement in most areas of HRM with the P/HR function still retaining a high level of responsibility for HR decisions. It was interesting to note that Irish-owned organisations appear less inclined to devolve HR responsibilities to line management.

EVALUATION

The role of the specialist P/HR function is a significant aspect of the nature of HRM in organisations. In Britain, Guest (1987) notes the well-established professional structure of personnel management whereby professional personnel specialists undertake responsibility for a range of human resource issues, and possess valued expertise in "core" HR areas such as selection, training, pay and employee relations. However, we have also noted that in so-called "strategic HRM" the major responsibility for managing human resources is assumed by line managers (Beer et al., 1984). The role of the specialist P/HR function is possibly the most commonly used indicator to evaluate the impact of HR considerations on strategic decision-making (see, for example, Legge, 1995; Thomason, 1984; Tyson and Fell, 1986). We have seen that, while the presence of a specialist P/HR function in organisations is of a relatively recent vintage in Ireland, its role was well established in most medium and large organisations by the late 1970s (Murray, 1984). However, this role was deeply rooted in the traditional pluralist model, with the specialist P/HR function primarily operating in a systems-reactive mode and concentrating principally on collective bargaining and related "industrial relations" activities (Monks, 1992; Foley and Gunnigle, 1994; see also Tyson, 1987).

The findings of this study provide prima facie evidence of the continuing importance of a specialist P/HR function in organisations. The evidence also indicates a considerable level of strategic involvement for HR, although this varies extensively between organisations. It also emerges that while employee relations remains an important aspect of HR work, the P/HR function is engaged in a broad range of activity areas, some of which are getting equal and sometimes more priority than employee relations. Of particular note is the extensive emphasis on training and development and payment systems. It is also clear that much of the responsibility for the execution of many of these activities is shared between the P/HR function and line management. However, the P/HR function continues to retain much authority in HRM.

The least positive aspect of the study findings was related to quantifying the role and contribution of the P/HR function. This is somewhat of an "old chestnut": for example, Legge (1995) noted the difficulties which personnel practitioners had in demonstrating their organisational worth through conventional quantitative and financial indices. In this study it was interesting that only 42 per cent of the organisations studied evaluated their personnel department's performance on a systematic basis. This figure suggests the absence of a systematic, quantitative approach to evaluating the P/HR function's contribution in organisations operating in Ireland. US-owned organisations were most likely to engage in such evaluation while Irish-owned organisations were least likely to do so. A similar picture emerged in relation to the extent to which HR data was systematically collected in organisation's. The findings suggest that while there was considerable emphasis on collecting data on absenteeism, a much lower proportion of organisations collected data on labour turnover and age profiles. The absence of a quantitative approach to issues such as staff turnover and age profiles places a major question mark against an organisations capacity to engage in comprehensive HR initiatives such as human resource planning, career development and other characteristics of "sophisticated" HRM. The low level of data collection on staff turnover and age profiles may also have more pragmatic roots: it probably reflects a degree of managerial complacency in relation to staff turnover and employee attrition arising from the loose labour market situation created by high unemployment levels and the large number of new entrants into the Irish labour market.

Employee Relations and the Role of Trade Unions

Employee relations has been identified as one of the key areas of change in HRM since the 1980s. The nub of such change has focused on a reduced role for collective bargaining and trade unions and a growth in non-union systems. In evaluating developments in Europe, Sparrow and Hiltrop suggest that the 1980s witnessed "a perceptible decline in the legitimisation and representativeness of trade unions" (Sparrow and Hiltrop, 1994: 135). In the US, Kochan et al. (1986) point to the decline in unionism and the extensive diffusion on non-union systems. Several commentators have traced changes in employee relations to developments in the broader business environment. For example, Salaman highlights the impact of developments in the economic and political environment in changing the relative power balance in employee relations and suggests that such change stimulated consequential shifts in management approaches to employee relations

(Salaman, 1992). This was clearly evident in the UK during the 1980s when a combination of economic conditions (increased competition) and government policies (market-oriented, anti-union) allowed managements to adopt tougher and more unitarist employee relations styles designed both to re-establish management prerogative and reduce the perceived rigidity associated with formalised collective bargaining arrangements (see Salaman, 1992; Sisson, 1991; Storey, 1989).

In the Irish context we have seen that the period 1980–87 witnessed a decline in trade union density. We have also noted some growth in non-union approaches. However, the aggregate evidence suggests that union membership in Ireland has held up comparatively well (see Figure 8.2) and collective bargaining remains a central aspect of Irish employee relations. A widely used explanation relates to the Irish socio-political environment which, it is argued, remains conducive to a strong collectivist orientation in employee relations. In specifically commenting on the political context and the implications for trade unions, Roche and Turner suggest that:

> The long established legitimacy of trade unions in Irish economic, political life has yet to be seriously and trenchantly challenged by any Irish Government, political party or any strong body of employer opinion. . . . In the absence of a strong anti-union ideology in Irish politics and business, trade unions still hold a relatively high, if probably declining, degree of legitimacy in the eyes of employees. . . . This pattern, combined with the high profile of leading union officials nationally, normalises unions and union membership in the eyes of employees to an appreciably greater degree than in the United States or even in the United Kingdom after a decade of Conservative Government opposition to trade union power and organisation (Roche and Turner, 1994: 745).

It is certainly clear that during the 1980s, Government policy in Ireland presented a stark contrast to the UK. Rather than adopting a policy of "market liberalism" combined with a forthright onslaught on trade unions, successive Irish Governments since the mid-1980s have sought to integrate trade unions into corporatist decision-making structures on economic and social policy (Gunnigle and Morley, 1993; Roche, 1989, 1994). The context for the analysis of change in Irish employee relations is quite different to that of the US and UK, from where much of the contemporary literature emanates. The most explicit manifestations of this difference include the widely accepted legitimacy of trade unions in Irish society, the maintenance of comparatively high levels of trade union density, high levels of centralisation of decision-making on pay and other aspects of economic and social policy, the related corporatist structures characteristic of Irish employee relations since the 1980s, and the absence of a strong anti-union ideology among any of the major political parties. These factors contribute to a social, political and economic context considered conducive to the sustenance of the traditional pluralist employee relations model by normalising divergent workplace interests and, consequently, trade union membership:

> The Irish industrial relations tradition and the wider Irish socio-political tradition with which it is meshed still provide a context that is conducive to . . . "divided loyalties" and multiple reference points, and probably to a greater degree than pertains in the United States and even the United Kingdom (Roche and Turner, 1994: 746).

However, this is not to say there is no evidence of the pervasive change in employee relations which characterises much of the UK, US and western Europe. For example, McGovern (1989) points to increasing employer opposition to trade union recognition, and studies of newly established firms point to the emergence of a vibrant non-union sector (Gunnigle, 1995b; Hourihan, 1996). There is also evidence of considerable change in employee relations in indigenous organisations, particularly in the semi-state sector. Hastings (1994) points to the extensive pressures for employee relations restructuring in many semi-state companies as a result of greater market competition and de-regulation. Hourihan (1994) also points to the significant employee relations implications of European Union initiatives designed to increase competition and reduce state monopolies.

Trade Union Presence and Influence

As discussed in the preceding chapter, the most widely used measure of trade union presence in a country is union density. Looking at workforce density in Ireland, we find that the proportion of the workforce who are trade union members fell from a high of 55 per cent in 1980, but currently would appear to be stabilising at approximately 43–44 per cent. This compares favourably with union density in the UK which is currently some 40 per cent, and is considerably higher than in the US where employment union density as a proportion of the non-agricultural workforce stands at approximately 16 per cent and is confined to a small number of industrial sectors such as the automotive and transport areas (see Figure 8.2).

Figure 8.2: International Union Density

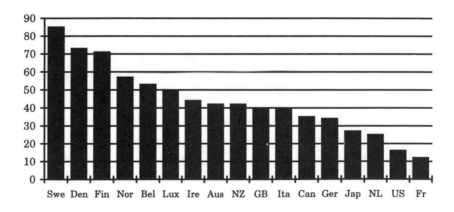

"Aus" represents Australia.
Source: OECD Outlook 1991.

The study findings on the levels of union membership among respondent organisations were reviewed in Chapter 6. These findings indicate a high level of union density: almost two-thirds of organisations reported that 50 per cent or more of their employees were trade union members. As might be expected, trade union membership was greater in larger organisations and in the public sector. On the impact of country of ownership, the findings indicate that levels of union density are lowest among US-owned organisations and greatest among Irish- and other European-owned organisations. While over half of indigenous organisations report that more than 76 per cent of their workforce are members of a trade union almost one-third of US organisations report having no union members in their organisations.

In evaluating contemporary developments it appears that trade union recognition has become an issue of some debate. In particular, there is considerable evidence of increased management opposition to unionisation in recent years, particularly among some multinational organisations and indigenous small firms (McGovern, 1989, Gunnigle and Brady, 1984; Gunnigle, 1992c, 1995b; Hourihan, 1996). It is therefore interesting to consider the key findings on union recognition in organisations operating in Ireland and to evaluate trends since our last study in 1992. The findings (reviewed in Chapter 6) indicate a high level of recognition: eight out of every ten organisations recognised trade unions for collective bargaining purposes. While this figure is marginally lower than in 1992, it presents a healthy picture of union recognition in Ireland. Recognition was more likely in large organisations or those in the public sector, whereas non-union approaches were more common among US-owned organisations.

While findings on the levels of trade union density and recognition provides vital factual information on the position of trade unions in Irish organisations, it is also useful to consider management perspectives on the changing role of trade unions. The study findings outlined in Chapter 6 suggest little change, with most respondents (71 per cent) suggesting that union influence has remained stable over recent years. However, where organisations reported a change in union influence this was significantly more likely to be a decrease (22 per cent) rather than an increase (7 per cent). Larger organisations and those from the private sector were more likely to report a decrease in trade union influence.

A Diminution of Industrial Relations Orthodoxy

In opening this chapter we argued that personnel management in Ireland has emerged in the context of what might be termed "industrial relations orthodoxy" (Gunnigle, 1996). Such orthodoxy was grounded in the belief that the key employer concern in workforce management was the establishment and maintenance of "stable industrial relations". Characteristics of this approach were trade union recognition, distributive collective bargaining and a degree of procedural formalisation. Essentially, the personnel function assumed responsibility for managing relations with the unions while also undertaking other related activities such as personnel administration, recruitment and training (see, for example Shivanath, 1987; Monks, 1992). While more reactive than strategic, this industrial relations role was nonetheless significant: it served to both define what personnel work involved and position the personnel management function as an important aspect of the managerial infrastructure.

Is there any evidence then, of a diminution of the orthodox industrial relations model? Four broad areas can be identified which appear to indicate some degree of change. Firstly, we can point to a decline in both the significance of employee relations as the dominant activity area in HRM, and in industrial relations orthodoxy as the dominant paradigm of the P/HR function. Increasingly, other aspects of HRM are taking priority, most notably those concerning training and development and payment systems. Secondly, it is also clear that in many organisations the P/HR role is heavily concerned with broader strategic issues such as organisational re-structuring and productivity improvements. Thirdly, these findings suggest that the P/HR function is solidly ingrained as an important dimension of the managerial infrastructure of Irish organisations. Finally, in the execution of personnel activities, much responsibility is shared with line management.

While the findings therefore point to the emergence of a broadly based personnel function, incorporating, in many organisations, a considerable strategic dimension, it is also characterised by old dilemmas. In particular, the lack of a quantitative focus points to the potential difficulty which the P/HR function may have in explicitly demonstrating its contribution to organisational performance. Of course, an alternative interpretation is that our findings on the lack of a quantitative orientation simply reflect a lack of top management concern that the P/HR contribution be demonstrated in hard terms. While this may be true, the authors feel it unlikely. As many organisations move to "leaner" organisational structures, all functional areas are likely to come under greater scrutiny. Given the substantial evidence of an increasing focus on costs and performance it seems more likely that organisations will seek to identify the demonstrable contribution of management activities (and expenditure) to bottom-line performance.

CONCLUSIONS

Our findings suggest that in Ireland's leading organisations most of the basic features of traditional pluralism are still well entrenched. However, the evidence on the growing range of personnel activities and the increasing focus on strategic dimensions, particularly in relation to performance enhancement, points to the changing role of HRM. A key HRM priority is in facilitating organisation change and the creation of organisation structures which are more cost-efficient, flexible and responsive to change. This is indeed a major challenge for HRM and particularly for the personnel function, especially given the P/HR function's traditional focus on more reactive and indeed mundane concerns. Research evidence again points to the robust nature of union presence in Ireland's leading organisations. However, there are some negative signals: particularly the fall-off in density and recognition since 1992 and the increase in non-union approaches in the private sector. Indeed our findings may understate this position. The evidence in this study point to a slight fall-off in union density and recognition since 1992. However, other studies, notably those based on new establishments, point to a more substantial decline in union penetration. It is likely that because of the "newness" and "smallness" of these companies, their impact to date on aggregate union density and recognition figures is limited. However, it should be noted that many of these greenfield companies are located in some of the fastest growing industrial sectors, such as electronics, software and business/financial services. In contrast, union penetration in this study was greatest in sectors which are either stagnant or declining in employment terms, such as the public/semi-state sector and traditional manufacturing. It is therefore likely that we will see some fall-off in union density and recognition as newer organisations grow and have a greater impact on aggregate union density levels. Trade unions clearly play a very significant role in Irish industry as evidenced from this study. However, it is likely that competitive pressures, high unemployment, the visibility of non-union models and a changing workforce profile will increasingly challenge this role at organisational level.

BIBLIOGRAPHY

Anastasi, A. (1982): *Psychological Testing*, London: Macmillan.

Anderson, A. (1993): *Successful Training Practice: A Manager's Guide*, Oxford: Blackwell.

Anderson, N. (1992): "Eight Decades of Employment Interview Research: A Retrospective Meta-review and Prospective Commentary", *The European Work and Organisational Psychologist*, 2, pp. 1–32.

Anderson, N. and Shackleton, V. (1986): "Recruitment and Selection: A Review of Developments in the 1980s", *Personnel Review*, Vol. 15, No. 4.

Anderson, N. and Shackleton, V. (1993): *Successful Selection Interviewing*, Oxford: Blackwell.

Armstrong, M. (ed.) (1992): *Strategies for Human Resource Management: A Total Business Approach*, Coopers & Lybrand, London: Kogan Page.

Armstrong, P. (1995): "Accountancy and HRM" in Storey, J. (ed.), *Human Resource Management: A Critical Text*, London: Routledge.

Arnold, J., Cooper, C. and Robertson, I.T. (1995): *Work Psychology: Understanding Human Behaviour in the Workplace*, 2nd edition, London: Pitman Publishing.

Ashton, D. (1984): "Current Issues in Line/Staff Relationships", *Management Education and Development*, Vol. 10, No. 2, pp. 105–118.

Atkinson, J. (1984): "Manpower Strategies for Flexible Organisations", *Personnel Management*, August, pp. 28–31.

Atkinson, J. and Meager, N. (1986): "Is Flexibility just a Flash in the Pan?", *Personnel Management*, September, pp. 26–29.

Bacon, N. and Storey, J. (1993): "Individualisation of the Employment Relationship and the Implications for Trade Unions", *Employee Relations*, Vol. 15, No. 1, pp. 5–17.

Bain, G.S. and Elsheikh, F. (1976): *Union Growth in the Business Cycle,* Oxford: Blackwell.

Barker, F. (1995): "The Flexible Organization: A Review of Current Practice with Particular Reference to the Flexible Workforce", *Management Bibliographies & Reviews*, Vol. 21, No. 2, pp. 2–12.

Beardwell, I. and Holden, L. (1994): *Human Resource Management: A Contemporary Perspective,* London: Pitman.

Beaumont, P. (1985): "New Plant Work Practices", *Personnel Review,* Vol. 14, No. 5, pp. 15–19.

Beaumont, P. (1986): "Management Opposition to Union Organisation: Researching the Indicators", *Employee Relations*, Vol. 8, No. 5, pp. 31–38.

Beaumont, P. (1992): "The US Human Resource Management Literature: A Review" in Graeme Salaman (ed.), *Human Resource Strategies*, London: Open University/Sage.

Beaumont, P. (1993): *Human Resource Management: Key Concepts & Skills*, London: Sage.

Beaumont, P. and Harris, R. (1994): "Opposition to Unions in the Non-Union Sector in Britain", *International Journal of Human Resource Management*, Vol. 5, No. 2, pp. 457–471.

Beer, M., Spector, B., Lawrence, P.R., Quinn-Mills, D. and Walton, R.E. (1984): *Managing Human Assets: The Groundbreaking Harvard Business School Program*, New York: The Free Press/Macmillan.

Beer, M. et al. (1985): *Human Resource Management: A General Manager's Perspective*, New York: The Free Press/Macmillan.

Block, P. (1990): *The Empowered Manager*, San Francisco, CA: Jossey-Bass.

Blyton, P. and Morris, J. (1991): "A Flexible Future: Aspects of the Flexibility Debates and Some Unresolved Issues", in Blyton, P. and Morris, J. (eds.) *A Flexible Future? Prospects for Employment and Organization*, New York: de Gruyter.

Blyton, P. and Turnbull, P. (1992): *Reassessing Human Resource Management*, London: Sage.

Blyton, P. and Turnbull, P. (1994): *The Dynamics of Employee Relations*, London: Macmillan.

Boyd, A. (1972): *The Rise of Irish Trade Unions 1729–1970,* Tralee: Anvil.

Bramham, J. (1989): *Human Resource Planning*, London: Institute of Personnel Management.

Breaugh, J. and Mann, R. (1984): "Recruiting Source Effects: A Test of Two Alternative Explanations", *Journal of Occupational Psychology*, Vol. 57, pp. 261–67.

Brewster, C. (1994): "The Integration of Human Resource Management and Corporate Strategy", in Brewster, C. and Hegewisch, A. (eds.), *Policy and Practice in European Human Resource Management,* London: Routledge.

Brewster, C. and Hegewisch, A. (1994): "HRM in Europe: Issues and Opportunities" in Brewster, C. and Hegewisch, A. (eds.), *Policy and Practice in European Human Resource Management,* London: Routledge.

Brewster, C., Hegewisch, A. and Mayne, L. (1994). "Flexible Working Practices: The Controversy and the Evidence", in Brewster, C. and Hegewisch, A. (eds.), *Policy and Practice in European Human Resource Management,* The Price Waterhouse Cranfield Study, London: Routledge, pp. 168–194.

Brewster, C., Hegewisch, A., Mayne, L. and Tregaskis, O. (1994): "Employee Communication and Participation", in Brewster, C. and Hegewisch, A. (eds.), *Policy and Practice in European Human Resource Management,* The Price Waterhouse Cranfield Study, London: Routledge.

Brewster, C. And Soderstrom, M. (1994): "Human Resources and Line Management", in Brewster, C. and Hegewisch, A. (eds.), *Policy & Practice in European Human Resource Management*, London: Routledge.

Buckley, R. and Caple, J. (1990): *The Theory and Practice of Training*, London: Kogan Page.

Burrows, R., Gilbert, N. and Pollert, A. (1992): "Introduction: Fordism, Post-Fordism and Economic Flexibility", in Gilbert, N., Burrows, R. and Pollert, A. (eds.), *Fordism and Flexibility: Divisions and Change*, London: Macmillan, pp. 1–9.

Burton, F., Yamin, M. and Young, S. (1996): *International Business and Europe in Transition*, London: Macmillan.

Carroll, S.J. (1991): "The New HRM Roles, Responsibilities, and Structures", in Schuler, R.S. (ed.), *Managing Human Resources in the Information Age*, Washington DC: Bureau of National Affairs, pp. 204–26.

Caudron, S. (1994): "Contingent Work Force Spurs HR Planning", *Personnel Journal*, July, pp. 52–60.

Clarke, P. (1989): "Payment By Results: A Review of Trends", *Industrial Relations News*, No. 8.

Clutterbuck, D. (1989): "Training: A World of Change", *Training and Development*, February, pp. 15–16.

Cook, M. (1993): *Personnel Selection and Productivity*, 2nd edition, Chichester: John Wiley.

Corcoran, T., Sexton, J. and O'Donoghue, D. (1992): "A Review of Trends in the Occupational Pattern of Employment in Ireland 1971–1990", Dublin: FAS/ESRI, Report No. 2.

Curran, J. and Stanworth, J. (1981a): "The Social Dynamics of the Small Manufacturing Enterprise", *Journal of Management Studies*, Vol. 18, No. 2.

Curran, J. and Stanworth, J. (1981b): "Size of Workplace & Attitudes to Industrial Relations in the Printing & Electronics Industries", *British Journal of Industrial Relations*, Vol. 19, No. 1, pp. 14–25.

Dale, M. (1995): *Successful Recruitment and Selection: A Practical Guide for Managers*, London: Kogan Page.

DeWitte, K. (1989): "Recruitment and Advertising" in Herriot, P. (ed.), *Recruitment and Selection in Organisations*, New York: John Wiley.

Dineen, D. (1989): "Changing Employment Patterns in Ireland — Recent Trends and Future Prospects", Final Report prepared for the Irish National Pensions Board, College of Business, University of Limerick.

Dineen, D. (1992): "Atypical Work Patterns in Ireland — Short Term Adjustments or Fundamental Changes?", *Administration*, Vol. 40, No. 3, Autumn, pp. 248–274.

Dobbs, J. (1993): "The Empowerment Environment", *Training and Development*, February.

Dobson, P. (1989): "Reference Reports" in Herriot, P. (ed.), *Recruitment and Selection in Organisations*, New York: John Wiley.

Donnelly, E. (1987): "The Training Model: A Time for Change?", *Industrial and Commercial Training*, May/June.

Due, J., Madsen, J. and Jensen, C. (1991): "The Social Dimension: Convergence or Diversification of Industrial Relations in the

Single European Market?", *Industrial Relations Journal,* Vol. 22, No. 2, pp. 85–103.

Dues Project (1992): Department of Industrial Relations, University College Dublin.

Easterby-Smith, M. (1986): *Evaluation of Management Education, Training and Development*, Aldershot: Gower.

Eichel, E. and Bender, H. (1984): *Performance Related Pay: A Study of Current Techniques*, American Management Association.

Elger, T. (1991): "Task Flexibility and the Intensification of Labour in UK Manufacturing in the 1980s", in Pollert, A. (ed.), *Farewell to Flexibility*, Oxford: Blackwell Business, pp. 46–66.

Farnham, D. (1984): *Personnel in Context*, London: Institute of Personnel Management.

Farnham, D. and Pimlott, J. (1995): *Understanding Industrial Relations,* 3rd edition, London: Cassells.

Filella, J. and Hegewisch, A. (1994): "European Experiments with Pay and Benefits Policies", in Brewster, C. and Hegewisch, A. (eds.), *Policy and Practice in European Human Resource Management,* London: Routledge.

Flood, P. (1989): "Human Resource Management: Promise, Possibilities and Limitations", Mimeo, University of Limerick.

Flood, P. (1990): "Atypical Employment, Core–Periphery Manpower Strategies — The Implications for Organisational Culture", *Industrial Relations News*, Vol. 9/10.

Foley, K., Gunnigle, P. and Morley, M. (1996): "Personnel Management in Ireland: A New Epoch?", *International Journal of Employment Studies*, Vol. 4, No. 2.

Foley, K. and Gunnigle, P. (1994): "The Personnel/Human Resource Function and Employee Relations" in Gunnigle, P. et al. (eds.), *Continuity and Change in Irish Employee Relations,* Dublin: Oak Tree Press.

Foley, K. and Gunnigle, P. (1995): "The Personnel Function — Change or Continuity" in Turner, T. and Morley, M. (eds.), *Industrial Relations and the New Order*, Dublin: Oak Tree Press.

Fombrun, C.J., Tichy, N.M. and Devanna, M.A. (1984): *Strategic Human Resource Management*, New York: Wiley.

Foulkes, F. (1980): *Effective Personnel Policies: A Study of Larger Non-Union Organisations*, Englewood Cliffs, NJ: Prentice Hall.

Fox, R. (1987): "Training of the Employed: Statistics for Ireland", *AnCo*, October.

Fox, A. (1974): *Beyond Contract: Work, Power & Trust Relations*, London: Faber & Faber.

Garavan, T., Costine, P. and Heraty, N. (1995): *Training & Development in Ireland: Context, Policy and Practice*, Dublin: Oak Tree Press.

Gill, D. (1977): *Appraising Performance: Present Trends and the Next Decade*, London: Institute of Personnel Management.

Goss, D. (1994): *Principles of Human Resource Management*, London: Routledge.

Grafton, D. (1988): "Performance Related Pay: Securing Employee Trust", *Industrial Relations News*, November.

Greenhaus, J.H. and Callanan, G.A. (1994): *Career Management*, 2nd edition, Orlando, FL: Harcourt Brace.

Guest, D. (1993): "Personnel Management Strategies, Procedures and Techniques", in Guest, D. and Kenny, J. (eds.), *A Textbook of Techniques and Strategies in Personnel Management*, London: Institute of Personnel Management.

Guest, D. (1987): "Human Resource Management and Industrial Relations", *Journal of Management Studies*, Vol. 24, No. 5, pp. 503–521.

Guest, D. and Hoque, K. (1994): "Yes, Personnel Does Make a Difference", *Personnel Management*, November, pp. 40–44.

Guest, D. and Rosenthal, P. (1992): "Industrial Relations in Greenfield Sites", Mimeo, Centre for Economic Performance, Industrial Relations Conference, London, March.

Gunnigle, P. and Flood, P. (1990): *Personnel Management in Ireland: Practice, Trends and Developments*, Dublin: Gill & Macmillan.

Gunnigle, P., Heraty, N. and Morley, M. (1997): *Personnel & Human Resource Management: Theory and Practice in Ireland*, Dublin: Gill & Macmillan.

Gunnigle, P. (1992a): "Management Approaches to Employee Relations in Greenfield Sites", *Journal of Irish Business and Administrative Research*, Vol. 13.

Gunnigle, P. (1992b): "Changing Management Approaches to Employee Relations in Ireland", *Employee Relations*, Vol. 14, No. 1.

Gunnigle, P. (1992c): "Human Resource Management in Ireland", *Employee Relations*, Vol. 14, No. 5.

Gunnigle, P. (1995a): "Collectivism and the Management of Industrial Relations in Greenfield Sites", *Human Resource Management Journal*, Vol. 5, No. 3, pp. 24–40.

Gunnigle, P. (1995b): "Management Styles in Employee Relations in Greenfield Sites: Challenging a Collectivist Tradition", Unpublished Doctoral Thesis, Cranfield School of Management.

Gunnigle, P. (1996): "The Personnel Management Function in Ireland: Models and Prospects", *Irish Business and Administrative Research*, Vol. 18, No. 2.

Gunnigle, P. and Brady, T. (1984): "The Management of Industrial Relations in the Small Firm", *Employee Relations*, Vol. 6, No. 5.

Gunnigle, P., McMahon, G.V. and Fitzgerald, G. (1995): *Industrial Relations in Ireland: Theory and Practice*, Dublin: Gill & Macmillan.

Gunnigle, P., Flood, P., Morley, M. and Turner, T. (1994): *Continuity and Change in Irish Employee Relations*, Dublin: Oak Tree Press.

Gunnigle, P. and Moore, S. (1994): "Linking Business Strategy and Human Resource Management: Issues and Implications", *Personnel Review*, Vol. 23, No. 1, pp. 63–84.

Gunnigle, P. and Morley, M. (1993): "Something Old, Something New: A Perspective on Industrial Relations in the Republic of Ireland", *Review of Employment Topics*, Vol. 1, No. 1, pp. 114–142.

Gunnigle, P. and Morley, M. (1997): "Strategic Integration and the Management of Industrial Relations in Greenfield Sites", in Skinner, D., Mabey, C. and Clark, T. (eds.), *Experiencing Human Resource Management: The Inside Story*, London: Sage.

Gunnigle, P. and Shivanath, G. (1988): "Role and Status of Personnel Practitioners — A Positive Picture", *Irish Business and Administrative Research*, Vol. 9, pp. 1–9.

Gutteridge, T. (1986): "Organisational Career Development Systems: The State of the Practice", in Hall, D. (ed.), *Career Development in Organisations*, London: Jossey-Bass.

Hamblin, A. (1974): *Evaluation and Control of Training*, Maidenhead: McGraw Hill.

Handy, C. (1984): "The Organisation Revolution and How to Harness it", *Personnel Management*, July, pp. 20–23.

Handy, C. (1989): *The Age of Unreason*, London: Business Books Ltd.

Hannaway, C. (1992): "Why Irish Eyes are Smiling", *Personnel Management*, May.

Harrison, R. (1992): *Employee Development*, London: Institute of Personnel Management.

Hastings, T. (1994): *Semi-States in Crisis*, Dublin: Oak Tree Press.

Hay Associates, (1975): *Survey of Human Resource Practices*, London: Hay Associates.

Hendry, C. and Pettigrew, A. (1990): "HRM: an agenda for the 1990s", *International Journal of Human Resource Management,* Vol. 1, No. 1, pp. 17–25.

Heraty, N. and Morley, M. (1994): "Human Resource Development in Ireland: Position, Practices and Power", *Administration*, Vol. 42, No. 3.

Heraty, N. and Morley, M. (1995): "Line Managers and Human Resource Development", *Journal of European Industrial Training*, Vol. 19, No. 10, pp. 30–38.

Heraty, N., Morley, M. and Turner, T. (1994): "Trends and Developments in the Organisation of the Employment Relationship", in Gunnigle, P. et al. (eds.), *Continuity and Change in Irish Employee Relations*, Dublin: Oak Tree Press.

Herriot, P., (1989): *Recruitment in the 90s*, London: Institute of Personnel Management.

Herriot, P. and Rothwell, C. (1981): "Organisational Choice and Decision Theory — Effects of Employer's Literature and Selection Interview", *Journal of Occupational Psychology*, Vol. 54, pp. 17–31.

Higgins, C. (1992): "Executive Search — An Essential Requirement for the 1990s", *Industrial Relations News,* No. 38, October 8.

Holden, L. and Livian, Y. (1992): "Does Strategic Training Policy Exist? Some Evidence for Ten European Countries", *Personnel Reviews*, Vol. 21, No. 1, pp. 25–38.

Hourihan, F. (1994): "The European Union and Industrial Relations", in Murphy, T. and Roche, W. (eds.), *Irish Industrial Relations in Practice*, Dublin: Oak Tree Press.

Hourihan, F. (1996): "Non-Union Policies on the Increase among New Overseas Firms", *Industrial Relations News*, No. 4, 25 January, pp. 17–23.

Hunter, J.E. and Hunter, R.F. (1984): "Validity and Utility of Alternative Predictors of Job Performance", *Psychological Bulletin*, No. 96, pp. 72–98.

Hyman, R. (ed.) (1992): *Industrial Relations in the New Europe*, Oxford: Blackwell.

Iles, P. (1994): "Developing Learning Environment: Challenges for Theory, Research and Practice", *Journal of European Industrial Training*, Vol. 18, No. 3.

Industrial Relations News (1995): "Trade Union Membership Rising, but Profile Changing", Vol. 14, April.

Institute of Personnel Management (1980): *Selecting Managers: How British Industry Recruits*, London: IPM, Information Report 34.

Irish Congress of Trade Unions, (1993): *New Forms of Work Organisation: Options for Unions,* Dublin: Irish Congress of Trade Unions.

Irish Congress of Trade Unions, (1995): *Managing Change,* Dublin: Irish Congress of Trade Unions.

Irish Industrial Relations Review (1993): "Trade Union Organisation in the Republic", Vol. 2, No. 7, July.

Irish Productivity Centre (1986): *A Guide to Employee Shareholding through Profit Sharing*, Dublin: IPC.

Kamoche, K. (1994): "A Critique and a Proposed Reformulation of Strategic Human Resource Management", *Human Resource Management Journal,* Vol. 4, No. 4, pp. 29–43.

Keating, M. (1989): "Personnel Management in Ireland", in *Industrial Relations in Ireland: Contemporary Issues and Developments*, Dublin: Department of Industrial Relations, University College Dublin.

Kelly, A. (1975): "Changes in the Occupational Structure and Industrial Relations in Ireland", *Management*, No. 2.

Kerr, A. (1989): "Trade Unions and the Law" in *Industrial Relations in Ireland: Contemporary Issues and Developments*, Dublin: Department of Industrial Relations, University College Dublin.

Kerr, A. and Whyte, G. (1985): *Trade Union Law*, Abingdon: Professional Books.

Kessler, I. and Purcell, J. (1992): "Performance Related Pay: Objectives and Application", *Human Resource Management Journal*, Vol. 3, No. 2.

Kirkpatrick, D. (1967): "Evaluation of Training" in Craig, R. and Bitten, L. (eds.), *Training and Development Handbook*, ASTD, New York: McGraw-Hill.

Kirnan, J.P., Farley, J. and Geisinger, K. (1989): "The Relationship between Recruiting Sources, Applicant Quality and Hire Performance: An Analysis by Sex, Ethnicity and Age", *Personnel Psychology*, Vol. 42, pp. 293–308.

Kochan, T., Katz, H. and McKersie, R. (1986): *The Transformation of American Industrial Relations*, New York: Basic Books.

Kram, K. (1985): *Mentoring at Work: Developmental Relationships in Organisational Life*, Glenview, IL: Scott-Foresman.

Lawler, E. (1986): *High Involvement Management: Participating Strategies for Organisational Performance*, London: Jossey-Bass.

Legge, K. (1995): *Human Resource Management: Rhetorics and Realities*, London: Macmillan.

Lewis, C. (1984): "What's New in Selection?", *Personnel Management*, January.

Locker, A. and Teel, K. (1977): "Survey of Human Resource Practices", *Personnel Practices Journal*, March.

London, M. and Stumpf, S. (1982): *Managing Careers*, Reading, MA: Addison Wesley.

Long, P. (1986): *Performance Appraisal Revisited*, London: Institute of Personnel Management.

Long, P. (1988): "A Review of Approved Profit Sharing (Trust) Schemes in Ireland and the UK", Unpublished Dissertation College of Commerce, Dublin Institute of Technology.

Marchington, M. (1982): *Managing Industrial Relations*, London: McGraw Hill.

Marchington, M. (1990): Analysing the Links Between Product Markets and the Management of Employee Relations, *Journal of Management Studies*, Vol. 27, No. 2, pp. 111–132.

Marchington, M. and Parker, P. (1990): *Changing Patterns of Employee Relations*, Hemel Hempstead: Harvester Wheatsheaf.

Marginson, P. (1991): "Change and Continuity in the Employment Structure of Large Companies", in Pollert, A. (ed.), *Farewell to Flexibility*, Oxford: Blackwell Business, pp. 32–45.

Marshall, R. (1992): "Work Organisation, Unions and Economic Performance" in Mishel, L. and Voos, P. (eds.), *Unions and Economic Competitiveness*, New York: M.E. Sharpe Inc.

Mayne, L. and Brewster, C. (1995): "Human Resource Management: The Role of the Line Manager", Proceedings of the Conference on European Competitiveness: The HRM Dimension, University of Limerick, May.

McBeath, G. and Rands, N. (1989): *Salary Administration*, Aldershot: Gower.

McCarthy, C. (1977): *Trade Unions in Ireland 1894–1960*, Dublin: Institute of Public Administration.

McGovern, P. (1989): "Union Recognition and Union Avoidance in the 1980s", in *Industrial Relations in Ireland: Contemporary Issues and Developments*, Dublin: University College Dublin.

McKersie, R.B. (1996): "Labour–Management Partnerships: US Evidence and Implications for Ireland", Fourth Annual John Lovett Memorial Lecture, University of Limerick, March.

McLoughlin, I. and Gourlay, S. (1992): "Enterprise Without Unions: The Management of Employee Relations in Non-Union Firms", *Journal of Management Studies*, Vol. 29, No. 5, pp. 669–691.

McMahon, G. and Gunnigle, P. (1994): *Performance Appraisal: How to Get it Right*, Dublin: Productive Personnel Ltd. in association with the IPM.

McMahon, G. et al. (1988): "Multinationals in Ireland: Three Decades On", *Industrial Relations News*, 11 February.

McMahon, G. (1988): "Personnel Selection in Ireland: Scientific Prediction or Crystal Ball Gazing?", *IPM News*, Vol. 3, No. 3, October.

McNamara, G., Williams, K. and West, D. (1988): *Understanding Trade Unions: Yesterday and Today*, Dublin: O'Brien Educational Press.

Millward, N. and Stevens, M. (1986): *British Workplace Industrial Relations: 1980–1984*, Aldershot: Gower.

Millward, N., Stevens, M., Smart, D. and Hawes, W. (1992): *Workplace Industrial Relations in Transition*, Aldershot: Gower.

Monks, K. (1991): "Understanding Personnel Management Practice: The Implications for Personnel Management Education", Unpublished Ph.D Thesis, Trinity College Dublin.

Monks, K. (1992): "Personnel Management Practices: Uniformity or Diversity? Evidence from Some Irish Organisations", *Irish Business and Administrative Research*, Vol. 13, pp. 74–86.

Morley, M., Brewster, C., Gunnigle, P. and Mayrhofer, W. (1996): "Evaluating Change in European Industrial Relations: Research Evidence on Trends at Organisational Level", *The International Journal of Human Resource Management*, Vol. 7, No. 3, pp. 640–656.

Morley, M. and Gunnigle, P. (1994): "Trends in Flexible Working Patterns in Ireland", in Gunnigle, P., Flood, P., Morley, M. and Turner, T., *Continuity and Change in Irish Employee Relations,* Dublin: Oak Tree Press, pp. 103–125.

Morley, M., Gunnigle, P. and Heraty, N. (1995): "Developments in Flexible Working Practices in the Republic of Ireland: Research Evidence Considered", *International Journal of Manpower*, MCB University Press, Vol. 16, No. 8, pp. 38–58.

Muchinsky, P. (1986): "Personnel Selection Methods" in Cooper, C. and Robertson, I.T. (eds.), *International Review of Industrial and Organisational Psychology,* New York: John Wiley.

Murray, M. (1991): *Beyond the Myths and Magic of Mentoring: How to Facilitate an Effective Mentoring Programme,* San Francisco, CA: Jossey-Bass.

Murray, S. (1984): *Employee Relations in Irish Private Sector Manufacturing Industry*, Dublin: IDA.

Nicholson, N. and Arnold, J. (1989): "Graduate Early Experience in a Multinational Corporation", *Personnel Review*, Vol. 18, No. 4, pp. 3–14.

Nollen, S.A. and Gannon, M.J. (1996): "Managing without a Complete, Full-time Workforce", in Flood, P., Gannon, M. and Paauwe, J. (eds.), *Managing Without Traditional Methods: International Innovations in Human Resource Management*, Wokingham: Addison-Wesley.

O'Brien, J.F. (1981): *A Study of National Wage Agreements in Ireland,* Dublin: Economic and Social Research Institute.

O'Brien, J.F. (1989): "Pay Determination in Ireland" in *Industrial Relations in Ireland: Contemporary Issues and Developments,* Dublin: University College Dublin.

O'Malley, E. (1983): "Late Industrialisation under Outward-Looking Policies: The Experience and Prospects of the Republic of Ireland", Unpublished Ph.D. Thesis, University of Sussex.

Ost, E. (1990): "Team-Based Pay: New Wave Incentives", *Sloan Management Review*, Spring.

Paauwe, J. (1996): "Personnel Management without Personnel Managers", in Flood, P., Gannon, M.J. and Paauwe, J. (eds.), *Managing without Traditional Methods: International Innovations in Human Resource Management*, Wokingham: Addison-Wesley.

Pearce, J. (1987): "Why Merit Pay Doesn't Work: Implications for Organisation Theory", in Balkin, D. and Gomez-Mejia, L. (eds.): *New Perspectives on Compensation*, Englewood Cliffs, NJ: Prentice Hall.

Pettigrew, P., Hendry, C. and Sparrow, P. (1988): "Linking Strategic Change, Competitive Performance and Human Resource Management: Results of a UK-based Empirical Study", University of Warwick.

Pfeffer, J. (1994): *Competitive Advantage Through People: Unleashing the Power of the Workforce*, Boston, MA: Stanford Graduate School of Business, Harvard Business School Press.

Piore, M. and Sabel, C. (1984): *The Second Industrial Divide: Prospects for Prosperity*, New York: Basic Books.

Plumbley, P. (1985): *Recruitment and Selection*, London: Institute of Personnel Management.

Pollert, A. (1987): "The Flexible Firm: A Model in Search of Reality (or a Policy in Search of a Practice)?", *Warwick Papers in Industrial Relations*, No. 19, December.

Pollert, A. (1988a): "Dismantling Flexibility", *Capital and Class*, No. 34, Spring, pp. 42–75.

Pollert, A. (1988b): "The 'flexible firm': fixation or fact?", *Work, Employment and Society*, Vol. 2, No. 3, September, pp. 281–316.

Poole, M. (1986): "Managerial Strategies and Styles in Industrial Relations: A Comparative Analysis", *Journal of General Management*, Vol. 12, No. 1, pp. 40–53.

Porter, M. (1987): "From Competitive Advantage to Corporate Strategy", *Harvard Business Review*, May/June, pp. 43–59.

Purcell, J. (1987): "Mapping Management Styles in Employee Relations", *Journal of Management Studies*, Vol. 24, No. 5, pp. 533–548.

Purcell, J. (1989): "The Impact of Corporate Strategy on HRM", in Storey, J. (ed.), *New Perspectives on Human Resource Management*, London: Routledge.

Randell, G. (1994): *Performance Appraisal in Personnel Management: A Comprehensive Guide to Theory and Practice in Britain*, Oxford: Blackwell.

Reilly, R. and Chao, G. (1982): "Validity and Fairness of Some Alternative Selection Procedures", *Personnel Psychology*, No. 35.

Rhodes, M. (1994): "Labour markets and industrial relations", in Nugent, N. and O'Donnell, R. (eds.), *The European Business Environment*, London: Macmillan, pp. 121–155.

Ripley, R. and Ripley, M. (1994): "CREAM: Criteria Related Employability Assessment Method: A Systematic Model for Employee Selection", *Management Decision*, Vol. 32, No. 9, pp. 27–36.

Robertson, I.T. and Makin, P. (1986): "Management Selection in Britain: A Survey and Critique", *Journal of Occupational Psychology*, No. 59.

Roche, W.K. (1989): "State Strategies and the Politics of Industrial Relations in Ireland", in *Industrial Relations in Ireland: Contemporary Issues and Developments*, Dublin: University College Dublin.

Roche, W.K. (1995): "The New Competitive Order and Employee Relations in Ireland: Challenges and Prospects", Paper presented to the Irish Business and Employers Confederation (IBEC) Employee Relations Conference, Dublin.

Roche, W.K. and Geary, J. (1995): "The Attenuation of 'Host-Country' Effects? Multi-nationals, Industrial Relations and Collective Bargaining in Ireland", Working Paper IR-HRM No. 94–5, Dublin: Graduate School of Business, University College Dublin.

Roche, W.K. and Gunnigle, P. (1995): "Competition and the New Industrial Relations Agenda", in Gunnigle, P. and Roche, W.K. (eds.), *New Challenges to Irish Industrial Relations*, Dublin: Oak Tree Press.

Roche, W.K. and Larragy, J. (1989): "The Trend of Unionisation in the Irish Republic", in *Industrial Relations in Ireland: Contemporary Issues and Developments*, Dublin: University College Dublin.

Roche, W.K. and Turner, T. (1994): "Testing Alternative Models of Human Resource Policy Effects on Trade Union Recognition in the Republic of Ireland", *International Journal of Human Resource Management*, Vol. 5, No. 3, pp. 721–753.

Roche, W.K. (1992): "The Liberal Theory of Industrialism and the Development of Industrial Relations in Ireland", in Goldthorpe, J. and Whelan, C. (eds.), *The Development of Industrial Society in Ireland,* Oxford: Oxford University Press.

Roche, W.K. (1994): "Human Resource Management and Unionisation in Ireland", Paper presented at the Second Annual John Lovett Memorial Lecture, University of Limerick, April.

Roche, W.K. (1997): "Pay Determination, the State and the Politics of Industrial Relations", in Murphy, T. and Roche, W. (eds.), *Irish Industrial Relations in Practice*, 2nd edition, Dublin: Oak Tree Press.

Rodgers, C.S. (1992): "The Flexible Workplace: What Have We Learned?", in *Human Resource Management*, Vol. 31, No. 3, Fall, pp. 183–199, by John Wiley & Sons, Inc.

Rynes, S. (1990): "Recruitment, Job Choice and Post-hire Consequences: A Case for New Research Directions", in Dunnette, M. and Hough, L. (eds.), *A Handbook of Industrial and Organizational Psychology*, Vol. II, Palo Alto, CA: Consulting Psychology Press.

Salaman, G. (1992): *Human Resource Strategies*, London: Sage/Open University Press.

Sargent, A. (1990): *Turning People On: The Motivation Challenge*, London: Institute of Personnel Management.

Schuler, R. and Walker, J. (1990): "Human Resource Strategy: Focusing on Issues and Action", *Organization Dynamics,* Summer, pp. 5–19.

Senge, P. (1990): *The Fifth Discipline,* New York: Doubleday.

Shivanath, G. (1987): "Personnel Practitioners: Their Role and Status in Irish Industry", Unpublished MBS Thesis, Limerick, University of Limerick.

Sisson, K. (1991): "Industrial Relations: Challenges and Opportunities", *Employee Relations*, Vol. 13, No. 6.

Smith, M. and Robertson, I.T. (1993): *The Theory and Practice of Systematic Staff Selection*, London: Macmillan.

Smith, M., Gregg, M. and Andrews, D. (1989): *Selection and Assessment — A New Appraisal*, London: Pitman.

Sparrow, P. and Hiltrop, J. (1994): *European Human Resource Management in Transition*, London: Prentice Hall.

Sparrow, P.R. (1994): "Redefining the Field of European Human Resource Management: A Battle between National Mindsets & Forces of Business Transition?", Manchester Business School Working Paper, November.

Sparrow, P. and Hiltrop, J. (1994): *European Human Resource Management in Transition*, London: Prentice Hall.

Spellman, R. (1992): "Gaining a Competitive Advantage in the Labour Market", in Armstrong, M. (ed.), *Strategies for Human Resource Management: A Total Business Approach*, Coopers & Lybrand, London: Kogan Page, pp. 61–79.

Stata, R. (1989): "Organisational Learning — The Key to Management Innovation", *Sloan Management Review*, Vol. 30, No. 3, Spring.

Statistical Bulletin (1996): Central Statistics Office, December.

Storey, J (1989): "Introduction" in Storey, J. (ed.), *New Perspectives on Human Resource Management*, London: Routledge.

Storey, J. (1992): *Developments in the Management of Human Resources,* Oxford: Blackwell.

Storey, J. and Sisson, K. (1994): *Managing Human Resources and Industrial Relations*, Buckingham: Open University Press.

Storey, J. (1995): *Human Resource Management: A Critical Text,* London: Routledge.

Streeck, W. (1992): "Training and the New Industrial Relations: A Strategic Role for Unions?" in Marino Regini (ed.), *The Future of Labour Movements*, London: Sage.

Thierry, H. (1992): "Pay and Payment Systems", in Hartley, J. and Stephenson, G. (eds.), *Employment Relations*, Oxford: Blackwell.

Thomason, G. (1984): *A Textbook of Industrial Relations Management*, London: Institute of Personnel Management.

Torrington, D., Weightman, J. and Johns, K. (1989): *Effective Management: People and Organisation*, London: Prentice Hall.

Tsui, A. (1987): "Defining the Activities and Effectiveness of the Human Resource Department: A Multiple Constituency Approach", *Human Resource Management*, Vol. 26, No. 1, pp. 35–69.

Turner, T. (1994): "Unionisation and Human Resource Management in Irish Companies", *Industrial Relations Journal*, Vol. 25, No. 1.

Turner, T., Dart, D. and Gunnigle, P. (1997): "Industrial Relations and the New Orthodoxy?: A Comparison of Irish and US Companies", *Industrial Relations Journal*, June.

Turner, T. and Morley, M. (1995): *Industrial Relations and the New Order*, Dublin: Oak Tree Press.

Turner, T., Morley, M. and Gunnigle, P., (1994) "Developments in Industrial Relations and HRM in the Republic of Ireland", *Journal of Irish Business and Administrative Research*, Vol. 15.

Tyson, S. (1979): "Specialists in Ambiguity: Personnel Management as an Occupation", Unpublished Ph.D. Thesis, London University.

Tyson, S. (1987): The Management of the Personnel Function, *Journal of Management Studies*, Vol. 24, No. 5, pp. 523–532.

Tyson, S. and Fell, A. (1986): *Evaluating the Personnel Function*, London: Hutchinson.

Tyson, S., Witcher, M. and Doherty, N. (1994): "Different Routes to Excellence", Cranfield University School of Management, Human Resource Research Centre.

Van Hilst, B. and Jansen, B. (1994): *Developments in Working Hours in the Netherlands*, Dublin: European Foundation for the Improvement of Living and Working Conditions.

Von Prondzynski, F. (1992): *Ireland: Between Centralism and the Market*, in Ferner, A. and Hyman, R., *Industrial Relations and the New Europe*, Oxford: Blackwell, pp. 69–88.

Walton, R.E. (1985): "From Control to Commitment in the Workplace", *Harvard Business Review*, March/April, pp. 77–84.

Webster, B. (1990): "Beyond the Mechanics of HRD", *Personnel Management*, Vol. 12, No. 3, pp. 44–47.

Wedderburn, A. (1996): "BEST Statistics and News", Dublin: European Foundation for the Improvement of Living and Working Conditions, No. 9.

West, P. (1994): "The Learning Organisation: Losing the Luggage in Transit?", *Journal of European Industrial Training*, Vol. 18, No. 11.

Wexley, K. and Latham, G. (1991): *Developing and Training Human Resources in Organisations*, New York: Harper-Collins.

Wiesner, W.H. and Cronshaw, S.F. (1988): "A Meta-analytic Investigation of the Impact of Interview Format and Degree of Structure on the Validity of the Employment Interview", *Journal of Occupational Psychology*, No. 61, pp. 275–90.

Wood, S. (1985): "Recruitment Systems and the Recession", *British Journal of Industrial Relations*, pp 103–120.

Zalusky, J. (1991): "Labor Seeks Security, Not Bonuses", *Personnel*, January.

Zenger, J. (1988): "Training for Organisational Excellence", *Journal of European Industrial Training*, Vol. 9, No. 7.